OLIVIA O'LEARY is an experienced writer and broadcaster who has worked in current affairs in Britain and Ireland for over twenty years. She has presented BBC's 'Newsnight', Yorkshire Television's 'First Tuesday', and Thames Television's 'This Week'. In Ireland she has fronted RTE's 'Today Tonight', 'Questions and Answers' and 'Prime Time' programmes. She has been parliamentary sketch-writer for *The Irish Times*, and associate editor and political writer for the *Sunday Tribune*. She was born in Co. Carlow, Ireland, in 1949 and now lives in Dublin with her husband and daughter.

HELEN BURKE is Professor Emeritus of Social Policy and Social Work at University College Dublin. She was head of that department for a number of years, a founder member of Women's Studies and an elected member of the Governing Body. She has been actively involved in the development of social policy in Ireland, as a Commissioner for Law Reform; as a member of the National Economic and Social Council, the National Planning Board and the Combat Poverty Agency. It was through a shared interest in social issues that she first met Mary Robinson many years ago. Her books include *The People and the Poor Law in Nineteenth Century Ireland*. She is married with three grown-up children.

For our families

MARY ROBINSON

THE AUTHORISED BIOGRAPHY

OLIVIA O'LEARY
& HELEN BURKE

SCEPTRE
LIR

First published in 1998 by Hodder and Stoughton
A division of Hodder Headline PLC
A Sceptre/Lir Paperback

A CIP catalogue record for this title
is available from the British Library.

ISBN 0 340 71739 4

Typeset by Palimpsest Book Production Limited
Polmont, Stirlingshire
Printed and bound in Great Britain by
Clays Ltd, St Ives PLC

Hodder and Stoughton
A division of Hodder Headline PLC
338 Euston Road
London NW1 3BH

ACKNOWLEDGEMENTS

The authors have called on many people in the putting together of this book, and are very grateful to Mary and Nick Robinson, and their families, especially to Dr Aubrey Bourke who was a constant and ever-patient source of information and of family photographs. We would also specifically like to thank Bride Rosney, political advisor to former President Robinson. While those interviewees we quote directly are acknowledged in the end-notes, others gave us essential background information. These include Fergus Armstrong, Denis Corboy, Barbara Sweetman FitzGerald, Pearse Colbert, Brendan Walsh, Tom Garvin, Maurice Manning, Edward Hughes and Ray Kavanagh. Thanks to Peter MacMenamin, Brenda O'Hanlon, Greg Sparks, and Tony Heffernan for access to precious presidential campaign papers; and to Dermot Gleeson S.C., Michael McDowell S.C. and John MacMenamin S.C. for their help – though they are not responsible for any opinions expressed in this book.

We are grateful to the *Irish Times* editor, Conor Brady, to the *Irish Times* reference and photographic libraries, and to Asia correspondent, Conor O'Clery; to the *Sunday Business Post* library and to editor, Damien Kiberd; to the *Irish Independent*'s Chris Glennon; to the *Sunday Tribune*'s newsroom and library; to the *Star*'s library; to the *Sunday Times* – Irish Editor, Rory Godson, and Jan Battle; to the RTE Dublin, London, and Belfast newsrooms, especially to Ed Mulhall, Michael Fisher and Charlie Bird, and to the RTE reference, television and radio archives libraries; to Eileen Finnegan of Gill and Macmillan; to Tony Donohoe, Chris Robson, Michael Forde and Henry Wills for particular help with pictures.

We would like to thank the very helpful secretariat at Áras an Uachtaráin; the press offices of the Department of Finance, Foreign Affairs, Office of Public Works; the offices of the Taoiseach; the Irish Embassy in London; the Seanad office, the Trinity elections office; the returning officer for presidential elections.

We thank, too, the libraries of the King's Inns, TCD and UCD, particularly the staff in the busy Law and Official Publications section; the libraries of the Oireachtas, the ILAC centre, and the National Library; Charles Coyle of IMS; Mike Chmura of Harvard Law School; Professor Binchy, Caroline Lewis, and Professor Ivana Bacik of the Dublin University Law School. We know that our book enters the field after excellent biographies by Michael O'Sullivan, Lorna Siggins and John Horgan; books on the presidential election campaign by Emily O'Reilly and Fergus Finlay; and a pictorial record of the Robinson presidency with text by Deirdre McQuillan. Where we have made use of their work, we have acknowledged it.

Olivia would like to thank her brothers and sisters, John, Art, Teresa, Elizabeth and Alice, for putting up with her – in particular, Mary for keeping her heart up, and Pat for finding the lost files; her friend, Eveleen Coyle, for her constant encouragement; and Richie Lennon of Canon for coaxing the computer. Most of all, she thanks Paul for his shrewd advice and his loving support, and Emily for keeping it all in perspective.

Helen warmly thanks her colleagues in UCD for their support and generosity, particularly her friends in the Department of Social Policy and Social Work, the Social Science Research Centre and the Women's Research and Resource Centre. Three must be mentioned by name: Professor Gabriel Kiely and Dr Margaret McCurtain for their wisdom and accessibility, Anne Coogan for her humour and never-ending patience with computer problems. Grateful thanks, too, to Dr Rachel Iredale, Kathleen McMahon and Aisling Byrne, who at different times helped with the library research. Finally, she wants to thank family and friends who sustained her on this journey: her sister Ann; her brother Dan; Maeve and Gordon; Greg, Iris and Heather; Maribel, Kate, Rita and Noreen; those fantastic daughters, Katie and Sara, and most of all her beloved Kevin.

Finally, the authors thank Sara Menguc of David Higham Associates, and Rowena Webb, Roland Philipps, and Angela Herlihy of Hodder and Stoughton.

CONTENTS

LIST OF ILLUSTRATIONS

Mary with Tessa (*Nick Robinson*)

Nan Coyne in Tenerife with William and Tessa (*Nick Robinson*)

Robinson children in France, 1987

Solicitor Nick Robinson and Mary on the day she takes silk (*Irish Times*)

Cartoonist Nick Robinson targets his wife (*Derek Speirs/Report*)

Bride Rosney (*Derek Speirs/Report*)

Campaigning against the amendment to ban abortion in the Irish constitution, 1983 (*Derek Speirs/Report*)

Addressing the Labour Party Conference, 1980 (*Derek Speirs/Report*)

Mary campaigning to save the Viking site at Wood Quay, Dublin, 1978 (*Derek Speirs/Report*)

Before: Mary with Dick Spring, on the day Labour nominated her for the Presidency (*Irish Times*)

After: Official campaign picture of the new-look Mary (*Conor Horgan*)

Mary on Inishmore, Aran Islands, 1990 (*Irish Times*)

Arriving at an election count centre with Ruairi Quinn, Aoife Breslin, Nick Robinson, Pat Rabbitte and Proinsias de Rossa (*Derek Speirs/Report*)

Accepting victory in the Presidential election (*Derek Speirs/Report*)

Inauguration day (*Derek Speirs/Report*)

Mary's family celebrate victory in Mayo (*Henry Wills, Western People*)

Bourkes in the early 1980s

Robinsons (*Derek Speirs/Report*)

President Robinson meets the Dalai Lama (*Louis Pieterse/PDI*)

Kathleen Power at Taylor's Hall, Dublin, 1995 (*Derek Speirs/Report*)

Welcoming all gay and lesbian groups to the Áras, 1992 (*Chris Robson*)

With Taoiseach Albert Reynolds and Peter Ryan (*Derek Speirs/Report*)

Chris McCarthy welcomes Mary to the Mercy Family Centre in Dublin

Mary and Nick in West Belfast (*Derek Speirs/Report*)

Prince Charles with Mary at Áras an Uachtaráin, 1995 (*Irish Times*)

With authors John B. Keane and the late Bryan McMahon at Listowel Writers' Week (*Liam Burke/Press 22*)

Mary meets children in a feeding line in Somalia, 1992 (*Eric Luke, Irish Times*)

Two presidents shaped by the civil rights movement: Bill Clinton with Mary in Ireland, 1995 (*Irish Times*)

Mary with Nelson Mandela on her state visit to South Africa, 1996 (*AP Photo/Guy Tillim*)

Meeting the Irish community in Manchester (*Rose Morris*)

Mary and Nick Robinson with the Duke of Edinburgh and John Major at the memorial service for the two boys killed in the Warrington bombing, 1993 (*Press Association*)

With Jim Rodgers and a group from the Protestant Shankill Road (*Lesley Doyle*)

Mary with children at Irish aid agency Trócaire's project in Rwanda (*Trócaire*)

Mary with protesting Bernadette McAliskey (*Irish Press*)

With Kofi Annan, New York, 1997 (*Reuters*)

Making history: President Robinson and Queen Elizabeth at Buckingham Palace, May 1993 (*Photocall Ireland*)

Seamus Heaney with Mary Robinson at Harvard, 1998 (*AP*)

No veil: meeting the Pope, 1997 (*AP*)

Time to go: Mary says goodbye to Áras an Uachtaráin, 1997 (*Irish Times*)

All illustrations are from private collections unless otherwise stated

INTRODUCTION

Their two faces said it all. Hers was open, expectant. His was closed, hooded eyes masking his defeat. On presidential election night 1990, Mary Robinson and Charles Haughey represented two different Irelands. She stood for change. He stood for none. She was the future. He was the past.

Mary's supporters could hardly believe what had happened. One tearful woman, a veteran of every liberal cause from contraception to divorce, repeated it like a mantra: 'She won. She won. You see, I never voted for anybody who won before.' After decades of rejection, it seemed at last that one could be both progressive and Irish. This election was allowing a new Irish identity and liberals could apply.

But the thousands who cheered and wept that night didn't know that the battle had only just begun. Charlie Haughey might well be the past, but the past in Ireland keeps a powerful hold. Mary Robinson, as President, would be under his thumb. Traditionally, that was how the Constitution had been interpreted. She would be a prisoner in her eighteenth-century residence in the Phoenix Park, a prisoner with a particularly hostile gaoler.

To become the active people's President she had promised to be, Mary knew she would have to break out of that prison. As a lawyer, she was sure that she could operate effectively within the Constitution, that tradition and precedent had been used to lock up previous Presidents, not the Constitution. She would have met resistance from any Prime Minister, but with Charles Haughey, it went further. He didn't like Mary. He didn't like what she stood for. And he didn't like Presidents. He was, in his own eyes, the political and symbolic leader of the nation. Mary's honourable and long-suffering predecessor, Dr Paddy Hillery, knew that only too well.

The Constitution gave Haughey the power to stop Mary travelling abroad and to vet her formal addresses to the nation. But he felt he had the constitutional right to stop her making any speeches, giving interviews to the press, making any public statement.

In her first month in office, while she kept dutifully silent, the media were awash with hostile news leaks about her staff changes at Áras an Uachtaráin, the presidential residence. She says Haughey did nothing to defend her. 'I was effectively shafted by Haughey,' she says. When she began to speak out, he got legal advice to try to gag her. Invitations issued to her were mysteriously withdrawn. He even refused her permission to visit Irish emigrants abroad. 'Not appropriate for the President', 'Not important enough to warrant the attention of the President' were the rubber-stamp phrases with which he grounded her. Once she started to ignore them, battle commenced. She didn't want to fight the government but she felt she had no choice. Finally, she took an irrevocable step. It was a battle of wills which went right down to the wire – and she won. By the time Haughey sank into retirement and subsequent disgrace, Mary had stamped her authority on the office. She had established a good relationship with government and the public service. But as she stretched the presidency to full capacity, politicians occasionally protested. It was inevitable. They were all competitors for public approval.

The tensions didn't amount to much with Haughey's successors, Albert Reynolds and John Bruton, but with Foreign Minister Dick Spring they were fuelled by a relationship of mutual suspicion. Mary and he shared the same basic beliefs. In the nineties, they helped to make Ireland a more liberal, caring society – she worked on public opinion, he, in government for four years, pushed through the policies. And yet they both admit to a long history of personal coldness they could never overcome.

'I think that Dick needed to have the capacity to rein in and control anybody who was going to work closely with him,' she says. Mary saw herself as belonging to the people, never to the man who had nominated her for the job.

Mary blossomed in the presidency. Those who knew her as a reserved, often abrupt lawyer were astonished at the real warmth with which she responded to people, the new confidence that public affection gave her. But there was steel behind the smile. Every move she made as President was calculated and considered, part of a strategic plan. She let nothing get in her way. She was ruthless in pursuit of the causes she believed in, relentless in her determination to keep her presidential promises. The people recognised her toughness, and they liked it. You don't argue, as Albert Reynolds said, with popularity ratings of 92 per cent.

She took risks, trusting that the people wanted her to be generous. They backed her when she visited famine-stricken Somalia, when she broke taboos and visited the Queen, when she visited Northern Ireland and, most controversially, when she visited republican West Belfast and shook the hand of Sinn Fein's Gerry Adams. Like all risk-takers, she had had to make herself vulnerable and the people responded to that.

The presidency carried its own price. Seven years of safeguarding the dignity and reputation of the office cut her off from many friends, and left her, she admits, institutionalised. Faced again with the ordinary world of hailing her own taxi, or finding her own way to meetings, she felt helpless.

When she finally became UN High Commissioner for Human Rights in Geneva, one of the few women to hold such a senior international post, she left behind an Ireland which had changed dramatically. Not only was it prosperous, it was more confident, more peaceful, more tolerant. A tide of change, dammed up for years, had swept aside the past. She represented this change triumphantly, not only for the Irish themselves, but for the world. She was confident and surefooted, as though she knew every step of this altered Irish landscape.

And well she might. She had worked all her life to create it.

1

THE BOURKES OF BALLINA

Will slipped quietly back inside. He'd long ago learned to avoid publicity. Outside on the steps of Buckingham Palace, his mother stood talking to Queen Elizabeth II as the frenzied photographers captured a piece of history – the first ever meeting between the Irish and British heads of state. Cameras flashed, smiles and hand-shakes were exchanged, the official cars rolled up, and suddenly Will saw his parents and the rest of the Irish delegation drive away. He was on his own. He was in deep trouble. He materialised in front of the Queen and put out a desperate hand. ''Bye now. Thanks very much,' said Will and ran to catch the end of the disappearing cavalcade. There might be a new welcome for the Irish in Buckingham Palace but young William Robinson didn't want to test it too far.

Queen Elizabeth and President Mary Robinson had made this tea party as relaxed as possible. The fact that it had happened now,[1] seventy-one years after the founding of the Irish state, was due not only to improved relations but to a President determined that her office would not be the last bastion of anti-Britishness. She overcame fierce political resistance to visit Britain in the first place. She caused officialdom to tremble when she said yes to the Queen. But when it came, the meeting could not have seemed more normal. About time, said Irish people in

Ireland and in Britain. Time to drop the baggage. Time to move on.

If Mary Bourke Robinson travelled light, there were good reasons. Like many Irish families, the Bourkes had long and varied connections with Britain and the Empire. Her father, Dr Aubrey Bourke, and all his family had been educated in Britain. Her uncle, Paget, had been a judge in the British administration in places as far away as Kenya and Cyprus.

Her great-uncle, Paget John Bourke, had been a member of Queen Victoria's bodyguard and, as children, Mary's brothers dressed up in his splendid uniform. All these connections meant, she said, that 'I had a complete lack of any sense of being second-class. I had a background of having a great-uncle who was the Queen's bodyguard at Buckingham Palace and all these uniforms and things. So, subconsciously, I had no sense of an Irish inferiority complex.'[2]

It was an interesting background, a good mixture of creeds and loyalties. There were those who rebelled against the Crown as well as those who served it. On her grandmother Eleanor Macaulay's side, Mary's great-uncle, Thomas Augustus Macaulay, was a member of the secret revolutionary organisation, the Irish Republican Brotherhood. After a number of incidents including the shooting of a man in north Co. Mayo, he was tried and convicted with others on 28 March 1884 on charges of conspiracy to murder. These members of what became known as the Crossmolina Conspiracy served between five and ten years in prison. Macaulay served eight years of a ten-year sentence in Mountjoy Jail in Dublin and was released in February 1892.[3]

The Bourke tradition was different. Mary's great-grandfather, William Orme Paget Bourke, was the son of John Bourke of Heathfield House, Ballycastle, Co. Mayo, and Elizabeth Paget. The family was Protestant and William and his brothers made their careers in the British army.

William was a captain in the Royal Irish Regiment, the last British regiment to leave Australia. His brother Oliver served with the 17th Regiment in Afghanistan, Baluchistan and the

Crimea and with the Queen's bodyguard, reaching the rank of major-general. Another brother, Paget John, was a captain in the Household Cavalry and served as part of Queen Victoria's royal bodyguard.

The Bourkes turned Catholic when William married Jane Morrogh, from a family of Catholic landed gentry in Co. Cork. Mary Robinson describes her great-grandfather as being of 'bigoted Protestant stock'. The tradition in those days was to bring up the girls in their mother's religion, and the boys in their father's. 'But Jane, without telling William, baptised them all, including my grandfather,' says Mary. 'I found it very unfair that a mother would baptise her children without telling the father. And I always had a sneaking sympathy for old William Orme, although neither his photographs nor anything about him was particularly attractive . . . I found it deeply repugnant that she would do that without asking. I did not think it was right.'

The family say that there was inevitable tension between William Orme and his wife, that William was unkind to her, dismissive of Catholic trappings like rosary beads, and that their son, Mary's grandfather, H.C. Bourke was fiercely loyal both to his faith and his mother.[4] He was surrounded by strong Catholic women. On his mother's side, there was Mother Arsenius, the pioneering Sister of Charity who founded the Foxford Woollen Mills. The Mayo woman he married, Eleanor Dorothy Macaulay, niece of the Republican rebel, Thomas Macaulay, and daughter of Dr Roger Macaulay, a Ballina GP, had first wanted to be a nun. Her sister, Mother Aquinas, helped establish the Jesus and Mary order in Ireland. Indeed, H.C. and Eleanor had two daughters who became nuns – Ivy joined the Sacred Heart order and worked in India, and Dorothy became a Jesus and Mary nun in England.

So this was a devoutly Catholic family, but one which, like many comfortably-off Catholic families of the time, maintained its links with Britain. H.C. Bourke was a well-known solicitor who had inherited not only from his father but from his uncle, Paget John, who had lived in some style in London. Like many middle-class Irish families of the time, Aubrey and his four brothers and two sisters were educated in England. Aubrey, at the age of ten, was sent to the Jesuit boarding-school, Mount St Mary's and from there he went to Edinburgh to study medicine. All the family, except Aubrey, were to end up living abroad. Hal became a doctor in England; Roddy lived in Australia; Denis became a writer, journalist and actor, and lived in Brazil. Aubrey's older brother, Sir Paget John Bourke, continued the tradition of service to the Empire. After studying law at Trinity he had a distinguished career as a judge, serving in Palestine, Kenya, Gibraltar and Cyprus. He was knighted by the Queen in 1957. In 1975, in retirement in Ireland he was kidnapped from his home – mistaken, it is thought, for a serving British judge. He escaped at a roadblock near the border with Northern Ireland.

So how did all these colonial connections affect Mary Bourke's sense of being Irish? 'I think my father felt quite strongly about having been sent to England,' she said, 'and when he came back, he was determined to live and work in Ireland. His father tried to stop him, saying there was no future in it. But he was adamant. So I got that determination very strongly from my father: I am Irish and I am proud of it: this is my country and this is where I live. It was extremely strong. He chose and fought to make his adult life in his home town.'

Dr Bourke's father offered to help him find a practice in England. 'He loved Ireland but in his head he still felt we were part of the Empire,' Dr Bourke says. 'But the fact that half my family was in England meant that England was part of us. That was important to Mary. She was never insular because the family was so broadly based.'

Aubrey Bourke had more than one good reason for returning to Ireland. In his fourth year as a medical student in Edinburgh he came to the Coombe Hospital in Dublin to get experience of delivering babies 'on the district' and there he met Tessa O'Donnell, doing her residency year in the Coombe after quali-fying in medicine at University College Dublin.

They were an interesting pair. He was tall, gentle, with some of the reserve of his British education. She was small, generous, gregarious, the energetic centre of any group and she knew the

Ireland he was coming back to a great deal better than he did. She had spent a lively and leisurely time getting her medical degree, captaining UCD in tennis and hockey, speaking at the Literary and Historical Society.[5] It was a smaller university then, but powerful, producing the new ruling caste of a new state. She knew the future consultants, barristers, judges, academics. She knew the rugby players and selectors. She knew how the world worked.

Tessa was the daughter of an O'Donnell and an O'Doherty, good Donegal names. Hubert and Winifred were shopkeepers in Carndonagh on the Inishowen peninsula. They must have been ambitious for their six children. All of them went to university and four became doctors – Jimmy in Derry and Florrie and Packie in England. Tessa practised for a few years – at one time she was based on Aranmore Island off Donegal.[6] In 1940 she married Aubrey Bourke, six years her junior, and settled to the busy life of a GP's wife in Ballina.

The Bourkes mattered in Ballina. Dr Bourke had to struggle to establish his private practice – he would have needed a knowledge of Irish for a state dispensary-doctor job – but the family had a certain position in the town. His father H.C. was a respected figure, now retired from his law practice because of ill-health. H.C. lived in some style at Amana, a low-fronted, eighteenth-century house in its own grounds on the edge of Ballina, overlooking the Ridge pool on the river Moy. As well as tennis courts and a large garden, there was a big stableyard where he could indulge the family obsession with horses. H.C. owned the winners of the Galway Plate and the Punchestown Cup; his horses won at point-to-points in Westmeath, Mayo and Galway. But it was Aubrey's mother, Eleanor, who was the horsewoman. She was a Macaulay. She rode side-saddle, competing in point-to-points and at the Dublin Horse Show and – almost unheard-of for a woman – she was Master of the North Mayo Harriers in 1910. She renamed her horse 'Tatler' after they both featured in the London society magazine. Aubrey hunted, too, was a keen race-goer and one of the rare breaks he and Tessa allowed themselves every year was to go to Cheltenham. The racing pages of the *Irish Times* and the *Telegraph* were combed keenly every day.

This then was the comfortable, sporting, professional background into which Mary (christened Marie Terese Winifred) Bourke was born in May 1944. She was the longed-for daughter after two boys, Oliver and Aubrey, and would later have two younger brothers, Henry and Adrian.

The family lived in Victoria House, part of a terrace overlooking the Moy and opposite the cathedral in the centre of Ballina. It was a busy house. Mary remembers patients coming and going and knew by the change in her father's voice whether the patients were old or young, from the country or the town. She sat under the table in the dining-room where she played with her brothers, and tried to work out what overheard words or conversations meant. She had a vivid imagination. One word, one incident could build to a drama. When a travelling circus came to Ballina, the clowns terrified her. When Miss Ruddy in her primary school said that emigration was a sin, she was distraught. 'I had all these uncles who were far away, and Aunt Ivy the nun in India whom we were writing to . . . why was emigration a sin?'

Mary and her brothers went to Miss Ruddy's private school which was at one end of the town. The public national school was at the other. 'There was a meeting point on the street,' says Mary's brother, Henry, remembering a lot of pushing and jostling. 'And you can imagine the kind of insults. "Snobs" was hurled at us and the word "culchie" was hurled back at the others. It was inevitable. To have a private school in a small town like Ballina was unusual in those days.'

The Bourke children didn't play around the streets of Ballina – they played at home. They had a nanny, Anne Coyne, whom Mary loved and who would long remain part of her life. As Mary grew, she took the lead over her two younger brothers, Henry and Adrian. They imitated the ceremonies in the cathedral across the river – elaborate funerals and weddings. Mary married Henry again and again with the Hallowe'en brack brass ring.

But it was when they moved into a new garden playroom at the side of the house that the games got tougher. Mary decided they would fly like Batman, and agreed that Henry, playing Robin, would go first. He leaped a whole fifteen feet from the playroom window on to the sandpit below and almost broke his ankle. 'Don't jump, Mary,' he groaned. 'Please don't jump.' 'All right,' said Batman cheerfully. 'I won't.'[7] Mary was imaginative and she was also, as she would be all her life, fiercely independent, even stubborn. The Sunday after the Batman flight, Mary and the younger ones were drilled out of the house for their usual afternoon walk. This Sunday Mary decided she was too old to be sent on walks. 'But she was ordered out,' said Henry. 'So she concocted this plan. "All right. If you want us to walk, by God, we'll walk ... to Enniscrone." That was seven or eight miles and it was a warm summer's day, so warm, and my feet hurt.' Henry, who had been afraid to tell his parents about his leap as Robin, begged mercy for himself and little Adrian. There was none. 'Keep moving,' she said. 'Keep moving.' They put sand in their pockets to prove they'd reached Enniscrone and when their father collected them, there was no recrimination. 'I think he was very proud of us, really,' said Henry.

When she got into trouble, Mary stood up for herself, more, she concedes, than children usually did then. Henry says: 'She would always be prepared to say, "Look, it's not the way you see it. We weren't in danger; you're blowing it up." She would make a case. She would stubbornly stick to her point instead of gracefully conceding. She would not concede and would suffer the consequences. No compromising.'

There were three dominant figures in Mary's young life – her parents and her grandfather. With her father she went on calls, learning something about the bleak poverty in rural Mayo. She noticed that her father would take time to listen, and began to realise that you could respect people by listening to them.

Very often they would be lonely old couples who had lost all their children to England or America, and Mary began to realise what Miss Ruddy had meant about emigration being a sin.

'There was a sense of hopelessness in that there was no choice but to emigrate. There was the extraordinary loneliness of families breaking up – at that time a visit home every two or three years was as much as there was', she says. 'I think I've been worrying about the issue of emigration ever since. Seeing the loss of it, learning at school and being aware of the devastation of the famine, but also feeling that it was part of an Irish demoralised sense of ourselves. That was the way it was. You got on the boat or plane or train. There was an inevitability about it.'

She remembered with her father coming across families split up by the tatie-picking: wives left at home for half the year while the husbands and older children lived the hard life of potato-pickers in Scotland. She remembered the sense of shame attached to emigrants, to people who went to the poorhouse, to tuberculosis victims – that they were all spoken of in whispers, as though they were to blame for their own misfortune. She questioned that. 'There was so much I couldn't accept. There was a lot I accepted on the surface that I didn't accept underneath.'

Her father worked hard to make a living. 'I was very conscious that we, particularly my mother, had a sense that we were one of the leading families, but we weren't wealthy like, for instance, the Murphys of the Mill. My mother was determined to keep up appearances but I was conscious that income had to be earned.'

But life had to be lived, too, and Tessa Bourke lived it to the full. She was generous to a fault, nothing was too good or too much trouble for the people she loved. She was warm, direct and a bundle of energy. When they were only seven or eight she took the younger boys up to see the All Blacks play in Dublin's Lansdowne Road rugby grounds. She had no difficulty getting into the smoke-filled reception rooms of the city's Shelbourne Hotel with 'all the selectors, and their wives and their cousins and their girlfriends,' says Adrian. 'She was a cigarette-smoking, whiskey-drinking lady.' She knew a whole influential generation from her time in UCD in the thirties and had no difficulty telling the selectors who should be on the team. She told them she'd seen a young solicitor's apprentice called Tony O'Reilly play at the Dublin Jesuit college, Belvedere, and then, says Adrian, 'she said, "It's time you put him on a wing or did something with him."'[8]

Tessa Bourke made things happen. 'She was everything I

wasn't,' says Dr Bourke. 'I was far too timid, quiet. She brought me out in every way possible.' She ran two households – her own and her father-in-law's house at Amana after her mother-in-law died. She organised birthday parties, picnics on Enniscrone beach, holidays with her own relations in Donegal where the Bourke children were allowed to help their grandmother in the dark, cool shop. Mary's memory of her mother is of two arms going around her. 'She was the earth mother, the centre of everything. She was very, very warm, dominant,' she says. 'She had very strong views on things, which could lead to clashes, but any potential clash was always outweighed just by her sheer loving generosity and a great sense of humour.'

They both had strong views and sometimes they did clash. Across the generation gap it seemed to Mary that her mother was sometimes 'very snobbish. She felt she had married into a family that was better than her own family, and that really was better than other families. It was one of the reasons I had such a commitment to equality.'

There were other differences. Mary's mother was sociable, talkative. Mary was growing to be reflective, enjoying her own thoughts.

'I was always accused of daydreaming,' says Mary. 'My mother would become irritated. She would become irritated even by my interest in literature and theatre. She really wanted me to be very good at hockey, so I was as good at hockey as I could possibly be!' Mary was later to play hockey and tennis for Trinity College Dublin.

'She loved so much that you had to respond. The first day she brought me to boarding school, she *wept*. And I thought she would never leave. And she *bawled* and I thought: God! Will she never go! She had this incredible strength of maternal love.'

'They clashed every now and again,' said Henry. 'My mother wanted so much more for her, wanted to spoil her if Mary would be spoiled. But Mary wasn't a clothes horse, wasn't interested in make-up, wasn't interested in the finer things some girls are interested in and which my mother wanted to lavish on her only daughter, and I think a certain wall built up on that score. My mother absolutely adored her and vice versa, but Mary's patience would run out.'

Mary needed to get away from Ballina. 'I couldn't wait to escape to boarding-school. I couldn't wait to escape to college. I couldn't wait to escape.'

Her first escape, at the age of ten, was to Mount Anville, a leading girls' school run by Sacred Heart nuns at Dundrum, Co. Dublin. Mary did well there and decided that she wanted to be a nun. There was a high-minded austerity about the nuns which appealed to her.

'The reserve and the high moral standards; the high principles of working for social justice. It was very interesting how strongly that came across to me. So to be a nun was to work to the highest standards, with a personal commitment to the poorest and the most vulnerable.'

But this was a school for the élite, where boarders were not allowed to speak to the day pupils, hardly a shining example of social justice. Mary says: 'I don't know why I didn't question that more. I questioned it, but I never really took it on.' Wasn't it a snobbish school? 'Yes, very definitely; as I say, we didn't mix with the day pupils – that was pure snobbery.' She can see the contradictions, looking back, and says she didn't send her own daughter to Mount Anville partly for those reasons. But at the time the great theological debate about real commitment to justice had begun to influence the thinking of the Mount Anville nuns, a debate which would later lead nuns to go to live among the poor. 'What Mount Anville did for me was to encourage idealism, high personal standards of integrity. I remember being concerned that my brothers in Clongowes were learning to be devious and the Jesuits seemed to be encouraging this. I was very judgemental about it and decided that I didn't like Clongowes and the Jesuits. Mount Anville placed great emphasis on being true to your word and not telling lies and taking your punishment if you did wrong.'

Schooldays weren't perfect. She was sent to hospital with scarlet fever and yearned for her mother who was nursing old Mrs Bourke at Amana. She had to fight for the right to read the *Irish Times*. She was ticked off when, with a broken leg in plaster, she walked on crutches along the sloping desk tops learning 'to be like Long John Silver'.[9]

But school gave her space to think. She read Camus' *The Outsider* in the school library and 'decided that I was the outsider. I was the great outsider for the last couple of years and that was my secret'. For most of her life she would feel like this.

'From the earliest stage I have felt like an observer and outsider in the very situation I was going through.' She was asking questions, at school, at home, and not getting answers. 'So in a way I was providing my own answers. I did at times ask questions and confront, but mostly I came to a realisation, very early on, that the better way to coexist was to have my secret outsider world.'

She questioned everything – class, religion, property – but not with her parents. More and more it was to her lawyer grandfather that she spoke. H.C. Bourke was a small, dapper man, with a passion for horses. Mary's brothers remember how he would study the racing pages and then set out, always impeccably dressed, for Paddy Moclair's betting office, his fancied horses noted on a small piece of paper. As Henry became interested in racing, he picked up tips from those pieces of paper. 'He usually got it right,' laughs Henry 'Financially, I missed him when his betting days were over.'

But Mary had different interests. She wanted to be a lawyer, the sort of lawyer her grandfather had been. H.C. had a formidable reputation in the courts of the west of Ireland as a defender of the underprivileged. 'He was a great fighter in court,' she says. 'You could never beat Harry Bourke. He would always come up with further arguments. I always had a sense of him as being very Irish – not Republican Irish, but very non-English Irish,' says Mary.

On their walks around Ballina, he spoke to her as an adult. He spoke about fairness, about the rights of the 'small man'. He explained about land rights, and tenants' rights and why it was proper that bigger landowners like the Bourkes should have had land taken from them and redistributed by the Congested District Boards, the Victorian forerunners of the Land Commission. 'It mattered very much to me that he had a moral approach. I was looking for very high standards at that stage.' Coming back from their walk, he would take out a box of Black Magic and they'd sit eating chocolates and talking about the books he read, a wide range of biography and a lot of religious books – he was a daily mass-goer. He would tell her how lucky he was, despite his Protestant father, that he had been baptised a Catholic. She wasn't so sure.

She remembers saying to herself, 'Why are they so certain that Catholics are absolutely right and the priests are right when, if it weren't for that circumstance, we wouldn't be Catholics at all?'

After all, Protestants questioned things, and Mary would question things all her life.

Old William Orme had left his mark.

2

ESCAPE TO PARIS

An Irish teenager going to Paris at the end of the fifties faced two great dangers. She could lose her virginity or she could question her Catholic faith. Mary Robinson settled for the second.

The culture shocks started early. Family friends delivered her to the Foyer du Sacré-Coeur in the Rue St Dominique where she would be staying for this post-school year in Paris. 'I rang the bell outside this very big wall and the door "pinged" open, which I wasn't used to.' She came into a courtyard and was greeted by a nun who showed her her room and then led her to a dining-room and a table set for one. It was Sunday, so all the other girls – eighteen French and one Italian – were out. There was a glass and a little carafe of wine and the sister began to pour the wine. 'And I was so shocked,' says Mary. 'And I said, "No, no, no!" And she said: "Petite, tu es anti-alcool?" She was as shocked that I was against drink, as I was utterly shocked to have a nun pouring wine. And I remember going into the chapel of the Foyer that evening and praying for myself because I had arrived at this place where even the nuns poured me wine. And here was I, a Pioneer up to the hilt.[1] And I remained all that year without drinking wine, even though I went through a transformation in other ways. I was very puritanical in those days.

'The Foyer was a hostel for nice girls attending Paris finishing schools. It was "snob" because it was Sacred Heart, but not smart.

17

But Mlle Anita Pojninska's on Rue de l'Amiral d'Estaing in the 16th Arrondissement was another matter. 'It was a finishing school for daughters of the wealthy,' said Mary. 'That was where you saw more visible signs of wealth. I managed from the beginning to be in the French stream but I think if I had been in the English-speaking stream I should have been really put off by the North American rich kids who came in their cars.'

Mlle Anita's focused particularly on literature and the arts. Mary was brought to the Louvre, to the Jeu de Paume, to the Museum of Modern Art. She discovered the delights of going to the cinema at ten in the morning – she saw *Jules et Jim*. She went to see Edith Piaf at the Odéon. 'It was almost frightening because she was rather like the clown in the circus, with a very severe white light focused on her very made-up white face. I loved her singing. I felt utterly uplifted by it: she was The Sparrow.'

Paris taught her early not to be ensnared by the Big City syndrome. Long before the rest of Europe began to talk about centralisation and regionalisation, the French were realising that the arts needed to be brought to the regions. 'This was an interesting concept to me. You didn't have art and culture only in the capital cities. The French were just about to establish a regional structure for galleries.' The girl from the remote west of Ireland was interested in that whole discussion. 'We always thought of Dublin as the place where you went to visit a gallery or a museum.' This whole cultural debate fascinated her. 'It was a wonderful opening up. I wasn't only ready for it. I was yearning for it.'

Mary had to work hard to progress from Moran's French Grammar[2] to proper spoken French, but her real leap was intellectual. In class and at the Foyer she was discussing philosophy, political thought and even theology. 'It was all possible! I was in a foreign country, speaking its language, where this was what you did. You challenged, you thought conceptually, you read.' It was heady stuff. 'Everything from Kafka to Camus, wonderful, wonderful, wonderful. I was a compulsive reader. Being in an intellectual environment was so nice, so different.' It was only then she realised that the country she had come from stifled intellectual thought. In Ireland, many of the authors she was reading had had their works banned as 'indecent or obscene'. The censorship had applied to books by André Gide, Jean-Paul Sartre, as well as Ernest Hemingway, John Steinbeck, Tennessee Williams, not to mention Samuel Beckett – and, of course, most notoriously, James Joyce's novel *Ulysses*, though never officially banned, was confiscated by customs officers in his own country for years.

She never felt more at home than she did in Paris, more comfortable with being the outsider, more comfortable with a culture that encouraged her to question everything. It was there that she made the first big decision of her life. At the age of seventeen-and-a-half she stopped going to mass regularly because she could no longer intellectually justify it.

'I was very angry at a lot of what the Church stood for at that time, at how religion could become power-play and oppressive, undermining the true sense of spirituality and the true ethical norms and standards that are the highest reaches of the human mind.' But only a year earlier, at school, she had wanted to be a nun, only months earlier she was shocked that a nun would encourage her to drink. Was Paris responsible for such a change? 'I was contemplating becoming a nun because religion was so important. But I was asking a lot of questions that weren't being answered. And then I came to Paris and I started to re-ask in a more fundamental way. I heard more profound arguments about religion itself, about spirituality, about the contributions of different religions, about different linkages between human beings.'

Mary's own spiritual inspiration came from her sense of justice. She has always admired spiritual people, whether religious or aesthetic, but her own source of creativity and idealism was primarily an ethical one. She looked to find others, from whatever background, who shared those ethical values. Some of those were within the Catholic Church. She didn't turn her back on Catholicism totally, but she knew that in those days good Catholics did not question the Church and she felt uneasy 'until I talked to Father Jack Kelly at UCD, and he reconciled me to the fact that probably for the rest of my life I would be questioning, and that that in itself was a way of seeking.'

It could also be said that for the rest of her life, there would be a bit of that lost nun in Mary – the slight public starchiness, the commitment to high ideals, the refusal to accept that the world could not be converted to new ways. It was what used to be called a sense of vocation, and it may well explain why it was often among those nuns and priests who fought for social justice that Mary would later feel particularly at home.

Paris woke her up intellectually but it woke her up in other ways, too. She remembers whizzing around on the back of a motor-bike with a well-off Canadian friend, Cherry Richards, 'who lived it up in no uncertain terms'. Paris made her less prudish, even appealed, she says, to a bawdy streak of humour that she inherited from her mother. It opened her eyes. 'It was the first time I had come across homosexuality. I was astounded because I hadn't even heard that it was possible. And yet through literature and lifestyles in Paris, it was something that I took on board with great interest at the time.'

There were no love affairs. 'I was a slow starter.' But she made another important choice. She had hoped to be a writer. 'I would love to have been a Camus.' She tried. She wrote some poetry but decided it wasn't for her. All around her on the streets of Paris was the backwash from the Algerian war – explosions, arrests, security clampdowns, the whole debate about the rights of a colonised people to their independence. It was fertile ground for a human rights debate. 'It raised so many issues, some of which were part of the reason I decided to study law.'

Mary knew that after Paris, life would be more difficult at home. Her ideas had changed so much, and perhaps the one person she might have been able to talk to was gone – her grandfather. While she was away, H.C. Bourke had died and for financial reasons, she hadn't been allowed to come home for his funeral. 'I was deeply lonely and distressed by my grandfather's death and hid myself away in my room for a week and caused great difficulty for everybody. I wouldn't eat. I literally mourned.'

She came back to spend a year in Ballina studying for a scholarship to Trinity College Dublin. When she could, she took her books up to her grandfather's empty house which was soon to be sold, a decision she resented fiercely. Amana held memories of him, but it also got her away from home and potentially sticky conversations. 'I had big problems of communications with my parents,' she says. 'I recognised early on that I had gone on a journey that they would never go on, that would distress them if I tried to bring them with me, and which, at the end of the day, just wasn't necessary. I had an extremely good relationship with my father and mother despite that. And I just decided that I would cease to try to have communication on that level because there was no purpose to it and it would hurt.'

This was a tough seventeen-year-old – sure she was right and sure there was no point in wasting emotional energy arguing with her parents. This is how she would be all her life – independent-minded and uncompromising, not one of life's natural mediators. It would be well into the presidential election campaign before she would realise the value of persuasion, of reassurance, seeing an opponent's point of view in order to better persuade him or her of her own.

But one thing never changed. She would rather be lonely than wrong. She was often lonely.

3

UNIVERSITY CHALLENGE

If it seems odd that Dr Aubrey Bourke would have to seek a bishop's permission for his daughter to go to Trinity College, it's worth remembering the power then wielded by a prelate of the Catholic Church. John Charles McQuaid, Archbishop of Dublin, could make decisions about people's very livelihoods and he did, every day. When the artist Maurice McGonigal wanted to send his son Muiris to Trinity, it was made clear to him that there would be a price to pay. Muiris's younger brother, Ciaran, then about fourteen, remembers the parish priest calling to communicate His Grace's displeasure. His Grace warned that there were divorced people in Trinity who were morally unsuitable to be in charge of Catholic young men; that if Mr McGonigal persisted, he would lose all Church commissions – he would never again paint a Catholic bishop, or a Station of the Cross, and there would be no place for his younger son at any Catholic school.[1] This was power one ignored at one's peril.

But, as often happens, power shouts loudest when it is most threatened. The Irish Constitution of 1937 gave the Catholic Church a 'special position' as well as reflecting its social attitudes, particularly on divorce. But by the 1950s the Church felt the need to come out fighting against what it saw as creeping socialism and secularisation – the welfare state, socialised medicine, increasing state control of education. The bishops helped to kill off the Mother and Child scheme, which would have provided a comprehensive and free scheme of mother and child health care, on the basis that the officials involved were not guaranteed to 'respect Catholic moral teaching'.[2] They returned to the pre-war denunciations of drink and dancing, opposing the extension of Sunday opening hours, and insisting in many dioceses that dances finish at midnight or earlier. Bishop Lucey of Cork declared that he and his fellow-bishops 'were the final arbiters of right and wrong even in political matters'.[3]

The Catholic bishops had always been deeply suspicious of Trinity College, which they saw rightly as a bulwark of the Protestant ascendancy in Ireland and a training school for Protestant divines. In 1927 they banned priests from recommending that young people go to Trinity. In 1944 John Charles McQuaid tightened the screw by specifically banning Catholics in his arch-diocese under 'pain of mortal sin' from attending Trinity. The ban was extended to the whole country in 1960 with John Charles as the only court of appeal competent 'to decide . . . in what circumstances and with what guarantees against the dangers of perversion, attendance at that college may be tolerated'.[4]

So Dr Bourke, whose elder sons Oliver and Aubrey had been able to enter Trinity with their local bishop's permission, found himself in 1963 beating a path to the archbishop's door.

As he drove to Dublin, Tessa read to him the newspaper reports of Dr McQuaid's latest attack on Trinity.[5] Dr Bourke knew he would never get to see the archbishop if he said he wanted his daughter to go to Trinity. So he gained access by pretending he had marital problems. The archbishop, once it was explained that Trinity was the family tradition, graciously gave his permission. It was a rigmarole Dr Bourke refused to go through again for Henry and Adrian. 'I'd grown up a bit by then. I said to hell with everybody!' and indeed the Catholic Church had given up that particular struggle by 1970 when the bishops asked Rome's permission to end the ban.

But the whole incident shows what a close stranglehold the Catholic Church had over ordinary people's lives. Without the archbishop's permission, the headmistress of Mount Anville could not have written the necessary letter recommending Mary for an entrance scholarship. In those pre-grant days, the Bourkes might have got by without a scholarship, but other families might not.

This was the power that Mary Bourke would take on, even as a student. The very laws of the country obediently reflected Catholic moral teaching, laws to be obeyed even by those of other religions or none, those who had no objection to contraception, divorce, the decriminalising of homosexuality. She would argue for the end of what was effectively a confessional state.

If Archbishop McQuaid feared the perversion of Catholic students at Trinity, then in Mary's case he was too late – the damage had been done in Paris. But Trinity was not under his control, whereas University College Dublin, the other big Dublin university, was, to quote Labour leader and former student radical Ruairi Quinn, a 'Catholic boys' academy'. At that time the archbishop's writ ran there. Monsignor Horgan, the much feared Dean of Philosophy and Sociology, was the archbishop's lieutenant in UCD. He ensured that during the 1950s and 1960s the major chairs in philosophy and the social sciences were held by priests. While most were well-qualified and some were liberal, they fulfilled the archbishop's need to ensure that sensitive disciplines like ethics, philosophy, politics, education, psychology and sociology were in Catholic hands. The big student societies were controlled by boys from the influential Catholic schools. This, after all, had been Cardinal Newman's Catholic University. It produced the ruling cadre which maintained conservative Catholic Ireland. Trinity, on the other hand, had few Catholic students and a large overseas contingent. Founded during the reign of Elizabeth I, it was often chosen as an elegant third option by students from England or the colonies who weren't accepted by Oxbridge. It was considered Protestant enough to be safe for Northern Unionists, like the former head of the Orange Order, the Rev. Martin Smyth. In what was almost a perfect Catholic monoculture, it was an island of dissent – somewhat languorous dissent to be sure, but independent enough at least to allow for a questioning mind.

It was also fun. And the Bourkes had fun. At Trinity, unlike any other university in the country except Maynooth, the Catholic seminary and university, students and staff lived on campus and social events were encouraged as part of college life. The Bourkes as good as lived on campus with their own house in Westland Row backing on to the college. The stories of Wilde House (it was Oscar's birthplace) are numberless.

Mary's elder brothers, Oliver and Aubrey, studied medicine and rugby, and partied. A fellow medical student remembers a party where they chased a sheep up the stairs of Wilde House. Then there was the junior doctors' party at the Adelaide Hospital where the brothers came with their own welcome, a plastic dustbin full of home-made beer. After the Bourkes arrived, the party took off like a bomb and eventually their Adelaide hosts found out why. The beer was generously laced with meths.

There was the famous Law Society party – Henry remembers that Mary was there – where the bath was filled with a mixture of gin, vodka, vermouth and beer, white lemonade and brandy as well. 'It was a great concoction,' he says. 'People were literally falling down. It was a dynamite of a drink.' The finishing touch was added when a senior academic sat fully clothed in the bath and fell asleep. Shane Ross, now a senator for Trinity, partied with the brothers. 'They were very well-off undergraduates,' says Ross, who, as a representative of the old Protestant tradition, made a conservative alliance with the younger Bourkes on the Student Representative Council. 'They were known as the Bourke mafia – four very large rugger-buggers roaming the place in a pack. I met them politically because of the SRC, when they were the right who provided some sort of opposition to the left wing culture of the time, led by the Maoist-inspired Internationalists. Henry and Adrian weren't only establishment – they were official Trinity's favourite politicians. They always wore pin-stripe suits as opposed to jeans. They were immensely self-confident, very good company, annoying, outrageous; they didn't quite feel the law of the land applied to them.'[6]

Adrian had replaced left-winger Alan Matthews as SRC president, and was then unseated in turn when the vote, which had been limited to SRC officers, was extended to the whole student body. 'Predictably he was beaten. Anyone who looked like a Tory MP was bound to be beaten,' says Ross.

Mary took little part in their revelries, he says. 'She was an adult, and they were children. She was a serious person, and they were hedonistic and not taking life seriously.' He remembers going back to Westland Row for breakfast after late nights on the town. Anne (known as Nan) Coyne, who had been sent up from the west to care for them, didn't keep them in order. Only their mother could do that. 'If their mother was in town, then they were under house arrest. They were very macho – not afraid of anyone, but they made it quite clear that if their mother was in town, they weren't coming out to play. They were scared stiff of their mother,' he says. 'I liked her. She was very definite. They kept her in the background because they didn't want people like me telling her things about them. She was the only one who could put the fear of God into them.'

Mary enjoyed the Dublin house, especially when all five of them were there. But there were things she didn't enjoy, such as the brothers' interest in horses and, she says, 'their hocking our furniture to pay for them.' Her brother Aubrey discovered in his pre-med year that veterinary students, in the pursuit of their studies, were allowed free into the races. He approached every vet he knew until he found one, Malcolm Argyle, who said he wasn't interested in racing. 'Okay,' said Aubrey. 'For the next year, I'm you.'[7] Mary, says Henry, could be cross and, particularly coming up to exams, could lay down the law. 'There were two dimensions that I had had enough of,' says Mary, who always had nine o'clock lectures. 'Firstly their coming in late at night, and secondly, the fry-ups. You'd come down in the morning to the very small kitchenette and you couldn't even get in the door for the pots and pans, and from time to time I would explode.'

Mary had her twenty-first birthday party at the house. It was a big affair, black tie and evening dress and everybody came. But her social life was quieter than her brothers' and she didn't share their politics. 'The elder brothers weren't interested, but Henry and Adrian had student political views and involvements that I wouldn't have shared. I was always seen as the leftie. I preferred to argue, not with them, but with my own contemporaries.'

One of those contemporaries was the poet Eavan Boland, who remains one of her closest friends to this day. 'I would love to have been able to write, to be a poet. That's why the friendship with Eavan was so important to me – she was the writer I couldn't be. The friendship was more than that, but what I loved about her was that she was the writer. She was doing it.'

They met as second-year students in the old coffee bar in the Rubrics in Trinity. Mary was the model student who had taken a first in her exams. Eavan, already a published poet, had dropped out of the honours school and felt disaffected by the whole academic regime. 'Trinity was very structured, with very small classes. I found it quite oppressive. I think Mary has always had slightly different attitudes to those things,' says Eavan. 'I was surprised at how much she was willing to go out of her way to challenge the structures that were there but yet always to remain within those structures, whereas I was much more alienated by them.'[8] Eavan later went on to have a brilliant academic career, but she remembers from that very first day how Mary, who would always work within the system, sympathised with those who felt alienated from it.

They became friends at that first meeting. 'She was shy, very pretty and graceful with a definite air, a great warmth.' Eavan admired a ring Mary was wearing with the motto in old French: 'Un Roi, Une Foi, Une Loi' (one king, one faith, one law), a family motto for the Norman Bourkes.

'She came from a background which would be considered landed – I suppose what in a Trollope novel would have been the squirearchy – whereas I came from a completely different background.' Eavan's mother was an artist, and her father a senior Irish diplomat who presided over the UN General Assembly.

Mary suggested lunch and Eavan agreed, presuming they were going to the students' Buttery. 'Of course, we went home to lunch at Westland Row. And what struck me was how very structured it was, how very orderly compared with the life I knew students to live.' Nan Coyne provided meals, and glasses of milk waited in the entrance hall to be drunk every morning. Food was sent up from Ballina, and they had an account at the local shop. Mary had her own room, and the brothers had theirs. Despite their differences,

Mary and Eavan would have a life-long friendship. 'I lived in the more Bohemian, literary side of college which, now that I look back, was always the more headily arrogant side. Mary was very involved in all those things like Trinity week which I wouldn't have touched with a forty-foot pole. Mary would put on her hat and go to the garden party – which I couldn't understand, and so would all her brothers,' says Eavan. 'She had a very cheerful sense of the forms of a society and went along and had a laugh and was very convivial.'

Mary and Eavan weren't such an odd couple, though. Joyce scholar and Senator, David Norris, who was at Trinity at the same time says: 'They had similar temperaments. Olympian qualities. They had a high-mindedness and a sense of destiny.'[9]

Nobody in those days would have called Nick Robinson Olympian. Even then he was a cartoonist, poking fun at the powers-that-be. He and Mary were friends for years, but Nick had a number of girlfriends, including broadcaster Ruth Buchanan. 'He was much thinner then, dark and very attractive. One of the lovely things about being a poverty-stricken student and going out with Nick Robinson, was that he was extremely well-off,' says Ruth.

Nick had an income other students envied. His weekly posters for college societies brought in a steady income. 'And he had a very generous father who sometimes let us eat Italian food and wine on his account in Bernardo's Restaurant. But for me, Nick was too nice. I think he is a perfect husband for Mary Robinson because he is very supportive. If he was ambitious, he never showed it.'[10] Nick was attracted to ambitious women, she says. Ruth herself was ambitious, 'and maybe he liked that. He would have backed me in anything I wanted to do.

'He wasn't wild like Henry and Adrian Bourke. He was a respectable Protestant young man,' she says. 'He knew about art.' She remembers Jack B. Yeats' paintings on the wall at the Robinson home, and visits to Victor Waddington, the art dealer, in London. She remembers Nick's musician brother, Andrew, teaching her to play the guitar. 'They were a cultivated family.'

Nick Robinson and Mary Bourke were in the same law class and both took first-class honours in their first year. Nick was friendly with Mary's brothers who helped add to the bill in Bernardo's Restaurant. He became more and more interested in her over the years in Trinity, but she held off. There were exams to be taken, causes to be taken up. In her second year in Trinity she won 'schol', a special scheme of undergraduate scholarships to honour Trinity's emerging 'scholars'. It entitled her to remission of fees and a quarterly salary of £45, plus £50 in lieu of meals in Commons which as a woman she couldn't attend. For Mary, these scholarships were flags of independence. This, after all, was a student whose mother wouldn't hear of her taking a summer job as a waitress. She hated being a burden on her parents, hated 'always being the recipient'.

She disliked the fustiness of Trinity traditions – no women allowed in the Hist or Phil debating societies, or in Commons – and she disliked the snobbery of societies such as Players, run in those days largely by the English contingent. Unlike most Trinity students who didn't deign to mix outside the college, Mary gravitated more and more to University College Dublin, co-editing a student law review, *Justice*, produced by both universities, and going to debates at the Literary and Historical Society.

'I was proud of that fact in a quiet way – it was a strange thing in those days to have a Trinity student visiting UCD at Earlsfort Terrace,' she says. 'I think, again, I was resisting any snobbery.' She also found debate in UCD livelier, more real – perhaps because UCD, for all its faults, was in the mainstream of Irish life. Trinity was not.

And yet, would a law student from a primarily Catholic university like UCD have dared to question the power of the Catholic Church in Ireland, as Mary Bourke did in her inaugural address as auditor of Trinity's Law Society in February 1967? Her chosen title was 'Law and Morality', her theme the separation of church and state, the argument that the Constitution and laws of the Irish state should not reflect the moral teaching of one church.

Mary knew she could hardly have chosen a more sensitive target, so in preparing her paper she went to Ireland's acknowledged expert on the Constitution, John M. Kelly, UCD's brilliant young

Professor of Roman Law and Jurisprudence. His reaction shattered her. When she told him the area she was going to address, he said: 'Ah no, I wouldn't. There's no law in that area of law and morality.' No law in addressing the constitutional ban on divorce and the laws against family planning? Mary was flattened by the reaction. She thinks he was trying to warn her off a clash with the Church. 'I think I was hearing John, the Catholic professor, at that time,' she says. 'It was a barrier I had to surmount intellectually, a terrible blow intellectually.'

John Kelly might well have feared for her, because Mary was about to engage in a battle that would rage for three decades, and with the greatest power in the land. She was about to plan a campaign that would dominate her legal career, her political career, but one that would cost her most grief in private. She might have the freedom of speech allowed to Trinity's Law Society Auditor and a future barrister. But in the end, Mary Bourke was a Catholic from Ballina and, in any battle with the Church, her parents could be held hostage.

She sent the paper to them, as Dr Bourke remembers. 'And Tessa read it. "Gosh, this is the end. She can't say things like this, about contraception and everything." Oliver and Aubrey said: "She's talking about the pill and she hasn't a hell of an idea what the pill is."'[11]

As to his own reaction: 'I nearly fell over backwards. I thought, she can't, she can't! She was to deliver this in a few days, in a Catholic country. I'm a Catholic, my parents – what am I going to do?' He consulted a priest friend, Canon McDonnell, later to be bishop, who told him that these were the thoughts of a young student talking to a closed university society and that he shouldn't worry. On this advice, he calmed down and, with Mrs Bourke, proudly attended Mary's inaugural address. Mother White from Mount Anville was there, along with Mother Stephenson who says gently that she feared Mary was in danger of being 'on the wrong track' in her thinking that night.[12] Mr Justice Kingsmill-Moore presided, and the respondent to her paper was Professor H.L.A. Hart of Oxford, a leading voice in the British debate on the role of law in relation to public and private morality.

31

Mary agreed with him that the preservation of morality did not require the legal enforcement of a society's moral code. 'I see a clear distinction between an ethical system from which I may draw my own values and philosophy of life, and the rules which I must obey under Irish law or incur criminal sanctions.' She argued that the ban on divorce should be taken out of the Constitution.

'It is possible for a Catholic majority to introduce legislation permitting divorce for those who feel justified in availing of this facility on moral grounds, without this in any way affecting their moral attitude towards marriage and divorce.'[13]

The law against contraceptives should be repealed as it was 'a legal infringement on the freedom of non-Catholics in this country'.[14]

She said that suicide, a mortal sin in Catholic Church eyes, should no longer be regarded as a crime and asked how Christian it was to retain capital punishment, or to offer imprisonment as the main sanction even for non-violent crimes.

Freedom, she said, required that there were residual areas of great importance where people felt free to act as they liked without being regulated by law, and in Ireland those residual areas were too restricted.

This would be the agenda for the next thirty years. Her life as a liberal campaigning lawyer was already mapped out. But she wasn't yet a politician. Harvard would see to that.

4

WE SHALL OVERCOME

It was 6 December 1995 and Bill and Hillary Clinton still glowed from the reception they'd received in Belfast the day before. Ireland was good news and they wanted more of it.

As they strolled with Mary and Nick Robinson in the grounds of Áras an Uachtaráin, they asked when the Robinsons would make their expected US state visit. No Irish President had made such a visit since de Valera in 1964 and Mary Robinson, by now a firm favourite with the US public, and with the Clintons, would be warmly welcomed. It would be good for US-Irish relations, good for business, good for everybody.

So Bill Clinton said: 'And you're going to come in June?'

'Well, I'm hoping to,' said Mary, 'but nobody's confirmed it.'

'Oh, but Hillary and I want you to come.'

The Clintons were puzzled, but President Robinson knew what was going on. John Bruton's government didn't want her to go to Washington. 'Washington was government turf still – that was the attitude of officials as well as government. It was too big a place and too important,' she says.

Successive governments had ensured that she had never made a state visit to Washington. It was the power centre of the world, jealously guarded by politicians and policy-makers, not somewhere to find oneself upstaged by the President. President Clinton's interest in the Irish peace process had ensured unprecedented access for the Irish to the White House. What Irish politician wants to share that limelight with an internationally known, popular Irish President?

'It wasn't really being pushed along. State visits have to be promoted,' she says. So Bill Clinton pushed it. In College Green in Dublin that afternoon, facing another ecstatic crowd, he declared that he was looking forward to Mrs Robinson's state visit. 'It wasn't happening up to then,' she says.

But no one ignores the US President. In June 1996, Mary Robinson went to Washington.

Even before that historic visit, the two couples had met frequently and got on well. They would exchange notes and Mary would often receive informal greetings through senior US figures – 'Hillary was asking for you.' The Clintons knew how to charm. And, after all, these were four lawyers, three of whom had been politicised in the Yale and Harvard law schools in the heady days of the late sixties. They remembered the songs, the sit-ins, the marches. In their way, all three had fought the liberal fight, and they had overcome. No Taoiseach (Prime Minister) could easily compete with the intensity of that shared experience.

Harvard was where Mary Robinson learned to fight. She knew how to question, thoughtfully, as a lawyer should. Now she would learn to challenge, to put up her fists and take on all comers. She would learn to be a politician.

Not straight away, however. She arrived at Harvard in 1967, late for the start of term, and fresh from exams from which she emerged top of her class and a qualified barrister. Waiting for her was a supper invitation from the President of the Law School, the formidable Dean Griswold, on whom John Houseman's character in the television series *Paper Chase* was said to be based.

Harvard took a keen interest in the foreign students to whom it had awarded fellowships and the faculty went to some trouble to entertain them. It expected that the students, in turn, would be duly conscious of their great fortune in being chosen by Harvard Law School.

No one is more formal than formal Americans, and Mary found herself standing in a stiff semi-circle of students in the Griswolds' sitting-room making polite conversation. Then, as if to put the final chill on the gathering, Professor Griswold asked each student to say a few words about themselves – why they had come to Harvard, and what they hoped to gain from it.

Mary remembers that the three or four people before her said things such as: 'It is the greatest moment of my life to have the privilege of coming to Harvard Law School . . . everything is wonderful . . . I will work very, very hard. When I go back to my country, because I am a graduate of Harvard, doors will open . . .'

Mary, fresh from easygoing Trinity College Dublin, where neither students nor staff took themselves too seriously, decided to lighten up the proceedings. 'I'm Mary Bourke from Ballina and I'm here to have a good time,' she said cheerfully. 'I hope I pass exams and get a degree but, in any case, I'm going to enjoy myself,' she finished. 'I suddenly realised that the Gris was looking at me with a baleful gaze. Nobody laughed or tittered at my joke. I froze. Afterwards there was a great deal of whispering. "You have a nerve!" And you know, it wasn't a nerve, it was innocence. I hadn't realised that this fellow caused terror in the hearts of everyone.' Professor Griswold told colleagues after that evening that this Mary Bourke was someone to be watched.

He was right – but then in the US in the autumn of 1967, there was a whole mutinous student body to be watched. A spirit of change was sweeping the country. Mary remembers: 'Vietnam was the key, Vietnam and the civil rights movement. They were questioning their whole society.' Already that year about 100,000 people, led by Dr Martin Luther King and the famous paediatrician, Dr Benjamin Spock, had taken part in New York's biggest ever demonstration against US involvement in the war between South Vietnam and communist North Vietnam. In October, large anti-war demonstrations in Washington and Oakland, California, led to outbreaks of violence. In December, Irish politician and intellectual, Dr Conor Cruise O'Brien, then Professor of Humanities at New York University, was arrested along with Dr Spock and the poet, Allen Ginsberg, during an anti-war demonstration in New York.[1] The campus at Columbia

University would erupt in this period, as would Berkeley. Even in the hallowed halls of Harvard Law School the sit-in meetings had begun and Mary was there.

'I sat in on endless discussions where we sat on the floor for the weekend, practically, and we slept through various discussion sessions on the morality of the war in Vietnam, the morality of America's participation, the morality of the draft. And then that led to discussions about the approach of the Law School itself, the teaching of law, the selection of the topics to be taught, the lack of equal participation.

'It was a time apart, a limited time, a window. I came in on this idealism: people avoiding the draft, lecturers sitting on the floor with students debating 'society' – heady stuff! I was lucky.'

It *was* an idealistic time. For all his stance on the Vietnam War, Lyndon Johnson was actually implementing the poverty and civil rights promises made by President Kennedy. Mary Bourke was impressed to find that the really bright lawyers in Harvard weren't bound for Wall Street but for the federal poverty programmes and civil rights programmes.

It was a different culture, a different set of attitudes from anything her legal education in Ireland had led her to expect. Professor Des Morton in Trinity had once dragged his class out to a travellers' camp, and made them question how the law could be used to change the poverty and discrimination they saw around them. 'That was one of the few exposures I had had to law interfacing with poverty. I was very disturbed by that lack.'

One of the courses she took in Harvard addressed those issues directly. Urban Legal Studies was a response to the growing problem of the improverished inner city ghettoes which developed as the middle-class fled to the suburbs, a problem Dublin would face within the decade. Professor Adam Yarmolinsky joined them at their weekend sit-ins and discussed the role of the law in an urban environment. Unemployment, inadequate health and social services, poor schools, bad housing – and the drug-addiction, crime, violence and family breakdown which went along with them – all these presented challenges to the law, demanded changes in the way the law was interpreted and applied.

In courses on the American Constitution, Harvard also taught her how a Constitution and a Bill of Rights, or, in Irish terms, a Constitution and the European Convention on Human Rights, could be used to bring about social change. This was the road she would travel, again and again, to force the granting of women's rights, gay rights, human rights. It taught her, years before Ireland joined the then European Community, to recognise how a federal system worked, and the conflict that can arise between international and state law. 'That was the first time I recognised the international dimension of making legal changes,' she says. 'I suddenly understood the potential of the international level influencing the national level.' Significantly, she did her Harvard thesis on the Rome Treaty, and competition law in the European Community. Part of the excitement of Harvard was that it brought in the outside world. Lecturers moved easily between the academic and the commercial and political spheres: Abram Chayes, who had been one of John F. Kennedy's legal advisers at the time of the Cuban missile crisis, taught international legal process, and used the Cuban crisis as a case study in class. Alan Dershowitz, now a famous trial lawyer, taught law and psychiatry as did Alan Stone. Archibald Cox, who later went on as an independent counsel to investigate President Nixon, taught securities law. These were political high-flyers from whom Mary learned to appreciate that law is practised in a political context.

And then there were the brilliant lecturers. Professor Paul Freund taught American constitutional law at Harvard. His was an extra course that Mary chose to sit in on, and she remembers 'at the end of his course the students stood up and gave him a standing ovation'.

A glutton for extra classes, she went across Harvard Square to the University itself to attend the course on the economics of India by quintessential East Coast liberal J.K. Galbraith. He had just returned as the Kennedy-appointed ambassador there. She had a letter of introduction to him and he gave her one of his books. 'I was very surprised at his lectures because he was still lecturing in the tradition that we were used to – the written lecture that he would simply read out. After the excitement and participation of the Law School,' she says, 'I wasn't that impressed.'

Harvard Law School made its students hop. Students were assigned a seat for the year so absence was noted. Lecturers had a chart of the class and could pounce suddenly on a chosen target. 'In Harvard you had such a competitive milieu that you never came in unprepared.' Unlike the self-deprecatory Irish, Harvard students were confident, confident to speak up and speak out, confident because they were prepared.

Harvard made her tough, but what she saw on the streets made her radical. She remembers feeling at odds with the sentimental 'greenery' of the Boston Irish, and even more at odds with their racism in districts like South Boston. She was appalled by the poverty of the black areas, and remembers Boston being brought almost to a halt the week in April 1968 when Martin Luther King was assassinated. 'There were riots in the black areas of Boston and we were warned not to go into Roxborough,' she says. 'It was very close, you know, the whole sense of a society that was very divided.' She was shaken by the depth of racial hatred, shocked that a man of peace should be the victim of such violence. The next shock was Robert Kennedy's assassination in June 1968, just after she had graduated. Her father was with her and as radio and television ran and re-ran the shooting in California, they 'went out on a boat tour around Manhattan to get away from the sheer awfulness of American violence'.

It was a hard lesson. Those who fight for political reform pay a price, but in doing it they can inspire a whole generation. In Northern Ireland that same summer, police batons would rain down on those marching for change. They sang the same song: We Shall Overcome. They had the same dream.

On the streets of Dublin that same year, students would join the Dublin Housing Action Committee to demand an end to slums and poverty. In Ireland, as in the US, the attitudes behind civil war and cold war politics were being challenged and the real enemies exposed – discrimination, injustice, want.

It was time to come home, time to join the battle, and Mary says that by summer 1968 Harvard had prepared her for it.

'I benefited from a kind of Harvard arrogance. You have the right to question. The fact that you're young doesn't stop you from having thoughts and developing them. Think on! That attitude was very much responsible for my questioning as to why Trinity senators always seemed to be elderly male professors and why I was ready to stand. That was the effect of Harvard assertiveness. Get up and do.'

She did. A year after her return from Harvard with a Masters (first class), Mary Bourke, part-time law tutor at UCD and apprentice barrister on the western circuit, decided she would run for the Irish Senate in the 1969 election. Trinity College had three seats in the Irish upper house and never in the history of the state had one of those seats been held by a woman, or by a Catholic. No one expected her to win.

'We didn't take her seriously,' says Senator Shane Ross whose father, John Ross, who lost his Senate seat in 1965, expected to take the seat now made vacant by the retirement of Professor William B. Stanford. It was assumed that Ross would be returned along with sitting senators, Owen Sheehy Skeffington and Dr W.J.E. Jessop. 'Here was this twenty-four-year-old *woman*. Our campaign was casual. There wasn't a lot done to oppose her,' says Shane Ross.

Mary set out the broadest possible stall for the Senate. She stood for a pluralist society which would recognise the 'validity of moral standards which differ in some respects from those held by the majority of the country'.[2]

She mentioned her Law Society speech which advocated the reform of the divorce and contraception laws and the ending of other constraints on individual liberty. 'As a modern European country, Ireland ought to introduce a certain flexibility in these areas, in order not to become isolated from accepted standards elsewhere.'[3]

And she made a demure play for the women's vote. Women were beginning, she said, to play a significant part in the political, economic and social life of the country. 'This achievement is a much more cogent achievement than the slogans of an aggressive feminist. The more we are ready to branch out and fulfil ourselves in the life of the country, the more doors will open in the face of quiet ability and feminine qualities of efficiency and good humour.'

Like all the other candidates, she amassed the most impressive Protestant support she could find. 'We all had this childish competition to get as many clergymen as we could,' says Shane Ross. She was proposed by Regius Professor of Law, Charles Bueno McKenna, then head of the Trinity law school, and seconded by Nick's father, financier Howard Waterhouse Robinson, a pillar of the Church of Ireland. Her list of nominators and her supporting committee included a great number of clergymen: the Archbishop of Dublin, George Otto Simms; Dr Donald Caird, Dean of Ossory; the bishop of Tuam, Killala and Achonry, the Rt Rev. Arthur Hamilton Butler; Rev. Professor Arthur Aston Luce, her father's friend in Mayo; the Dean of Killala, Very Rev. J.E.B. Ashton; Rev. S.R. Auld, and Dean Buchanan of Kildare, father of broadcaster Ruth Buchanan. Also on the list were a school of Trinity professors: the eminent medieval historian, Professor Jocelyn Otway Ruthven; mathematician Professor David Spearman, as well as Professors Chubb, Dawson, Greene, Heuston, Henry, Lydon, Moody, Moran, Murdoch, O'Meara, Rice, Ryan, Walton, Wormell, and Wright. She had the support of poets, Professor Brendan Kennelly, her friend Eavan Boland, and Micheal O Siadhail; and she had Thekla Beere, then the only woman to have penetrated the higher levels of the civil service.

'She went to immense lengths to market herself,' says Shane Ross. 'She was identified so much with the liberal issues of contraception and divorce – anti-Catholic-hierarchy issues fashionable among Protestants. Protestants were comfortable voting against John Charles McQuaid and his ban on Catholics attending Trinity. And they felt it was extra liberal and extra fun because *she* was a Catholic.'

Mary had no instant election team, or rather she had – her family. The Senate election is by postal vote of Trinity's graduates, so she broke down the list of electors into personal contacts. Oliver and Aubrey canvassed the doctors; Henry and Adrian and herself the lawyers and SRC connections; Nick mobilised his family's Trinity contacts and, having just returned from London, any Trinity graduates there. And Mrs Bourke recruited any Trinity friends in the west and then came up to Westland Row and ran the election canteen. Mount Anville girls were drafted in to stuff envelopes and Ann Lane, later to be Mary's secretary, who was then working for Adrian on the Trinity SRC, organised the office.

There was a lot of hard work and there was some luck. Mary had sat the examination for the Reid Professorship in Trinity, then a five-year, part-time lecturer's post in Penal Legislation, Constitutional and Criminal Law, and the Law of Evidence (1888). The title was impressive.

'She was one of the most brilliant minds of her generation,' remembers Shane Ross, who was working on his father's campaign. 'And she won the Reid. I'll never forget that awful moment when I picked up the *Irish Times* and there she was with her new title of Professor Mary T. Bourke – right in the middle of a Senate election campaign!'

The day of the Senate election count, 12 August 1969, was the day that brought the Troubles in Northern Ireland to full crisis point. The Protestant Apprentice Boys' march in Derry provoked Catholic riots.[4] For two days the crowds fought the Royal Ulster Constabulary in the now famous Battle of the Bogside. The Irish Taoiseach, Jack Lynch, said the Republic could not stand by and he called for a UN force to keep the peace. The British Home Secretary, James Callaghan, warned that within twenty-four hours there could be civil war in Northern Ireland and an invasion from the Republic. British troops were sent in to replace the police. Suddenly it seemed as if anything could happen. The old certainties had gone. Senator Owen Sheehy Skeffington, pacifist, humanist, socialist and so relaxed about his own re-election that he had disappeared to France on holidays – was desperate to keep up with the turbulent events at home. He stretched his radio aerial as far as he could to pick up the news from RTE, Ireland's state broadcasting service.

He listened through the crackling static until the newsreader came to the Senate count. 'Surprise result in the Trinity election, a new senator, Mary Bourke, elected,' announced the radio and promptly died. Sheehy Skeffington was open-mouthed. Which candidate had she pushed out? Was it he?

As it happened, it was John Ross, who would never run for the Senate again. A new voice had entered politics, an awkward voice asking awkward questions. The answers would be a long time coming.

5

MR AND MRS ROBINSON

When Mary Bourke married Nick Robinson, there was no room for doubt. 'I was going to have to leave my family to commit myself,' she says. For a while, her family cut off all contact. 'Even then, I felt, it's a good thing for me that I'm having to pay a price to marry Nick because I have to be terribly sure.'

She'd had plenty of time to make sure. They'd been friends since first year at university and stayed that way throughout Nick's romances with various girlfriends. Then he became serious. As Mary Bourke pursued her studies, Nick pursued Mary Bourke. 'He became more strategically determined to distract me from my po-faced hard working. And he would come to the library with a rose and say: "Come on, now. You've done enough."' she says. 'And on the morning I was sitting my finals in the King's Inns, he presented me with an orchid and said: "I dare you to wear that for the finals." So I put it on and wore it . . . He knew that side of me that wanted to let the hair down and have fun and he always managed to draw it out.'

They had gone to Lamb Doyle's, a restaurant in the Dublin Mountains, to celebrate their first-year exams. Mary liked Nick best of the group, all of whom had taken first-class honours. But Nick wasn't interested in remaining a model law student. 'I didn't see myself becoming a lawyer at that stage. I saw myself as a journalist or a cartoonist. Looking back now, I could well have read history, or history of art. I painted. I worked for *Trinity News* and *TCD Miscellany*. I was exhibited in Trinity exhibitions. I had a young creative mind and I felt I had been frog-marched into the law.' His father had studied law at Trinity, his grandfather had been a barrister, and Nick was bright enough to do well. He would become auditor of the Law Society, and win the Law Society's Vincent Delaney medal in his final year in Trinity, and go on to become a solicitor in the seventies. But the law never sustained his interest. He took after his artist mother, Lucy Douglas.

After college he worked as a cartoonist in London for a time and then did cartoons for the *Irish Times*. All his life he would have the cartoonist's eye for the pompous and the ridiculous.

Nick's father Howard Waterhouse Robinson was a successful accountant and financier who started his own bank – the City of Dublin bank. The Waterhouses, who had come from Sheffield at the beginning of the nineteenth century, were jewellers and silver-smiths to the Irish Lords Lieutenant – the famous Waterhouse clock in Dame Street marked their business premises. The Robinsons, who came from England in the eighteenth century, were originally coopers. Like the Bourkes, they served the British Empire through the generations and two of Nick's uncles were Spitfire pilots and were killed in the Second World War.

Nick's mother died when he was ten and he and his three brothers Andrew, Peter and Michael were brought up by their father. Howard Robinson was a forceful, unconventional figure and he held the family together as a close unit. They called him Boss, as he had called his father. The boys went as weekly boarders to Mountjoy School and spent weekends and holidays with Howard, who once took them all on a camping tour of Canada and the US. He remembers that they were camping in the Grand Smokey National Park in south Virginia, when the nice American family next to them warned they would need guns to defend themselves against attackers. Howard says he could see that the younger boys, Nick and Andrew, were looking a bit nervous. So he said: 'Aw, that'll be no trouble to us. We're used to this sort of situation, so we always have a few bottles of stout and if anyone stops us we'll just take the bottle by the neck and break it off like that and they'll be gone in no time.' There was a big laugh among the boys and next thing the Americans got up and moved their tent.[1]

Howard Robinson used his financial skills to help the Church of Ireland. He joined the board of the Incorporated Society for Protestant Schools, was then on the finance committee of the Church and then became a member of the Church's General Synod. He was also a director of the *Irish Times*.

He lived well, with a superb collection of Jack B. Yeats paintings in his home in Monkstown. There was family property in Clare Street and Wellington Place and he had a holiday home in Tenerife. Howard lived colourfully and generously, and Nick's girlfriends remember being brought for dinner to Dublin's best restaurants – Jammet's and the Red Bank.

Nick's success as a cartoonist and increasing disinterest in the law, however, didn't impress Mary's parents. During the courtship the Bourkes asked them to separate for a while. Her year in Harvard had kept them apart anyway, though Nick used to call on Anne Coyne in Westland Row for news of Mary. Not long after Mary came home, they agreed to another six-month separation and Nick worked as a cartoonist in London. On his visits home, they would meet, and one night when he pressed her to marry him and she still wasn't sure he said: 'You know, when you jump, you're going to jump into my field.' First she laughed and then she thought, 'You know, he's right'. After that, she began to think seriously about marrying him, 'whereas he had been serious all along. Part of my recognition then was just how serious he was, and for how long.'

Her family were not pleased. 'I think they knew he'd had a number of girlfriends. I think they felt I could do better for myself by marrying somebody who was established in a profession, a good doctor, a good lawyer, a good something, and – less important – preferably a Catholic.'

Her parents were always very hurt by the suggestion that more than anything else they didn't want her to marry a Protestant, says Mary. 'Because we had so many Protestant friends and relatives, after all, that that was never really the issue. But from an early stage, because we all wanted to batten down the hatches on what had been a very hurtful time for us, it seemed the easiest formula. To try to explain the situation was simply to give it air-time.'

So what was the real reason? 'I think over-love and possessiveness was a large part of it. I was really very conscious that my parents loved me and wanted to save me from what was in their judgement a mistake.

'I think they loved me so much they wanted to make that important decision for me, too,' she said. After all, she had been the precious daughter in the middle of four boys. She'd had a brilliant academic career. She'd become a professor and a senator. 'And then one of the most important things: who will this daughter marry? And they wanted to influence that, too.'

In the autumn of 1970 she decided she wouldn't wait any longer. 'I'd already postponed the wedding, We'd put it off for quite a long time.' Her family decided they would not attend. Adrian, the youngest, remembers how it was.

'There is no point in my saying now that I wanted to be there. I did not want to be there. My mother's decision was no. Now, of course, I would kill for it. But I won't pretend I felt otherwise then.' Why?

'I probably felt she shouldn't have gone against family opposition. There were cultural differences, religious differences, town and country differences. That was the propaganda that we believed inside ourselves. Of course, we were totally wrong.'[2]

This was a close family, and loyalties were divided. Henry remembers that he wanted to attend and was told not to by his elder brother Oliver. The night before the wedding, Mary came to collect something at Westland Row, and Henry and his wife Barbara both told her they were coming 'She came in and we announced it,' says Henry. 'She was distraught, very angry, uptight. Her attitude was, "I bloody don't want any of you at this stage." It was as much pre-wedding nerves as anything else.' Henry regrets to this day that he didn't turn up anyway. 'I knew afterwards she would have welcomed us there.'[3] Mary didn't encourage her brothers to come because she didn't want to divide the family. She doesn't talk about her wedding day.

She was married from her friend Eavan Boland's house. Mary's cousin, Mary O'Donnell, was her bridesmaid, and she was given away by Mr Justice John Kenny. Her friend, Father Jack Kelly S.J., organised the archbishop's permission for this mixed marriage, and with Dean Tom Salmon of the Church of Ireland, he performed the ceremony at the Dublin airport church early enough for Mr and Mrs Robinson to catch their honeymoon flight to Paris.

'And I never had any doubt that afterwards all would be well. I knew that I had to go through with this and if I had to, to pay this price,' she says. 'Nick was fantastic, you know, he literally, he . . .' she laughs, 'he was so *pleased* to be marrying me.'

Wiser heads in the family knew this stand-off had to end. Mother Aquinas, Mary's now ageing great aunt, wrote to tell them all what 'nonsense' it was. Finally, it was a car accident on the road to Belfast that persuaded Mary to take the first step towards reconciliation. She was to appear on a television programme with British Labour Minister, Barbara Castle. 'And we skidded and spun round and round and into a ditch, and as luck would have it, didn't a tractor arrive with a rope and pull us out.' She did the programme and on the way home said tearfully to Nick: 'Imagine if one or other of us had been killed. Imagine if I had died, what it would do to my parents. I'm going to ring my mother tomorrow!'

She did. 'And we met the following day and we never looked back. We never looked back, but we never talked about it,' she says. 'Nick adopted a generous moving-forward attitude. And we never did go back over it. It was much more "Come and see our house, come and see where we live." We just moved on.'

Family opposition cemented this marriage but in fact, for the life she would lead, Mary Bourke had chosen extraordinarily well. First of all, she loved him. 'He was unashamedly romantic . . . he had an extraordinary capacity to express love.' Then, he was generous. 'Nick was the first to want me to get back to a good relationship with my parents and was very generous about the whole thing, and formed a wonderful relationship with my mother in particular because the two of them were keen to spend money!'

Nick encouraged her in her career – he admired her ambition and accommodated it. 'As she accommodated me. We were very compatible,' he says.[4] Mary always found him as bright or, in some areas, brighter than she was, but she was intrigued by the difference in their approaches.

'He has an extraordinary mind but isn't particularly driven to self-achieving.' She says that's partly a self-doubt that she sees in some other members of his family. 'It is a lack of belief in yourself, and therefore sometimes the compromise is to do something in a way whereby you achieve the objective, but you don't do it in the way that somebody more ambitious would try to do it.' Nick, who has a lifelong commitment to preserving Ireland's architectural and physical heritage, could, she says, have made money out of the projects he ran and the bodies he helped set up, but he preferred to do it as part of a group of volunteers.

Mary has usually been the main breadwinner in the family and, unlike many men, Nick has never felt threatened by that. It's been accepted by their three children, Tessa, William and Aubrey, though not without some questions. 'For William at a certain stage, Nick was a bit of a problem because I was the main breadwinner,' says Mary. 'There was a kind of a joke: "What exactly do you do, Dad?" "Well, actually, I'm a German spy."'

After practising as a solicitor, Nick became administrator of the Irish Centre for European Law, based in Trinity College. But he always used his particular talent for organising and ordering a home. He has always overseen the decoration and furnishing of the house. 'He's visual, I'm not,' Mary says. 'I love his taste and choices. I learn a lot from him about how to look at things. He's made all the choices in our lives to do with things visual or physical. I wouldn't have the slightest idea how to choose curtains or furnish a room and I wouldn't even notice it if he did it.' She remembers dashing out to work past the builders one morning and realising mid-afternoon that something had been different about the house. 'And then eventually it struck me. There was no front door. They'd taken the front door off.'

Nick has an eye for the physical world that she lacks. He will come into a room and notice everything, from the paintings, to the carpet, to a visitor's leather handbag. She will remember the people and what they said, but little more. He handles a car well, is physically at ease. She, according to her brothers, used to have arrows pasted on either side of the steering wheel to remind her which was her right and which her left. He has good taste in clothes and used to choose her evening dresses. She wore them cheerfully, not at all interested, but trusting that he had chosen well.

He introduced her to a whole world of form and beauty, of architecture and history and archaeology. He was an early member of An Taisce, the national heritage preservation group, and campaigned with them and the Irish Georgian Society against the wholesale destruction of Georgian Dublin. In the early seventies the brash new property developers, and the traditionally nationalist Fianna Fáil government, wanted to build for the future, not to preserve the hated colonial past. In many ways, there was only one official past – nationalist, Celtic and Catholic – anything else could be consigned to the skip.

Mountjoy Square had more gaps than a set of rotting teeth. St Stephen's Green had been severely ravaged and round the corner in Hume Street, students squatted in beautiful rundown buildings in a desperate attempt to fight off the demolition crews. They had little political backing for their protest except from Garret FitzGerald of Fine Gael, Independent Noel Browne and from the fearless Senator Owen Sheehy Skeffington and his great admirer, the new Senator Mary Bourke.

She remembers getting a phone call from the protesters. Would she address their meeting that day? Senator Owen Sheehy Skeffington had agreed to do so, but he had died that morning. She paid her tribute to him by climbing on to the back of a lorry and denouncing those who were destroying the people's heritage – a heritage for Irish Catholics and Protestants, one which should unite them, not divide them. It would unite herself and Nick, too.

'I suppose you could argue that Georgian Dublin was my heritage,' said Nick, whose people had been in business in Dublin since the eighteenth century. 'But it was Mary's, too. And we were both conscious of alerting people to the fact that this was a shared heritage. Each of us as part of a mixed marriage was eager to defend the heritage of the other.'

For Nick the destruction of the past is wasteful. Once when he saw workmen on a site about to destroy a great cut-stone triumphal arch, he asked the works foreman to cost the building of it in today's money. 'When he costed it it was enormously valuable, so why was it being destroyed? There was a big public opinion battle to be fought, to warn people that there was a difference between pastiche and the real thing. We in Ireland had a finite number of these things. Were we doomed to repeat the mistakes that others were repenting of?' asks Nick.

Nick tried desperately to stop Irish institutions selling off the family silver. When the Benchers of the King's Inns (the educational and supervisory body for the Irish Bar) tried to sell off 120,000 irreplaceable books and documents at Sotheby's in London, Nick and Mary helped to mount a protest campaign through the newspapers. An Taisce established that it was illegal to export some of the older books, thereby stopping their sale, and going on to acquire some of them for Irish libraries. In case an attempt might be made to sell others, Nick went to London to keep a watching brief at the sale, helped by Mary Polland from Trinity College Library.

But Mary and Nick's biggest rescue mission was the Viking site at Wood Quay. The arguments that raged over Georgian Dublin were intensified in the great campaign to save this tenth-century site on the banks of the Liffey in the centre of Dublin. Politicians who scoffed at preserving the 'British' past were equally enraged at being asked to respect the heritage of the pagan invaders, the 'Viking hordes'. An enormous job had to be done to educate public opinion to the fact that the Vikings founded the city of Dublin.

They were the first urban settlers – traders, merchants, crafts-people, entrepreneurs, true heroes of Ireland's capital city. Once again, Mary and Nick Robinson helped to fight that battle both on public platforms and in the courts. Once again, she says, Nick was the one who appreciated the historic value of the site. 'I was involved in the issues and the principles, but almost as though he was briefing me.'

Ironically, what threatened Wood Quay, the ancient centre of Dublin, was a new municipal centre, a block of civic offices for Dublin Corporation. When planning permission was granted in the early seventies, it was on condition that the archaeologists be given time and facilities to 'record and recover matter of archaeological interest or value'.[5] The somewhat outdated approach of the National Museum at the time was that archaeology was about recovering artefacts and putting them on display. But the younger archaeologists working on the site, including the present Director of the Museum, Dr Pat Wallace, had quietly moved to the international view that the site itself was vitally important and revealed more about its own history than did mere artefacts in a museum.

Laid bare beside the Liffey were the foundations of a wooden city, with post and wattle house walls a foot high and wattle paths running in between.[6] The preservation of the actual site became the focus of the campaign by historian Father F.X. Martin of the pressure group, Friends of Medieval Dublin. In his long battle through the courts, Father Martin would be represented by junior counsel, Mary Robinson, and Donal Barrington, senior counsel, instructed by solicitor Nick Robinson. In the High Court, they won a judgement from Mr Justice Hamilton declaring a large section of the site a National Monument which should therefore be preserved.[7] It was a victory welcomed on all sides. But Dublin Corporation found a legal way around it. If they could get the Minister in charge of National Monuments to give joint permission with the Corporation for the demolition of a National Monument, then it could be done.

On 25 August 1978, the then Fianna Fáil Minister gave his permission for the destruction of Wood Quay. There was public outrage. Many of those on the massive protest march from Leinster House to Wood Quay on 23 September 1978 had never joined a public demonstration before. Office-workers, schoolgirls, mothers with prams, and fathers 'whose children had a year's supply of tinfoil swathed around pudding-bowl helmets and ice-cream cone horns'.[8] They were beginning to realise they had one thing in common, however. They were Dubs, and this was Dublin's heritage. Senator Mary Robinson had fought their battle in court – now she was fighting it on the streets. 'This peaceful protest is part of the lifeblood of democracy,' she said, speaking to the massive crowd outside Leinster House. 'And its very size shows the pulse is strong.'[9]

But democracy wasn't enough. As protests poured in from all over the world, the archaeologists on the site were reduced to standing bodily in front of the invading bulldozers. Father Martin, whose own legal team worked for free, faced massive legal costs awarded against him as well as substantial compensation for the delays he caused. In a desperate last effort in June 1979, a group of protesters occupied the site, sleeping in tents and cooking on campfires. Three weeks later, as Dr Pat Wallace remembers, a breathless Mary Robinson came running from the Four Courts across the river Liffey to warn them that the Supreme Court had granted an injunction and they must leave.[10] Mary herself had just been elected to Dublin Corporation on a Labour and Wood Quay ticket, and there were still hopes that this new Corporation would save Wood Quay. But official threats that they would each personally be levied with a huge compensation bill discouraged the councillors. Councillor Mary Robinson pushed for more excavation time, and the archaeologists stayed on until March 1981 when one of Europe's finest Viking sites was levelled to the ground.

The long, wearisome battle had ensured at least that the site was excavated. It alerted public opinion in Ireland and in Europe to the wealth of Viking remains still to be found in Ireland.

Mary was again to play a part in protecting the national heritage, this time on behalf of the state when in 1986, led by T.K. Liston SC, she helped win a landmark case establishing the state's right to treasure trove and to the priceless Derrynaflan hoard of sacred vessels found by amateur treasure hunters.[11]

Wood Quay also forged one crucial alliance for the future and for the presidency. Occupying the Wood Quay site in the summer of 1979 was Bride Rosney, a Dublin schoolteacher and Friends of Medieval Dublin activist. Through the campaign Rosney and the Robinsons had become friends, but Bride's first reaction to Mary was cool. 'I remember seeing her on a television programme and saying to a friend, "Isn't she cold and hard?"' The first time she really saw Mary's human side was during the interminable Wood

Quay court cases. Nick was away. They were walking over to the Four Courts for a difficult hearing and Mary suddenly stopped and said: 'I wish that big hairy man was here. I really need him.'

Bride was surprised. 'I think it was the first time I realised what a force in her life he was.' She was even more surprised to get a phone call from Nick early one morning to ask her to be godparent to their third baby. 'I didn't realise that the friendship was as deep as she saw it,' says Bride. 'But for me that upped the ante. If someone asks you to be godparent, they are saying: "Stay around in our lives."'[12]

Bride Rosney would stay around in their lives for quite some time.

6

HOLY WAR AND FAMILY PLANNING

'He was a bully of the Church,' says Mary Robinson. 'I hate bullies.'

She had driven to Dundalk to visit the Catholic Primate of All Ireland, Cardinal William Conway. It was three months after her wedding, weeks after her reconciliation with her parents and she was at the centre of a blazing row with the Church over family planning.

The Church would fight again on abortion and on divorce, but never with the arrogant display of raw power it would use to keep contraception out of Ireland. On 26 February 1971, Senator Mary Robinson notified the Senate that she had prepared a Bill to legalise contraception – it was called the Criminal Law Amendment Bill 1971. The following month she asked for it to be printed and distributed. Immediately she found herself, her Senate supporters and, what was worse, her mass-going parents in Co. Mayo, the target of public abuse.

'I had just regrouped with my parents,' she says. 'And here I was tabling a Bill which my Donegal mother and Mayo father did not think was a good idea, especially when it was denounced in the church in Ballina. It was hard times.'

So she entered the lion's den, for her parents' sake, rather than her own. She was hoping that the cardinal would at least accept the integrity of her position and that this could be conveyed to

Ballina. 'I was only looking for a small concession . . . "We agree to disagree but I accept your integrity". I was hoping this would help my parents, that I could tell my parents first of all, and that maybe the cardinal would send a message to the local bishop.'

Cardinal Bill Conway was a big man, calm, distant – not one to engage in small talk, certainly not to Senator Mary Robinson and her new husband. 'He was a bully of the Church. He took me to a room and tried to bully me, and Nick was left sitting in the car outside. It was most uncourteous and bullying. I'm sorry, but it was. He refused to do what I'd hoped, which was to say "I accept the integrity of your arguments, and as far as I'm concerned you have integrity in your arguments and I don't have a problem with that." That's what I was looking for, but he wasn't giving me any space.'

The cardinal's attitude merely brought out the stubborn streak in Mary. 'But I remember being disappointed – bitterly disappointed from a family point of view because it mattered a lot. I came away with no warmth, no joy, and then Archbishop John Charles McQuaid said it – contraception would be and would remain a curse upon the country – thanks very much!'

There has always been something of the innocent about Mary Robinson – this may account for her success. Only a trusting person would have taken the risks she has taken. But only a very trusting woman indeed would have approached an Irish cardinal in 1971 expecting to establish an atmosphere of mutual intellectual respect. It would be an exceptional priest, let alone a bishop or cardinal, who regarded any woman, or indeed any lay person, as having the right to disagree with the Church on moral matters – and Cardinal Bill Conway was not exceptional.

This, after all, was war. Senator Mary Robinson had challenged the Catholic Church in the crucial area of sexuality. The Church taught that the sexual act was for the purposes of procreation within marriage. To separate sex from its physical consequences was to encourage promiscuity. Sex for mere pleasure, sex outside marriage, was a sin, but what was even worse was to make sin painless. The wages of sin, the Church vowed, must be paid.

Before the women's movement gathered strength, no one worried too much that those paying were women – no one except a few enlightened doctors and family planning activists, a few protesting voices from the minority churches, and a few politicians like Mary Robinson. To appreciate the full audacity of her challenge, one has to appreciate the zeal with which the Church ruled women's lives.

Two decades earlier when the bishops had helped smash attempts to introduce a free mother and child health scheme, it was largely for fear of contraception. Explaining the hierarchy's opposition, Bishop Browne of Galway said the bishops were concerned that the scheme gave the state the right to educate women about motherhood, 'for education in regard to motherhood and in regard to health means instructions in regard to the sacred and delicate subjects of sex, chastity, marriage, childbirth and family life. This is moral teaching which belongs to the Church established by Christ. The state had no right to interfere in this sphere. It has no right to tell girls or women how they shall act or behave in regard to the most important and sacred matters of conscience and of spiritual salvation.'[1]

The subject was not to be discussed, even in the sixties. One devout Catholic at her wit's end from too many pregnancies asked her confessor about the natural family planning method of which the Church reluctantly approved. She was severely rebuked for thoughts that would 'lead her poor husband into sin'. She was told to go home and do her Christian duty.[2]

Women who did just that, as Dr Michael Solomons, an eminent Dublin gynaecologist, remembers, 'found themselves pregnant annually with no let-up until menopause or death'.[3] He tells of a colleague who pulled back the bedclothes after a home delivery to find another baby in the bed. Knowing he hadn't delivered twins, he stared at it until the woman said: 'That was last year's, doctor.'[4] Women with high blood pressure or eclampsia were warned to be careful about having another baby, but the law and the Church gave them no choice. 'For them, pregnancy was to be a death sentence.'[5]

Hope was high among Irish women in the sixties that the new spirit of the Vatican Council would help change Church thinking on contraception. A Papal Commission appointed in 1965 actually recommended such a change, but Pope Paul VI decided to reject it. His 1968 encyclical, *Humanae Vitae*, restating the Church's ban on all forms of artificial contraception, closed the debate. Rome had spoken. Official Ireland would submit. And the hierarchy were there to ensure that it did.

This was the atmosphere of renewed zeal into which Senator Mary Robinson launched her first family planning Bill in 1971. The law saw contraception as a crime, to be linked with prostitution. Prostitution and contraception were banned under the same law, the Criminal Law Amendment Act of 1935 which made it an offence to sell, offer, advertise, import or attempt to import any contraceptives. It was no accident, then, that women campaigning for a change in the law at the time were regularly labelled as 'whores and prostitutes'.[6]

This was the level of response which met Mary Robinson when on 3 March 1971 she placed on the order book of the Senate her first private members Bill to change the law. Supported by Senators Trevor West of Trinity and John Horgan of the National University of Ireland, she proposed to repeal section 17 of the Criminal Law Amendment Act 1935 and the Censorship of Publications Acts 1929 and 1946. As John Horgan remembers, she wasn't even able to get the six Senate votes which would have ensured at least the publication of her Bill.[7]

Even known liberals like Dr Noel Browne, the Minister who had resigned over Church interference in the Mother and Child Scheme, thought she had gone too far. 'He was very nervous about her introducing these Bills,' says former Taoiseach Dr Garret FitzGerald who recalls Browne saying to him: 'She would need to be very careful about that. This is a theological issue. The bishops have a right to speak about this. You've got to be very careful.'[8]

And the bishops were quick to assert their rights. After all, mutiny was breaking out not only in the Senate but now on television. Three days after Mary's Bill, the Women's Liberation Movement was launched on the Irish public on the all-powerful *Late Late Show*. Members discussed women's rights, including the right to contraception, and their legal adviser that night was Senator Mary Robinson. Six days later the bishops launched a broadside from Maynooth. 'The bishops fully share the disquiet, which is widespread among the people at the present time, regarding pressures being exerted on public opinion on questions concerning the law on divorce, contraception and abortion. These questions involve issues of grave import for society as a whole, which go far beyond purely private morality or private religious belief. Civil law on these matters should respect the wishes of the people who elected the legislators, and the bishops confidently hope that the legislators themselves will respect this important principle.'[9]

The cardinal himself went on the radio programme *This Week* two days later, and warned that a change in the law could mean children under eighteen being prescribed contraceptives. The war was on. Two weeks later John Charles McQuaid, the ever-vigilant Archbishop of Dublin, issued a ringing challenge to the legislators. 'Given the proneness of our human nature to evil, given the enticement of bodily satisfaction, given the widespread modern incitement to unchastity, it must be evident that an access, hitherto unlawful, to contraceptive devices will prove a certain occasion of sin, especially to immature persons,' he said. 'It may well come to pass that in the present climate of emotional thinking and pressure, legislation could be enacted that will offend the objective moral law. Such a measure would be an insult to our Faith. It would without question prove to be gravely damaging to morality, private and public. It would be, and would remain, a curse upon our country.'[10]

If he had stuck an effigy of Senator Mary Robinson on every church door and invited the people to stick pins in it, he could hardly have targeted her more precisely. For her Catholic parents, that Lenten period of 1971 was a nightmare. Bishops all over the country condemned her attempts to introduce a family planning Bill. In St Muredach's Cathedral in Ballina, the Bourkes' friend, the newly-elected Bishop McDonnell, made his own attack, albeit in more moderate language. If one had to cater for minority codes, then should one make divorce, abortion and even pornography legal, too – was that what people wanted, he asked?

People, he said, should 'make their wishes known to their public representatives and not have it appear that the clergy are the only people concerned about this.'[11] People made their views known to Mary's father, to Mary's mother. When Mary's Bill was attacked from the altar, 'my parents left the church, which they had never done in their lives, and they left because they were humiliated.' The national newspapers made much of the fact that Mary's local bishop had attacked her Bill. Archbishop McQuaid wrote to congratulate him. The bishop wrote back saying that, unfortunately, Senator Robinson was a Ballina girl, but he reassured the archbishop that she was of excellent Catholic parents.[12]

Mary remembers her mother on the phone from Ballina 'in tears'. Mrs Bourke didn't agree with Mary on contraception, which made it doubly difficult for her when people in the town walked up to her to complain. Recalling it all twenty-seven years on, Mary is visibly moved. 'It was, for her, shaming and humiliating and yet it was not going to divide us again. She coped very well,' she says. 'When they started to think things through as doctors, it didn't remain a problem between me and my parents. It became a big problem how difficult it was for them publicly in a town like Ballina, where they were both pretty well daily mass-goers.'

There was some clerical glee at the discomfiture of the very respectable Bourkes.[13] One senior local cleric jibed that it was a pity Mary's mother hadn't practised family planning in her day. As for Mary herself, she was given a lot of unsolicited advice about 'the importance of humility', but there was worse. Through the post, in among the rosary beads and miraculous medals and warnings about eternal damnation, came a crop of rubber fingers cut from garden gloves – crude imitations of condoms. The letters were vitriolic to the point of obscenity. 'I was affected by the hate mail I was getting. Nick knew it and we destroyed a lot of the letters. But I remember walking down Nassau Street one day and consciously trying to avoid people's eyes because I felt they were looking at me,' she says. 'It was outside my range of fairly limited experience to be so hated. I was quite affected by it and then toughened by it.'

Mary always saw contraception not as a feminist issue, but as a civil right for women and men. She did not take part in the now famous Contraceptive Train outing to Belfast in May of that year when members of the Irish Women's Liberation Movement bought condoms north of the border and dared the Irish Customs officials in Dublin to arrest them for breaking the law.[14] She doggedly stuck to her legislative last in the Senate.

Her first Bill was refused a first reading. Two years later, on 14 November 1973, her second Bill, again supported by Senators West and Horgan and some Labour members, passed its first stage.[15] It did at least force the first full debate on contraception in the Irish parliament in February 1974.[16] But by then, as was so often the case in Ireland, the courts had forced the government to act. The Supreme Court decided on 12 December 1973 that Mrs Mary McGee, a fisherman's wife, had the right to import contraceptives for her own use and that the law that stopped her doing so was unconstitutional – an invasion of her right to privacy under Article 50 of the Constitution.

Now the curtain rose on a decade of pure farce. First came the Cosgrave government's Bill in 1974 which was defeated when the Taoiseach himself and his Education Minister, both conservatives, voted against their own Bill.[17] Then in 1979 the Dáil passed Fianna Fáil Health Minister Charles Haughey's even more restrictive Bill limiting sale of contraceptives to married people with a doctor's prescription, what he memorably called 'an Irish solution to an Irish problem'.[18] It would be 1985 before Labour Health Minister, Barry Desmond, would remove most restrictions, but for Mary Robinson, Haughey's Bill did two worthwhile things. First, despite its limitations, it made contraceptives available. Secondly, it was a Department of Health, not a Department of Justice Bill, something she had been pushing for in her own Family Planning Bills in 1974 and 1978. 'I remember feeling how worthwhile all our persuasion had been to have it moved into the health area. It was a women's reproductive health issue. It isn't a matter of the criminal law – it's about women's health and choice.'

Moving contraception from the area of crime (and sin), to the health arena was a major cultural change. Even in the late seventies, books giving information about contraception were still banned as 'indecent and obscene'. When an Irish Family Planning Association booklet on contraception was banned, Mary, representing the

IFPA, pursued the Censorship Board to the Supreme Court and won. Mr Justice O'Higgins in his judgment said: 'Far from being pornographic or lewdly commercial or pandering to prurient curiosity, it simply aimed at giving basic factual information on a delicate topic as to which there is genuine concern.'[19]

Mr Justice O'Higgins was reflecting the extent to which public opinion had leaped ahead of officialdom. Women had been choosing for years to get the pill from co-operative doctors as a menstrual cycle regulator. Women had been choosing to obtain contraceptives, in return for a voluntary contribution, from the family planning clinics who could, after the McGee case, import but not sell them. Women were getting on with their lives while the government still pretended that there was no contraception.

Public Ireland dressed itself in many figleaves over the contraceptives issue but none so shameful as the pious pretence that only married women had sex. When Haughey's contraceptive law was finally introduced it was limited to married people, pandering to the Church's obsessive fear of extra-marital sex. That's how it had always been. The myth of pure Irish womanhood must be maintained and those who endangered it, such as single mothers and their babies, would be hidden away or banished. When Mary Robinson started to help the single mothers' organisation, Cherish, in the early seventies, organiser Maura O'Dea, herself a single mother, remembers how terrified the women were that their parents would find out about their pregnancies.

'Always the terror of who might have the heart attack, or of the father who might die, or of the somebody who might die if this girl didn't disappear. They didn't tell their parents anyway. I remember the terror and how everything had to be hidden.'[20] Many ran away to England, and to understand why, one has only to read what an Irish mother wrote to a Catholic priest in London: 'Tell my daughter never to set foot in Ireland again and that she has disgraced her family and her country.'[21]

The letter was quoted in Michael Viney's fine series of articles on single mothers in the *Irish Times* in the mid-sixties. When Viney told a prison doctor he was going to write the articles, he was told:

'If you go besmirching the name of Irish womanhood, you won't be forgiven.'[22]

By the early 1970s, Maura O'Dea decided it was time to come out, and come out fighting. Maura was in her thirties and her parents were dead, so she felt able to be the public face for Ireland's hidden mothers, demanding housing and an allowance, as well as changes in the law on the establishing of maintenance rights, and the law on illegitimacy. On all of these issues she demanded and got advice from Mary Robinson. 'I remember Mary coming to talk to us about the law. She was pregnant with William, and she was tired, and she probably should have been at home, but she wasn't. She was with us,' says Maura. Mary was to remain the president of Cherish for seventeen years, from December 1973 until her inauguration as President. More than anything else, Mary said, she admired them.

'At the core of it was that they were doing it for themselves. Maura O'Dea going on the *Late Late Show* (Ireland's leading television chat-show), looking Gay Byrne in the eye and saying I'm here, I'm real, I exist and I'm doing it for myself.' Maura was just as direct in her approach to Mary. 'You're fucking well going to be our president because we need you for respectability.'

For Mary's critics, it was only one more proof that she was irredeemable. She remembers their reaction. 'Typical! Typical of her. She's not only for the contraceptives, but she's helping women who are sinful.' For Mary it was a total commitment. She raised funds for them and got others to do so. She phoned powerful friends. She phoned students. Deputy Eamon Gilmore, then head of the student body in University College Galway, donated the proceeds of UCG rag week.

She went to every Cherish Christmas party with her children. She dropped in a cheque, every Christmas, for the staff party. But most of all, she helped to change minds. Cherish's aim was to ensure that women, if they wanted, could keep their own babies, that they did not have to deny their own experience. It was quite common for women to arrive up from the country on a week's holiday, wanting to have their baby and return home without it. It was quite common for a woman to wake up after giving birth to find her baby gone with no explanation – or in the case of a woman Mary knew from Cavan, to find a nun stealing away with her baby girl, presumably for adoption, and having to fight tooth and claw to hang on to her.

Anna Lee, Cherish social worker for many years, remembers that one of her jobs in the beginning was to provide English postal addresses, so that women who were going to mother-and-baby homes in Ireland could pretend to their parents they were working in England. 'They were encouraged and helped to feel that they had never been pregnant.'[23]

Cherish lobbied during the 1973 election campaign and as a result won their most famous victory – the granting of the unmarried mother's allowance by the 1973 coalition government of Christian Democratic Fine Gael and the centre-left Irish Labour party. The allowance was a vital recognition that unmarried mothers existed. 'While there was no official state provision,' says Maura O'Dea, 'you could pretend there were no unmarried mothers.'

Mary Robinson's real value to Cherish was that she fought a two-handed battle for them in parliament and in the courts. She pushed politically for – and won – the eventual abolition of the cut-off period for paternity and maintenance claims. Then she helped win vital court cases which forced the government to make long overdue changes in the law. Children born outside marriage still bore the stigma of illegitimacy. In the Johnston case, a couple with a child challenged the insecure status of their unmarried family under Irish law. Representing them, Mary took the case as far as the European Court of Human Rights in Strasbourg which found that their child should be placed legally and socially in a position akin to that of a legitimate child.[24] This forced the government to end discrimination by introducing the Status of Children Bill – bitterly opposed by the right and by those worried about equal inheritance rights. It was a famous victory for Mary and for Cherish, but the Bill introduced one clause that worried her slightly. It gave automatic parental rights to the unmarried mother, but not to the unmarried father. To many in Cherish, given that unmarried mothers had been left to carry the whole responsibility for their children, this seemed only fair. But Mary could see that it was short-sighted. If unmarried fathers were to take on their responsibilities, then they had to have rights.

In the Keegan case, she represented a single father who wasn't consulted before his child was placed for adoption. They lost in the Irish courts, but the European Court in Strasbourg found that his rights had indeed been infringed.[25] This changed adoption practice – efforts are now made to contact and consult the natural father.[26]

Not everybody in Cherish cheered, and Mary knew they wouldn't. 'It wasn't too easy to take that case,' she says. 'He was a good young father who wanted a relationship with his child, and the mother wasn't interested. It wasn't easy because the predominant view in Cherish was – don't give rights to fathers. And yet it was through Cherish that I learned how important it was for fathers to have that relationship, and how important for children. We're still underestimating it.'

Mary believed in individual rights, not just in women's rights. The fact that natural fathers had behaved irresponsibly in the past did not mean they should be counted out for the future. Attitudes change, societies change, even bullying churches can change. Indeed, it is perhaps a measure of how far Ireland has come in its attitudes to single mothers that a Catholic priest and commentator, Father Colm Kilcoyne, was moved to admit in Lent 1997 that it was the Catholic Church which forced families to throw pregnant girls out of home. 'We, the priests, told people to drive the daughter out if she got pregnant. I don't think any mother ever wanted to do that. I don't think she *could* want to do that. We created the atmosphere in which it was acceptable to do that.'[27]

7

FREE WOMEN

President Mary Robinson drove in to the Vatican, through court-yard after courtyard, and drew up in front of a brilliantly dressed guard of honour. There were the striped doublets and glinting helmets of the Swiss guard and the decorated lines of Papal Knights. 'What was very curious was that *they* were very colourfully dressed with medals and stiff white collars and plumes and you name it. But when I got out of the car, it was quite clear they were surprised *I* wasn't dressed in black.' Queen Elizabeth had come in penitent black with a veil. It was assumed that the President of Catholic Ireland would do no less. Yet here she was in a smart green dress and coat with a cheeky sprig of Women's Day mimosa – bareheaded. Some critics would later say – barefaced.

The Pope's men were astonished. 'When I recognised that, I was delighted I had taken the decision that I had. Far from feeling awkward about it, I felt that this was what I was about. This is International Women's Day, and I am an elected woman head of state and it is right that I should walk along and inspect this elaborate male guard not wearing a veil and a black dress!'

President and Pope met as two heads of state with shared interests and a sense of mutual respect. Unlike the encounter with Cardinal Conway twenty-six years earlier, this was a constructive meeting. Times had changed since the days when she had challenged the power of the Church over women's lives and won. Contraception liberated women to fight for all the other freedoms. Mary Robinson had helped establish a new status and a new confidence among Irish women and her election was the very symbol of it.

She was not, however, an ardent member of the early women's movement. 'It took me a while, I remember, to be comfortable with calling myself a feminist because I had an image of this strident and almost required lesbianism,' she says. She had read a lot of American feminist literature and found it theoretically sterile. 'It was that sort of aggressive, anti-man attitude, almost anti-ordinary-woman, too, that I was very unenamoured of,' she says. 'It was like UN-speak. It was feminism-speak.' As for the Irish Women's Liberation Movement, she says: 'I didn't want to join the IWLM because I found some of the discussion frankly boring. It was just going round in circles, boring and whingeing.'

But she was their loyal legal adviser, as Nell McCafferty remembers. Between Nell McCafferty, radical feminist from working-class Derry, and Mary Robinson, well-bred academic reformer, there has always been a wry affection. When Nell described in her *Irish Times* 'In the Eyes of the Law' column the scenes of misery and injustice played out every day in the courts, Mary gave her a plaque representing the scales of justice. Nell was touched. Somebody, she felt, understood what she was saying. They are both reformers, but Nell has always accepted that Mary needed to go the orthodox, legal route to change. Mary admires the outrageous side of Nell and hates the notion that she should ever become too respectable.

Nell remembers a meeting in Dun Laoghaire in the early heady days of the Women's Liberation Movement. 'Mary looked like Dilly Dream. She wore awkward clothes. Mary Kenny was there in hot pants, Máire Woods was looking elegant, June Levine was as sexy as a radioactive field, but wee Mary Robinson . . . ! I remember Mary going on about the law, saying it was all going to take years. And we all listened – despite the fact that she wasn't hysterical. She gave a sense of stability, an assurance that it could be done. Good old Mary! After we'd delivered all the revolutionary calls, there she was, deeply respectable, not like me, not like Máire Woods; she was no rowdy. She was sweet, respectful of people.'[1]

Nell remembers that Mary didn't come to the early Women's Liberation meetings held in Gaj's restaurant in Baggot Street, a radical students' haunt, nor to the sessions in the pubs, nor join in the required discussions about sex. Sex was a forbidden subject at the time, particularly for women, so the early feminists made a point of talking freely about it. Nell remembers trying hard to get Mary to join in. It was her own thirtieth birthday lunch – Emer Philbin Bowman, Mary, and her friend Eavan Boland were there. 'As the lunch got rowdy, we talked about sex as we always did. But Mary said: "Sex doesn't bear description. One has to adopt such absurd positions, you couldn't talk about it!" But she giggled while the rest of us talked about it.'

The consciousness-raising which was so vital to feminist activists at the time didn't seem so important to Mary Robinson. She had always thought of herself as equal, had come from a highly competitive family where she had been expected to achieve in the same way as her brothers. She saw the task as a practical one, changing the law – and she knew the law. When Eavan Boland phoned her from a Women's Liberation meeting in a journalist's house to ask her for seven examples of how the law discriminated against women, Mary said: 'Why only seven, Eavan?' Eavan, who needed the information quickly, said impatiently: 'Look, stop arguing, seven will do!' Mary remembers writing out seven laws that discriminated against women, and then venturing: 'If you want a few more, now . . . ?'

'No,' said Eavan. 'Seven will do!'

The legal inequities were listed in the manifesto of the Irish Women's Liberation Movement, *Chains or Change*, published early in 1971: women were not called to serve on juries; women had no statutory right to equal pay; a married woman had no legal domicile other than her husband's and almost no independent right to make financial arrangements; if a married woman paid tax, her husband got the rebates; he also got the children's allowance money; he was also the legal guardian of the children. Injustice in the workplace was as bad. Women had to leave public sector jobs once married. Women workers earned 54.9 per cent of men's wages.[2]

Women's Liberation hit the Irish public in March 1971 in a

now famous *Late Late Show*. Mary Robinson went on the popular television programme not as a member of the movement but as a lawyer, pointing out the extent of legal discrimination against women and the fact that it was probably unconstitutional. She also reminded women that they were equal in the ballot box and should use their voting power.

The show and the women on it caught the public imagination, and when the Irish Women's Liberation Movement was launched as a mass movement on 14 April 1971, at the Dublin Lord Mayor's residence, the Mansion House, the hall was packed beyond expectations – a crowd of about 1,000 turned up.

Nell McCafferty (Mary Robinson remembers joining her on the platform as legal adviser) outlined the six demands of the movement: equal pay, equality before the law, equal education, contraception, justice for deserted wives, unmarried mothers and widows, and one family per house. Sixty people spoke from the floor during an enthusiastic three-hour meeting. Elections were organised to select representatives for the first delegate meeting of the IWLM some weeks later.[3] That was when they organised the Contraceptive Train to bring banned contraceptives back across the border and challenge the authorities to arrest them for breaking the law. Mary didn't go.

'I approved of it but I knew as a practising barrister I couldn't be part of it. I wasn't prepared to be ridiculed.' In order to be effective as a lawyer fighting for women's rights, she had to stay within the law, she says. The Law Library (the practising Irish barristers' professional organisation providing for them a shared working place at Dublin's Four Courts) was a conservative, chauvinist place in those days, already hostile enough to the causes she was adopting. 'It would have been a battle from the inside which I wasn't prepared to fight . . . the boring prospect of trying to convert the Law Library into a progressive force for change! That would be a lifetime task and I had other things to do. If I'd gone on that train, I would have exposed myself to ridicule. If I was going to be effective, I had to avoid getting out on the end of a branch and being chopped off. And going on that train would have given them an easy target.'

On other occasions, Women's Liberation demonstrated outside

Leinster House, the Irish parliament building, when she was trying to introduce her family planning measures. On one occasion they broke into the building and were led out singing 'We shall not conceive' to the tune of *We shall overcome*. It wasn't necessarily the sort of support Mary Robinson wanted at the time. 'I remember the meetings outside – I went out to meet them beforehand – and being slightly uncomfortable with the populist element, particularly at that time. I'd be more comfortable now . . . But I was shy and I wanted the lawyer–senator approach. I didn't want the exhibitionism.'

She wouldn't break the law, but she would defend those who did. The squalid housing conditions which still existed for the poor in Dublin in the early seventies had led Máirín de Burca, who came to feminism from her left wing background in Sinn Féin (the old nationalist party then becoming increasingly socialist after a split creating the aggressively republican Provisional Sinn Féin), to take action. Máirín and her feminist colleague, Mary Anderson, organised protest squats in empty houses. Housing, they insisted, was a feminist issue. When the government countered this with tough legislation, the Forcible Entry Bill, which was passed by the Dáil in August 1971, Máirín and Mary Anderson protested by pushing closed the great wrought-iron gates of the parliament building on ministerial cars as they left after the debate. They were arrested for obstruction and elected to go for jury trial because, as Máirín says, 'between anti-Vietnam war and anti-fishing rights protests, we had been up in court so often that this time we were in danger of going to jail again.' A jury might be kinder than the district court judge.[4]

Meeting Mary Robinson at a party, Máirín asked her how she could protest about the scandal of all-male, property-owning juries judging a property-related case against two women. Mary explained that it would require a constitutional case challenging the Juries Act. Máirín took one, with Mary Robinson as her junior counsel and Donal Barrington as her senior. The case held up Máirín's obstruction charges for so long that finally they were dropped. In the meantime, history was being made. The High Court's dismissal of her case in June 1973 by Mr Justice Tom

O'Higgins indicates the conservatism of the time. He said that he must assume 'that the members of an all-male jury will not disregard their oaths simply because the defendant is a woman, and that a jury composed of property owners will not be prejudiced against a defendant who happens to have little or no property.' The Supreme Court thought differently and on 12 December 1975 the tradition of all-male, ratepaying juries was brought to an end.[5]

Making history costs money, though, and after the failed High Court case, Máirín remembers telling Mary and the legal team that she didn't expect them to carry on working for nothing.

They did, however, so Máirín went to the then increasingly middle-class Women's Liberation movement and demanded – 'I demanded, I didn't ask' – that they raise some money for the lawyers fighting this path-breaking women's battle. None, it seems, was forthcoming.

Mary admired Máirín de Burca's determination to change things. 'I felt she was very strong, very committed and generous.' She understood why Máirín's anger against injustice led her deliberately to flout the law, why her anger against the Vietnam war led her to throw an egg at the visiting Richard Nixon. The egg-throwing incident led to some confusion with an elderly patient in Mary's father's Ballina surgery. Mary's and Máirín's maiden names – de Burca, Bourke – are the same and the old lady, looking at the photograph of Mary on the wall said: 'Ah, Dr Bourke, I so admire your daughter – in jail again for Ireland!' – which, as Mary says, 'I was very careful not to be!'

Mary encouraged the women's movement early on to look to process and procedure, not simply to protest. In April 1970 she told them that equal pay for women would have to come once Ireland joined the EC, because the Rome Treaty required it.[6] She would turn to Europe again and again in her efforts to reform the law, and indeed when the Fine Gael–Labour coalition in 1975 tried to get away with postponing equal pay, despite an EC directive that it had to be introduced by February 1976, Mary knew what to do.

'Mary said, "Here's who to write to,"' says Máirín de Burca. 'We all sat down and wrote letters of complaint to the person in the Commission.' Within months, Brussels had refused permission to derogate and the government had to give in.

'We had embarrassed the hell out of them!' says Mary. 'That government, which had come in on a commitment to reform, were awful in this area and were very chauvinist. They didn't buy equality really, and they were quite happy for economic reasons to postpone it in certain sectors if they could get away with it. And I was quite determined that they wouldn't.'

Mary was patient. Some of the injustices listed by the women's movement in 1971 would take years to change. But she believed in the slow, sure processes of the law. In 1980 in the Supreme Court she won equal tax treatment for married couples in the Murphy case – previously they had had to pay more tax than two single people on the same incomes.[7] This ruling meant that spouses, whether working outside or inside the home, got full tax-free allowances. She took the Hyland case, in which the Supreme Court in 1988 backed the High Court decision that married women and their husbands should get the same social welfare benefits as if they were single people.[8] She helped represent Mary Murphy and twenty-eight women workers in their equal pay case against Bord Telecom Eireann. After going through the Irish Labour Court and High Court, they finally won the day in the European Court of Justice in 1988.[9] Improvements in pay and conditions had made the workplace more welcoming for women and the number of women at work in Ireland rose from 34 per cent in 1971 to 46 per cent in 1993.

The law had proved to be an instrument of change for women – but lawyers themselves were another matter. Attitudes in the Law Library were so chauvinist in her early years there that Mary regarded it as a lost cause. When she went there at the beginning of the seventies, there were six women barristers, only four of them practising. Mary didn't warm to the culture. Good barristers such as the present Miss Justice Mella Carroll, whom Mary admires, took on the system from the inside and indeed Miss Carroll went on to become chairman of the Bar Council. 'But we were heading at that time in completely different directions, because she was showing that she could do better than any man within that culture,' says

Mary. 'I felt much happier being an outsider to the system while cracking it. I didn't care enough about them to let them worry me or, like Mella Carroll, to try to become chairman of the Bar Council and work to change it from inside.'

Mary's independence wasn't appreciated by all her women colleagues. 'I had been wearing this very smart pin-striped trouser suit in the Law Library. I went up to the loo one day – by this stage there were twenty women barristers at most – and there was a printed notice saying: "At a meeting of the ladies of the Bar, it was decided that trousers would not be worn". I took out my Biro and amended the notice to read: "At a meeting of *some of* the ladies of the Bar'.

The macho culture of the Bar in those early days was not something she bothered to confront very often, but she remembers letting fly after one incident. It was at a legal do for a departing colleague. A song, innocuous in itself – 'There is nothing like a dame' – was sung in a suggestive way, and a remark was made after it which she found offensive. 'I knew I could respond heavily. There was singing, and a remark afterwards, and I pounced!' she says. 'I got very uptight and I took on a couple of them. I was probably saying fairly ordinary feminist things that were absolutely rootedly shocking to them. I felt very angry.'

The Senate was no more congenial. The anti-woman culture of the political system was legendary. Its hours were impossible for anyone who had a family, as was the expectation that one would join the boys at the bar. And Mary had her academic commitments, her court cases and her family. Fianna Fáil Minister, Mary O'Rourke, was in the Senate with Mary for a short period and remembers for the first time seeing the family woman when Mary came in flustered and late for an adjournment debate. 'She was full of apologies. She'd had a birthday party for her child and she had the new baby, Aubrey, and I remember thinking, well, she's not just the cool academic I thought she was. She said to me as she ran into her seat "I've just had a birthday party for twenty four-year-olds," and I just thought this was the human side of her.'[10] But the real proof of parliamentary attitudes was evident in the Oireachtas (Irish parliament's) pension scheme which extended only to the widows of male parliamentarians – the spouses of female parliamentarians didn't count. Mary decided to take the matter to the Labour Court on behalf of her husband – her union representative was Pat Rabbitte, then a SIPTU (Services Industrial Professional Technical Union) official, now a member of the Irish parliament. She won.

Mary was to find that Labour, with its traditional working-class views, was just as much a male club as any other party. She still remembers with anger the male gang-up in the Dublin Corporation to elect a Labour Mayor in the eighties. As a Labour councillor herself, she had become very friendly with colleague Mary Freehill. 'Mary should have been the candidate on one particular occasion, but it was the boys, the lads, who fixed it up between them. She was outstandingly the better candidate. She would have brought the party great kudos.'

Indeed, it was Mary Freehill, she says, who helped her put her working life in perspective. The Corporation's answer to everything was to form a sub-committee, she recalls. 'I remember sitting beside Mary Freehill at one of these endless meetings and saying, "It's all very well for you, but honest to God, it's very hard when you are a mother of children!" Mary Freehill said, "You don't know how lucky you are. I don't have a family like that so I don't know when to stop." And she stopped me in my tracks. How lucky I was that I had a home to go to, and kids! And she was going on to yet another meeting and another meeting and she didn't have that distraction. And I never complained again!'

For Mary, feminism had to come out of the real lives of ordinary women. It had to encompass motherhood, home and family, as well as the world of work and politics. In her first election address to Trinity voters, she welcomed the fact that women were beginning to play a significant part in the political, economic and social life of the country. 'This concrete achievement is a much more cogent argument than the slogans of an aggressive feminist.'[11] As late as the mid-seventies she told the Catholic magazine, *The Word*: 'I think the Women's Movement is too radical', and also 'I don't believe in suffragette-type activity'.[12] She embraced the term feminist later on when she was able to define it herself. 'Feminism is about realising the full potential of women because we are all enhanced by both men and women achieving their full potential. To do that, men have to adjust, particularly in recognising the values of home-making, child-rearing – a partnership approach. It enhances a marriage, partnership, a family, if what a woman can contribute is realised in balanced terms to what a man can do.'

Her own family, her own children, are central. 'With Tessa, my first, I couldn't believe the joy I felt on learning I was pregnant. I had had this sense of not necessarily being the sort of person who's capable of having a child.' She says she is as obsessive as her own parents were. 'My children are, with Nick, the centre of my life and know they are. It has been happily a wonderful relationship. I absolutely adore my three and it's reciprocated', she says. 'They have managed to be very private about having a very public mother. They don't want to be public, but have never been anything less than really supportive of me in what I'm doing.'

Her pride in her children was something she shared with her own mother, even if only for the six months between Tessa's birth in October 1972 and Mrs Bourke's death in March 1973. Mary still cherishes one of their last conversations. Mrs Bourke had come up to Dublin to visit Adrian's wife, Ruth, who had given birth to a new baby, Elizabeth.

'I remember my mother coming out of the hospital and saying, "That's a beautiful baby, but nobody will be as nice as your Tessa."' Twenty-five years later, Mary Robinson, feminist and proud mother, can't suppress a grin.

8

HARD LABOUR

'Let's be very blunt about it,' says Dick Spring, former Tánaiste (deputy Prime Minister) and Labour leader. 'Not that one wants control over the office of Attorney-General, but Mary Robinson as Attorney-General would have been a free agent and ahead of the political agenda of the day.'[1]

This was a criticism. Mary Robinson was too progressive, too liberal and too independent to be the Irish Labour party's Attorney-General, the job for which she seemed to be ideally suited. Indeed, Mary Robinson may simply always have been too progressive, too liberal, and too independent for Dick Spring and the Irish Labour party. Party politics needs compromise. It cannot value independence. It didn't value Mary Robinson.

Independence is what defines her. She was comfortable as an Independent Trinity senator and successful as an independent President. So, many people were surprised when this independent voice joined Labour in 1976. Despite the 1969 intake of intellectuals like Conor Cruise O'Brien, David Thornley, and Justin Keating, Labour's radicalism was blunted by its solid block of country TDs (members of parliament), traditional working-class men who distrusted change. It was unlikely Mary would have joined the country's biggest party, nationalist Fianna Fáil, founded by Eamon de Valera. But people could have understood it better if Mary had waited a year until her friend Garret FitzGerald took over Christian Democratic Fine Gael. Garret himself was more a social democrat, he was progressive and welcomed women. Fine Gael was Mary's family tradition, after all. Her grandfather, H.C. Bourke, had spoken on party election platforms.

'I had no interest in joining Fianna Fáil or Fine Gael – though I was asked,' she says. 'I'd gone a long way on the independent agenda. My political interests had deepened. I got angrier. Through Cherish and other involvements, I became interested in issues of empowerment and justice. Of the existing parties, Labour was nearest to addressing the issues I wanted to address.' She was influenced by the fact that John Horgan, the Independent senator who had campaigned with her on almost every reformist issue in the Senate, had decided to join Labour. 'If we could get into the Dáil (Ireland's lower House, equivalent to the House of Commons), we could achieve together a change in Irish society in relation to resources and distribution, equality and education. Despite everything, I'm glad I did make that choice.'

But Labour distrusted middle-class intellectuals. 'For someone coming from her background, it was difficult to be accepted by party-men who were not university graduates, who had come up through the trade union movement, up from labouring positions to parliament,' says Dick Spring, whose own father had been first a trade unionist, then a TD. 'They represented conservative, rural Ireland.' These people need patient persuading to take on new ideas, says Spring. 'One of my criticisms of Mary and the intelligentsia in the party was that they didn't spend the time, even if it seemed futile, to persuade those coming from other echelons of society, from the other side of the street. They should have given them the time and respect which was necessary in order to bring those people with them.'[2]

Current Labour leader, Ruairi Quinn, remembers her from the Senate as 'clinical, cold and distant, a political sole trader. She would make a devastating speech but wouldn't stay around to tease it out with individual party members. She didn't try to persuade you. She would make her point at parliamentary party meetings but she wouldn't stay on to persuade people.'[3]

Mary accepts the criticism. 'Usually before going into the

Senate, I would have been to a parliamentary party meeting and they were deadly . . . except for the funny moments with Frank Cluskey or Conor Cruise O'Brien. But, let's face it, it prepared me for the UN. It was all horrifically long-winded, and there would be some item on the agenda that I wanted to discuss and we would never get to it, and if we did, they weren't interested. Yes, I'm sure I didn't explain. I was probably doing too much to have time to explain. I was probably trying to get to a lecture or meet a commitment for a client in court in the morning, or to get home to my family.'

Brendan Halligan, the then party secretary who organised Mary's entry to the party, says that she was badly treated by Labour. 'They should have recognised what they had. She should have been warmly supported and protected. As far as I was concerned she was a princess. She was everything we could have wanted.'[4]

Mary called herself a socialist, but the ideological clothes never quite fitted. Her friend, Garret FitzGerald, who was happy to see her join Labour, says she was a liberal social democrat like himself – she never teased out the economic implications of socialism, he says.[5]

Ruairi Quinn agrees. 'In economic terms, she was very strong on issues of poverty and of marginalised groups, but in terms of the collectivised economy, or of using the state in an interventionist way, that wasn't her interest. Economics basically didn't interest her.'[6]

Indeed, the public associated Mary with pluralism and with social justice, so it came as a surprise to see her declare in a 1982 interview with *Irish Times* journalist Mary Maher: 'The task is now the use of the existing pressures to build the socialist movement . . . we need to be tougher about our own policies. We want employment . . . we have to cost it. We want banks nationalised, taxation reformed, building land controlled.'[7] It didn't really sound like Mary Robinson and indeed, the comment about the banks came back to haunt her during the presidential election. Did she ever really believe it?

'Yes, I believed it at the time.' Did Nick believe it? 'I doubt it. He never challenged me on it. He knew how strongly I felt about equality and social justice and didn't have to agree with me on the small print . . . I remember, a couple of times, his scepticism and my growing doubts.'

The truth was that Mary, so expert in other fields, was not trained to develop an acceptable set of economic principles to address inequality. So she embraced socialist economics whole and undigested. In other areas she was able to work out her position from first principles but not where economic issues were involved.

As the years went on, she became increasingly disenchanted. For someone like her, a liberal who believed in individual rights within a community context, socialism was too big, too centralised, too dogmatic, she says. 'And it didn't address the motivations of people, what makes people respond – whereas the market addresses part of the motivation of people but leaves out the unmotivated, as if they don't count. That's the cruelty of the market . . . Yes, I miss that economic training. I recognise that I have a weakness there.'

Labour left-winger, Michael D. Higgins, saw her as a lonely figure. He co-sponsored her legislation for contraception and the abolition of illegitimacy in the Senate, and admired her because her sense of injustice didn't stem from her own background. 'There was a kind of intellectual loneliness to her position. Some of us would have been able to discover a sort of comradeship out of social activity in the more lumpen backgrounds we had come from, but that wasn't available to her. Her practice and commitment had come out of intellect rather than emotion and rage. In my case the emotion and rage at the waste of human life had preceded the intellectual framework. She did it the other way around.'[8]

Michael D. respected the fact that Mary had emerged from a privileged background to become a champion of social justice. Others were more critical, pointing particularly to Mary's membership since the early seventies of the executive committee of the Trilateral Commission.

The commission, which was made up of politicians, academics, trade unionists, businessmen and journalists from North America, Europe and Japan, was branded by suspicious left-wingers as right wing because its members included top executives from Coca-Cola, the Wells Fargo Bank, Rio Tinto Zinc, General Electric and Rolls-Royce. Even more damning in the eyes of the conspiracy theorists, it included former NATO Chief, Lord Carrington and the great hate figure of the left, Richard Nixon's secretary of state, Henry Kissinger. The membership also included Dr Garret FitzGerald, Dr Ken Whitaker, former governor of the Central Bank, Michael O'Kennedy of Fianna Fáil, Myles Staunton of Fine Gael, and Justin Keating of the Labour party. The commission, Mary says, was regarded as a left-wing conspiracy in the US and a right-wing conspiracy in Europe. 'It's a conspiracy theorist's godsend.' She was on the left of the commission with politicians like William Rodgers then of the British Labour party, later of the Liberal Democrats. She enjoyed meeting powerful people, she says, and learned not to be fazed by them. 'The Trilateral Commission was a learning process in that I met powerful North American, European and Japanese counterparts in countries and contexts that were extraordinarily interesting.' It was an influental network and Nick didn't want her to abandon it. Mary had co-produced a report on North/South issues with Governor Scranton of the US, and the then Japanese chairman Michio Watanabe. When it had no impact, Mary resigned. 'I felt I was beginning to be mildly corrupted and when I couldn't wield influence, well, I said goodbye.'

When the 1977 election came, Brendan Halligan had packaged four candidates – himself, Pat Carroll, Michael D. Higgins, and Mary Robinson as representing the young radical voice of the party.

He had to do something to improve Labour's liberal credentials. The outgoing government of which Labour was a part had voted down its own contraception Bill and two years earlier when Labour formally committed itself to introducing divorce, no parliamentary party member would go on air to defend it, says Halligan. He had to do it himself.[9]

Mary was seeking a nomination in the right Dublin constituency, and Rathmines West was considered progressive enough to suit her. Selection is done by delegates from constituency branches and two new ones were formed, dominated by women members who supported Mary Robinson. Two branches each were also controlled by two Dáil hopefuls already on the scene, local labour councillor Michael Collins and left-winger David Neligan. But there was a problem. By the time the election was called, the pro-Robinson branches had been in existence slightly less than the six months necessary before delegates could vote at a selection convention. So Roddy Connolly, then party chairman, backed by Halligan, decided that lunar, rather than calendar months should apply, and claimed that Robinson's branches qualified. Halligan makes no apology for his lunar logic. 'You use your discretion,' he says. 'I regarded her as a flagship. It was a great coup that she ever joined the party and I was glad I played even a little part in that.'

The selection meeting decided, however, that it was wiser not to let Mary's branches vote. She wasn't selected but was added to the ticket later by party headquarters, prompting David Neligan to withdraw in protest.

So Mary headed into a campaign where the Labour camp, as ever, was riven; inflation and unemployment were high; and the outgoing government of which Labour had been part was extraordinarily unpopular.

Then came the smear. 'The night before the election, every pub in Rathmines was leafletted with the claim that I was a Robinson of the pharmacy chain, Hayes, Conyngham and Robinson, and that I was getting a penny on every contraceptive pill sold, and that was why I was backing contraception,' Mary recalls. 'That was a blow – but the bigger blow was that we didn't pull together, because that seat was eminently winnable.'

Mary lost by about 400 votes. Fianna Fáil returned to office with a massive seventy-seven seats and Labour retired to opposition. When Mary went back to her Trinity electorate not as an Independent but as a Labour Senate candidate, they punished her – she scraped in third.[10] The next years were tough and disillusioning. Brendan Halligan guessed she was thinking of leaving the party and asked her out to lunch to beg her not to go. She told him that she was pregnant with her third child and that she felt she could do more outside than inside politics.

Still, when the 1981 election was called by Fianna Fáil Prime Minister, Charles Haughey, she agreed to run for Labour in Dublin West. 'I allowed myself to be persuaded against my better instincts.' She had just had her third baby, Aubrey; she was beginning to question her role in the party; and this was the wrong constituency. It was largely working class, a wasteland of half-built new housing estates and roads where many of Ireland's travelling families had established temporary camps. In some places there was tension between the new estates and the travellers, and Mary Robinson had championed the travellers. Irish politics has little room for such champions. In the catch-all game of the single transferable vote, you mustn't alienate anybody, and champions always do.

Mary had taken on an unpopular issue – travellers were culturally and socially different; they obeyed their own rules; settled people didn't want to live beside them. Because travellers were nomadic, they rarely voted, so Mary was one of the few politicians who took up their cause.

Mervyn Ennis, then an Eastern Health Board social worker, remembers bringing her to see travellers in the seventies and making her park her green Saab outside the site. Mervyn had no time for those he saw as intellectual middle-class Labour politicians. The site was a mudbath.

'I wanted to give her the experience of walking up through the mud and dirt. The travelling women have to come up through the mud after going out to get water maybe three miles away, to get water in a churn to bring back home, or they are dragging up bales of turf briquettes in an old pram. I remember saying to myself: I wonder if she'll come up through the muck? But she did.' She talked to the families; she went to the schools, to the training centres. 'So she saw it from all sides. She is the only politician I know who ever did that.'[11]

The previous summer, on 23 July 1980, she had helped the travellers win a famous legal victory. Rosella McDonald lived in a caravan on the almost completed Tallaght by-pass road with a sick husband and ten children aged between six months and fifteen years. On 14 May 1980, she was officially given three days to move on, without being offered anywhere else to go. Mary Robinson

SC, instructed by Greg O'Neill, solicitor, won an interlocutory injunction preventing Dublin County Council from evicting her. The case was appealed to the Supreme Court and in a famous 1980 judgement, Mr Justice Tom O'Higgins pointed out the duty of local authorities to provide alternative accommodation before evicting people.[12]

After the judgement, local authorities could no longer afford to ignore travellers' housing needs and, even before the statutory recognition of such needs in 1988, they started to provide both housing and halting sites, despite fierce resistance by local residents.[13] Among the areas where resistance was fiercest was Dublin West, where Mary found herself fighting an uphill battle as the travellers' or, more colloquially, the 'knackers' friend. Opponents were quick to capitalise and very soon the leaflets were out: 'Want a knacker for a neighbour? Vote Labour!'

For Mary and Labour, it was an exhausting campaign, during which she breast-fed her four-week-old-baby, Aubrey, in safe houses as she canvassed. She remembers Nell McCafferty, who came to write a piece on the campaign, being fascinated by the breast-feeding. 'She'd keep asking. "Are ye empty? D'ye feel empty?" She'd never seen anyone feed a child before and from the point of view of my own privacy I was terrified she was going to write about it, and also because it wouldn't do me any good on polling day.'

As a pre-election publicity stunt, Mary had reluctantly agreed to be photographed with baby Aubrey in Holles Street Hospital, but the 'new baby' angle did not help her among the working-class voters in Dublin West.

'It was not only no use to me, it was a positive disadvantage in places like Ballyfermot. They disapproved of me running for election with a new baby. They said it on the doorsteps – "Haven't you a young baby?" Whereas in a middle-class area I probably would have got reasonable support.'

Mary didn't win, and journalist Mary Maher of the *Irish Times* remembers her fighting back tears at the election count as her second defeat was announced. That was her last Dáil bid. She won back her Senate seat easily in 1981 and twice in 1982 after two quick elections in a row.

The women at the doors in Ballyfermot had a point. How did anybody manage two careers, one in politics and one in the law, as well as bringing up three children, one of them a baby? Mary's secretary, Ann Lane, from Millstreet in Co. Cork, remembers that Mary, like any working mother, made do from day to day. Sometimes she had someone helping at home. When she didn't, Ann would help out. 'Once I looked after a two-week-old baby here in the office,' says Ann. 'The notion of Mary as a cool, organised career woman is not valid. It was hit and miss. We muddled along.' Then Mary's nanny, Nan Coyne, came back from England and life settled down. Nan ran the house and the children and, for Mary, she was a personal support, a highly intelligent and forthright woman. Mary loved and respected her. When Nan became fatally ill, it was Mary personally who nursed her. After all the years, it mattered very much to Mary that she would be the one to care for Nan. 'To me, it was very important. It was the completion of the cycle.' When Nan became fatally ill, Laura Donegan, who would eventually go with Mary to Áras an Uachtaráin, helped with the children and the house.

In 1984 it seemed as though politics was finally going to find the perfect role for Mary Robinson. Labour had formed a coalition government with Garret FitzGerald's Fine Gael two years earlier. Now the Attorney-General, Peter Sutherland of Fine Gael, had become a European Commissioner and Labour claimed the right to nominate his replacement.

Mary Robinson looked like an obvious choice. She was Labour's best-known lawyer, she was a senior counsel and a friend of the Taoiseach. She was not, however, a friend of Dick Spring's.

The prickly relationship between Robinson and Spring had many origins. There was the matter of legal rank – she'd taken silk, he hadn't. There was background – she came from the professional upper-middle classes – he, despite his Trinity education and barrister's training, was loyally the trade unionist's son from Kerry.

There were the differences – albeit good-humoured – between himself and the Bourke brothers in student politics, where he helped engineer his friend Joe Revington's defeat of Adrian as Student Representative Council President. 'Of course we beat him,' says Spring. 'Sure, we're from Kerry.'

But there was a more important clash – one of values. Spring, the supreme politician, valued loyalty above all. Mary Robinson valued independence. Each distrusted what the other held most dear. They were bound to disagree.

Spring spoke to her about the job and she was interested – so interested, says Ruairi Quinn, then Minister for Labour, that, unusually for her, she looked for support. 'She canvassed me in relation to the A-G slot and not very comfortably, in the vicinity of the Members' bar. It was, in an indirect way, letting me know she would be interested in it.

'She was clearly the best qualified person around,' he said. 'But she was too taken up with campaigning to make a good A-G. I can say that now.'

Spring wanted to appoint his friend, John Rogers, then a junior counsel. 'From my point of view at the time, I needed an A-G whom I had an intimate working relationship with. My relationship with Mary Robinson would never have reached that scale. Maybe there's fault on both sides. I don't think we're the cuddly types.'

Spring says that for the first time the position of Attorney-General was going to be a Labour party resource and he chose Rogers on that basis, a choice, he says, which came to be regarded as 'one of the best appointments we've had in the state'. Indeed, despite his youth, Rogers was generally recognised as having carried out his job as the government's legal adviser in exemplary fashion. Spring says he didn't have to find negatives for not appointing Mary Robinson because he was going to appoint John Rogers. 'I know that there were others who would have been saying that Mary Robinson as Attorney-General would cause fierce problems for the party, for the state. Mary wouldn't take the state line. If an issue came in that she had been fighting for for the previous 15 years, irrespective of whether the state could afford it

Bourke family seal and motto: un roi, une foi, une loi (one king, one faith, one law)

Mary's great-uncle, Thomas Augustus Macaulay of the Irish Republican Brotherhood, convicted for conspiracy to murder

Mary's great-uncle, John Paget Bourke, a member of Queen Victoria's bodyguard

Mary's uncle, Paget John Bourke, and his wife Susan, are presented to Princess Elizabeth and Prince Philip, Nairobi 1952

Above left Mary's grandfather, H. C. Bourke, and Mary's father, Aubrey, lead in the winner, at a Westmeath point-to-point. Frank Boland on horseback

Above right Young Tessa O'Donnell, Mary's mother, and her mother, Winifred

Left Mary's paternal grand-mother, Eleanor Macaulay Bourke, joint master of the local hunt, sits side-saddle on Tatler, in front of her home, Amana

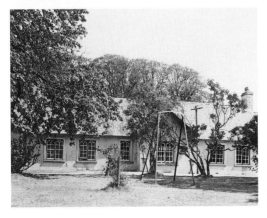

Amana, home of H. C. and Eleanor Bourke

Dr. Tessa
O'Donnell and
Dr. Aubrey
Bourke at his
conferring

Below Occasionally,
Dr. Bourke did his
calls on horseback

Mary on her rocking-horse

Mary in action on Billy

Oliver in uniform of great uncle John Paget

Bourkes at the beach: *back left to right*: Oliver, Mary, Aubrey; *front left to right*: Henry and Adrian

Mary Bourke, outgoing Auditor of the TCD Law Society, hands over to her happy successor (*lower right*), Nick Robinson

A Paris bridge: Mary on honeymoon   A Paris bridge: Nick on honeymoon

Sharing a cigar – Mary and
(below) her father

Mothers-to-be: Mary (expecting Aubrey), and her
sister-in-law, Louise Bourke, married to Oliver,
outside the Robinson's home in Wellington Place,
1981

Mary and her father-in-law,
Howard Robinson, Tenerife 1971

Mary and her friend, the poet, Eavan Boland at
Enniscrone beach, Co. Mayo

Mary on Enniscrone beach

Mary on holiday in the US

Mary on holiday in Tenerife

Above right Mary with Tessa

Nan Coyne in Tenerife with
William and Tessa

Robinson children in France,
Easter 1987 *Left to right*:
Aubrey, Tessa, William

A legal team: solicitor Nick Robinson and Mary Robinson on the day she takes silk

Cartoonist Nick Robinson targets his wife; Mary lectures on 'Crowd Control and the Criminal Law' – to an empty hall

Bride Rosney

or not, I think she might go down and say: "I support this motion, my Lord". People were saying that sort of thing,' he says.

It was a blow to Mary. 'I think I was disappointed because I felt the reason he didn't appoint me was that he couldn't control me . . . He would know that I would have to be true to the issues and my principles and I think Dick liked to have the capacity to rein in and control anyone who was going to work closely with him. Very shortly afterwards, I was relieved, because I recognised that the way the Anglo-Irish discussions were developing was causing me immense concern, and if I had been appointed I would have had to resign as Attorney-General.'

Mary's differences with Dick Spring would continue even into the presidency. They would always disagree most sharply over the North, the issue which, more than any other, dominated her political life. Again and again, when Mary went to the edge – and, in Dick Spring's opinion, over it – it would be because of Northern Ireland.

9

A RESIGNING MATTER

It was Easter 1998 and Ireland was celebrating. A historic agreement had been arrived at after thirty years of the troubles in the North. Former loyalist paramilitary Billy Hutchinson was asked on radio why Unionists could accept this agreement, but not the 1985 Anglo-Irish Agreement. 'Because this time we were consulted,' said Hutchinson.[1]

Consulting the northern majority about their future would seem like the democratic thing to do. It wasn't done when Garret FitzGerald and Margaret Thatcher signed their deal at Hillsborough in November 1985, and only one member of the Irish parliament cared enough about the sidelining of Unionists to resign from the government back benches – Senator Mary Robinson.

She was a classic liberal. She believed that any political development had to have the involvement of both communities. She believed that both Unionist and Nationalist views, even at their most extreme, had a right to be heard. Since the dominant political culture in the Republic was a nationalist one, she found herself pleading most often for a hearing for Unionists. They were a major concern, but not her only one. Northern Ireland splits people into camps and Mary didn't belong to any. She enraged traditional nationalists by pointing to the bigotry of the twenty-six county state. She irritated all nationalists, even progressive ones, by insisting that Unionists had to be consulted.

She infuriated Unionists, and the law-and-order lobby in the Republic, by criticising security measures that infringed civil liberties. She believed in a liberal society north and south, and refused to retreat behind tribal or ideological barricades.

This created tensions with those who might have been political allies. Conor Cruise O'Brien is an example. Mary and he had soldiered together for a pluralist Ireland – he was one of her Senate supporters in the 1973 election. But in 1974, they crossed swords heatedly over a civil rights issue.

Mary felt that governments reached too easily for emergency legislation in response to security problems and she had protested, as had Conor himself, over the speed with which the anti-terrorist measure, the Offences Against the State (Amendment) Act, had been rushed through parliament after two bombs exploded in Dublin in 1972.

But by 1974, Conor was himself Minister for Posts and Telegraphs and became increasingly security conscious, hardening up the broadcasting ban on the IRA and their political apologists, Provisional Sinn Féin, under Section 31 of the Broadcasting Act (whose provisions Mary fought right up to the European Court of Human Rights).[2]

Internment without trial had been introduced in Northern Ireland in August 1971 and was still operating in 1974. In October of that year, Mary Robinson addressed a meeting in Dublin's Mansion House condemning internment, as she had from the beginning,[3] and arguing for a return to the due process of the courts.

She was in turn condemned by Conor Cruise O'Brien for not referring to the difficulties the courts had in dealing with armed conspiracies, for not condemning the murder of judges by the IRA, and for casting an aspersion on the integrity of judges. She hit back on RTE radio, refusing to allow her liberal voice to be silenced because of attempts to align her with the Provisional IRA. 'He said I condemned the integrity of judges. In fact, I condemned the collective silence of the legal profession, including the judiciary, at the operation of internment. They operate side by side with a system which undermines the legal process and is a fatal flaw in building up society, creating confidence and building, in an alienated minority, trust and faith in the system.'

North or south, Mary believed in respect for the law, faith in the system. That meant ensuring that the system and the law deserved such respect. The bringing down of the power-sharing executive in the North months earlier by an illegal Ulster Workers' Council strike had led nationalists to argue bitterly that law-breaking was the only way to get results.

Ten years of failed political initiatives led to increased support for the IRA, and in 1983, in an effort to provide a forum for constitutional politics, the Irish government set up the New Ireland Forum. It was open to all parties, but only constitutional nationalists attended and they set about finding common ground and an agreed initiative to present to the British government. Mary Robinson, who travelled constantly to Northern Ireland, who had contacts in both communities through Trinity and her own family, and through her interaction with the Irish Theological Commission, was an ideal representative for Labour on the forum.

Northern Ireland had figured heavily in all her Senate election addresses since 1973. She was looking for peaceful reconciliation, for functional and economic north–south links within a European framework.[4] In 1977 she was warning that people mustn't give up on the North because they were sickened by the brutality, and she challenged them to look into their own hearts.

'Despite public avowals of horror, we continue to brutalise the situation by assuming inflexible cultural patterns and dogmatic notions of Irishness,' she said. 'We can and should be looking for a flexible and generous interpretation of nationality for the whole of this island which by removing rigid definitions of identity would remove the necessity to fight for and against such definitions.'[5]

This is what she was hoping for at the New Ireland Forum: an island solution which had room for all traditions, all beliefs. Pluralism in the Republic would be a good place to start, she thought, so she took on the Catholic bishops at the Forum with their legal adviser, Belfast-born lawyer, Mary McAleese, later to be elected President. Their vision of a new Ireland was very different.

Mary Robinson tackled Bishop Cahal Daly's claim that he understood Northern Protestant fears of any new political settlement and his avowal that 'we would raise our voices to resist any constitutional proposals which might infringe or might imperil the civil and religious rights and liberties cherished by Northern Protestants'.[6]

Conscious of church resistance to any change in the Republic's laws on divorce, Mary asked: 'Why are you not raising your voices now in relation to the Protestants and others who are not of the Catholic faith, in this part of the country? Surely they, too, are entitled to full civil and religious liberties?'[7]

She did not get a direct answer. Earlier, when she asked how progress could be made towards a new Ireland unless the rights of minorities were recognised and guaranteed, Mary McAleese argued that pluralism was about more than divorce and said, 'If divorce and contraception are seen as the hallmarks of a liberal society, then Northern Ireland was a very liberal, pluralist society a long, long time ago.'[8]

Later, Mary Robinson moved on to education. Accepting that the Catholic/Protestant division in the school system was not the cause of Northern's Ireland's problems, she asked about the development of inter-denominational schooling and the possibility of promoting greater understanding among young children who would be the adults of the future.

Mrs McAleese was quick to disabuse her. 'I often hear this catch-phrase in the Republic. "Why do you not all get together and integrate the schools – would that not help the problem somewhat?"' she said. 'The notion that consensus comes from contact or even that understanding comes from contact is wrong. It is a dubious and simplistic notion. It would be nice if it were right.' She then went on to tell of her own experience growing up in Belfast's Ardoyne. 'It was a mixed area as I was growing up. I had tremendous contact with Protestant neighbours, played with them. They were in and out of my house but it did not stop one of them from becoming a member of the UDA and now doing a life sentence for killing five Catholics.'[9] Catholic parents in Northern Ireland, she insisted, appreciated their Catholic schools, for which they had to pay extra.

If flexibility had been expected from the Catholic Church, it wasn't forthcoming. Mary's questioning had exposed the fact that the bishops preferred to make promises about the new Ireland rather than make changes in the present one. Dick Spring praised her understanding of canon law and described her contribution to the Forum as 'quite mould-breaking'.[10]

But the Forum Report, when it came, wasn't mould-breaking enough for Mary. The political need for a unanimous report forced a concession to Charles Haughey's ultra-nationalist views. Despite Garret FitzGerald and Dick Spring's reservations, the Forum members agreed to state that the 'ideal' solution would be a unitary Irish state, though the Forum was also open to other proposals such as federation or confederation.[11]

Mary objected strongly to the categorising of the unitary state as 'ideal' – as did Frank Cluskey, former Labour party leader. She and Cluskey had always pushed for an understanding of the Unionist viewpoint. She had voted for him as leader in 1977 and was close to him. 'He could be terrible when he was the worse for drink. But I loved him dearly, I mean *loved* him. I remember sitting beside him at the New Ireland Forum and somebody would be droning on and Frank would turn to me and say "Rivettin'!" I remember when he had the awful growth in his throat and I said it must be a terrible pain in the ass. "No, Mary, wrong part of the anatomy, wrong part of the anatomy."'

Dick Spring says that perhaps he should have consulted with his Forum team more, including with Frank and Mary. 'Her point was valid but compromise was the order of the day.' Cluskey was her ally, too, on the Anglo-Irish Agreement. Just as with the Forum, Mary was almost a lone dissenting voice, and now she was criticising what would probably be regarded as her friend Garret FitzGerald's greatest political achievement, an agreement which would give the Irish Republic for the first time a consultative voice in the running of the North.

'The interest and involvement and concern with the North is

probably one of my strongest motivating factors ever since I started in political life, and over a long period of time I had built up a very considerable range both of church and other contacts, and through twenty years in the Senate and my time in the New Ireland Forum I knew the political figures very well. I was really desperately concerned about the cobbling together of the Anglo-Irish Agreement,' she said. 'I respect Garret FitzGerald enormously. I have a great *grá* (love) for him, a great sense of him. Garret desperately needed something in the bag, as did John Hume, and it was terribly difficult. It was one of the most lonely and difficult times for me,' she said. Unionists had been kept in the dark about the negotiations and felt betrayed, not only by Prime Minister Margaret Thatcher, but by Garret FitzGerald, who, only a few years earlier, had said he would never do a deal over their heads.

'It was so evident to me that the Unionists felt resentful, excluded, that the Agreement couldn't achieve the framework envisaged. I had more discussions with Dick Spring then than at any other time – before the publication of the Anglo-Irish Agreement. I not only got no satisfaction, but I couldn't believe some of the things he said to me – that within a month all the Unionists were going to accept it! I don't know whether he really did believe that or whether it was part of his persuasion tactics. Part of my problem was that I was completely failing to get my concerns across and I was being given the most optimistic scenario on what was going to happen.' Mary knew what would happen and indeed few people will ever forget the massed crowds of Unionists in Belfast protesting against the agreement and their cheer as Jim Molyneaux and Ian Paisley vowed: 'Never! Never! Never!' Mary got nowhere with Spring at private meetings, so she made her opposition known at the joint meeting of the coalition government parliamentary parties. Frank Cluskey and Donegal TD, Paddy Harte, objected with her to what she angrily called 'the brouhaha, *ruaille-buaille* (fuss) and glory and celebration of the Anglo–Irish Agreement'. But official accounts of that meeting on the television news claimed the agreement had been supported unanimously. Angry and disillusioned, Mary Robinson promptly resigned from the Labour party.

Dick Spring remembers it like this: 'She felt Unionists should have been more represented. On the other hand, as we said to her many times, we assumed that Margaret Thatcher was looking after the Unionists – that wasn't our brief.' He's not convinced that the Anglo-Irish Agreement was her real reason for resigning from the party. 'It was the stage of her career she was at. If she was somebody who had intended to contest the following Dáil election or try to move on in politics, I think she could have overcome her reservations.'

He didn't try to stop her leaving. In the macho world of party politics, Dáil seats were what counted and Mary had failed to deliver.

In time, she would deliver a vote which would set Spring and the Labour party rocking on their heels but, for now, she felt she could achieve more in the courts or as an Independent.

Her family didn't mind. She often told a story during her Labour years about her son William. The children had welcomed her back greedily after one of her general election campaigns and William, then four, was dismayed to see her open a letter with the familiar Plough and Stars masthead. 'But Mum,' he wailed, 'I thought the Labour party was over.'

It was now.

10

ABORTION AND DIVORCE

Since the 1992 Supreme Court judgment which makes abortion at least technically legal in Ireland, Mary Robinson has believed in facing the facts. 'I would make abortion available in this country in limited circumstances.' She believes that Ireland must address honestly the needs of more than 4,000 women who annually seek abortions in Britain.

'It would be healthier to be more mature about ourselves, more honest. Even for a country that regrets and feels a great sense of loss at the termination of life, it would be a preferable situation. It would be a kind of coming to terms with the problem, instead of exporting it and moralising about it.'

This is not a view Mary Robinson could ever have expressed as President. Indeed, when she was accused during the presidential election campaign of being pro-abortion, she protested vigorously that she was against abortion and had been all her political life. Abortion is a crime in Ireland under the 1861 Offences Against the Person Act, but a controversial 1992 Irish Supreme Court judgment has now, at least technically, changed that.[1]

Mary never joined in the condemnation of abortion. She did something more useful – she tried to ensure there were alternatives. More Irish women chose abortion than did their English counterparts, she argued in 1977,[2] because they did not have other options. Contraceptives were not available and, as she knew from her work with Cherish, at that time single mothers and their children were shunned by society and ignored by the state. 'I consistently said that we need access to contraception to reduce the abortion rate. That was partly because I knew through Cherish the terrible fear, financial burden, humiliation, lack of self-respect involved in taking the train and the boat to Liverpool. And it wasn't middle-class women I was talking about,' she said. 'It was the woman who has no choice, who is trapped in a terrible situation which is horrific for her, and she hasn't the money to resolve the issue.' She asked again and again for proper housing, child care and income support to alleviate the pressures.[3] But it suited almost everybody if a woman took the lonely abortion trail to England. The main task for the Church and most of the political establishment was to keep Ireland an abortion-free zone.

In 1981, with the liberalising influence of EC membership and the creeping availability of contraception – the Catholic Church had always linked contraception and abortion[4] – there were conservative fears that abortion was on the way. Politicians were neatly skewered before the June 1981 election when an anti-abortion alliance called the Pro-Life Amendment Campaign extracted a promise from both major parties to introduce an abortion ban in the Constitution.[5] Abortion was still a word that could frighten grown men in their beds. 'It still is the "A" word,' says Mary. 'Look at the US. Look at the arrears for the UN! That's what's holding it up – abortion. It takes a disproportionate hold on political calculation.'

Once again Mary was to find herself sharply at odds with her friend Garret FitzGerald. He was facing a knife-edge election, and he was pitted against his bitter political enemy, Charles Haughey. For both, it was their first general election as party leaders, FitzGerald as leader of centrist Fine Gael, which sits with the Christian Democrat group in the European Parliament, Haughey as leader of the more nationalist Fianna Fáil. Every vote counted, and abortion swings votes.

'Garret was shanghaied on it,' Mary says. 'I remember being very cross. He shouldn't have considered putting it in the Constitution at all, but he was too far gone and he was too near the election. Some of the Protestant Churches had come out and said they didn't agree with the proposal. He had a formula if only he'd used it – "I'm not going to change anything over the heads of a minority church".'

Garret FitzGerald tried to retreat from the absolutist formula but in the end he was defeated. Rebels from his own party joined the opposition, and the formula approved by the Pro-Life Group was to be put before the people: 'The State acknowledges the right to life of the unborn and with due regard to the equal right to life of the mother, guarantees in its laws to respect and, as far as practicable, by its laws to defend and vindicate that right.'[6]

Anyone who accuses Mary Robinson of being cold, detached, or a reluctant feminist, should read what she said about this Eighth Amendment to the Constitution Bill in a marathon two-and-a-half hour speech in the Senate.[7] At times, her anger was close to grief. The measure offended her as a lawyer, as a liberal, but above all it offended her as a woman. This Bill equated the life of a woman with that of a fertilised ovum, nothing more. Fianna Fáil were voting for it. The largest government party, Fine Gael, were going to sit on their hands and, as she put it, 'heroically abstain'. Of the main parties, only Labour were opposing it and Mary led the charge in the Senate.

'We are witnessing the forces of the Catholic Church moving in on a political debate, taking sides in it and using the resources of the Catholic Church to advance those sides,' she said. 'The problem with this Constitutional amendment is that it is the Catholic way of doing things. One is morally right and therefore one puts it into the Constitution, asserts it, and that is the end of it. The Protestant ethos, and the ethos of the Chief Rabbi on behalf of the Jewish community, and the ethos of the other groupings in the state would be one of the freedom of the individual, that it is a moral issue which one does not put in any form into a Constitution for cultural or religious reasons.' The Bill indicated a closed, pre-emptive society which was going to prevent freedom of conscience, make certain citizens feel less citizens of this state, she said.[8] She described some of the thousands of women who went to the UK that year for abortions and mentioned the comment from agencies there that the Irish were the most disadvantaged because they were the most ignorant.

'There have been graphic descriptions of women arriving at Euston Station asking a taxi-man, or carrying an advertisement with a PO box-number in their handbags and asking if anybody knows where this address would be, and so on. This is a terrible indictment of us.'[9]

Where were the women who should protest about this, she asked, frustrated? 'We don't have a sufficiently organised feminist movement to counter this kind of proposal.'

Even though Cherish, the Rape Crisis Centre and the Council of the Status of Women had opposed the Bill, it showed what little power they had in affecting the process, she warned. If men's lives were being equated with a fertilised ovum, she said, it would be another matter.

Instead, women were being put at risk and men were sniggering at a debate 'of prime social, medical and emotional concern to women. Men on the whole get embarrassed. I heard a few jokes downstairs in the bar about my contribution on the other amendment and the detail I had gone into. They were snigger jokes. It was a matter for nudge, nudge, snigger, snigger, all that talk about the fallopian tubes and so on – imagine that on the records of the Seanad (Senate)!'[10] She finished with a blistering attack on a measure which even government ministers had accepted could pose 'a direct life threat to pregnant women in certain circumstances. It comes very close to a kind of licensed murder.'[11]

It was Mary Robinson's finest ever parliamentary contribution and it was remembered not only because it was passionate, but because it was prophetic. The Irish people put an abortion ban in the Constitution on 7 September 1983 by a majority of three to one, and realised ten years later to their horror that Mary's forecasts had all come true. In her detailed legal demolition of the Bill, Mary had made two predictions: that someone would use it to stop a woman travelling abroad for an abortion – 'that is not far-fetched, that is not unreal' – and that it could violate Irish commitments under the European Convention for the Protection of Human Rights and Fundamental Freedoms.[12] She also warned the Labour party at a parliamentary party meeting that the amendment could, because of its ambiguity, actually open the door to abortion.[13] In all cases she was to be proved correct.

First she established that actions pursued under the new amendment would put Ireland in contravention of the European Convention on Human Rights. The issue was the right to information. There were many groups in Ireland who gave women information about abortion or referred them to English clinics. The Society for the Protection of the Unborn Child now set about using the new amendment against such groups. Mary helped defend the groups. She helped represent the leaders of the student bodies in the Supreme Court when SPUC successfully stopped them giving abortion information.[14] In the Supreme Court, too, she helped represent the Dublin Well Woman Centre, which joined with Open Door Counselling in their appeal against the High Court decision on 12 December 1986, when the Attorney-General and SPUC won an injunction which meant the WWC and ODC were 'perpetually restrained from counselling or assisting pregnant women within the jurisdiction of this court to obtain further advice on abortion or to obtain an abortion'. The decision was upheld unanimously in the Supreme Court on 16 March 1988. Mary will never forget that day.

'I felt I was being slapped on the face with a wet dishcloth "Whack! Whack! Whack!" as I listened to the judgment.' It was rare for her, she says, to have such an emotional reaction in court. 'I felt the Supreme Court had tried to do God's work. I remember feeling physically crushed taking that judgment because I felt, this is not a court of law. They're doing the wrong job.'[15]

It would be 1992 before the European Court of Human Rights finally ruled on the Well Woman case which Mary had brought to Europe, even while fighting her presidential campaign. The court found that the denial of information constituted an interference with the applicants' freedom of expression under Article 10 of the Convention.[16] Mary had been proved right.

What proved even more spectacularly true were her warnings that pregnant women would be pursued in court and that the whole constitutional ban was a legal quagmire which would actually allow the introduction of abortion. On 17 February 1992, almost exactly as she had predicted, a fourteen-year-old rape victim was legally prevented by the High Court from leaving the state to procure an abortion in Britain. As a result of what became known as the X case, the Irish abortion law was condemned internationally as barbarous and Irish women of child-bearing age realised they they could lose their right to travel. They felt they had been betrayed by the institutions of the state. They felt no one was listening, and President Mary Robinson chose, as she would at other times of crisis, to ease that sense of hurt by expressing it. She could hardly have chosen a more sensitive subject, but on this occasion there was a feeling that she had spoken for the whole country.

It had been a difficult week for women and girls in Ireland, she said, and she called for a more compassionate society: 'Although as President I have no role in relation to either possible constitutional or legal changes, in a curious way as President I am very much in touch with what women and girls all over the country are feeling – and not just women, because there are very many men who are as troubled as women.' The Irish people were experiencing a very deep crisis, she said. 'I hope we have the courage which we have not always had to face up to and look squarely and to say this is a problem we have got to resolve.'[17]

The courage hasn't been found yet. On 5 March the Supreme Court, which had by then allowed the teenager to leave the country, decided that abortion should be permitted where the life of the mother was at risk, as in this case, from suicidal inclinations.[18]

Once again, Mary was proved right. A case taken under the anti-abortion ban has effectively legalised abortion, but the legislators are still running. At the time of writing, a law regulating abortion has not yet been introduced.

Because of the X case, the Irish government was forced to ask the people once again to vote on the abortion issue. In a constitutional referendum in 25 November 1992 the people voted to keep the ban on abortion but to make two new amendments upholding the right to abortion information and the right to travel abroad for an abortion.[19] Mary Robinson remembers as President signing the new amendments into the Constitution. 'I felt a terrible sadness when the amendments to the abortion issue came up, because I felt we had wasted so much time unnecessarily on a contortion of the Constitution instead of addressing the real pressures on women and families. We still haven't addressed that issue properly.'

There is a real price to be paid when politicians dodge reality. Campaigners for divorce, like Mary Robinson, knew that political timidity had caused real pain. Without divorce, thousands of people were forced into a state of limbo.

Clara Clark married when she was eighteen and fled her violent husband five years later, in 1974, with two small children. From then on, she says, she ceased to exist as far as the state and society were concerned. Because she had taken the initiative, she didn't qualify for a deserted wives' allowance, and for the same reason an unsympathetic court three years later granted her a paltry £15 a week maintenance. The tax authorities still taxed her at the penal rate which applied to married women.

As far as the authorities were concerned, she was married. She couldn't afford an expensive legal separation and by the time Mary Robinson won the right for civil legal aid for separation cases, Clara had a small business and no longer qualified for such aid. Even twelve years after she left him, she had to get her estranged husband's permission for passports for her children. She was his prisoner. She couldn't travel abroad without his permission, and emigration was out of the question. Even when she had a child by her new partner, she had to get her husband's permission to have the baby registered as the child of his real father. Every child born to a married woman was automatically, in the eyes of the law, the child of her legal husband.

The law reflected social attitudes and socially, she says, she was shunned. 'The danger of the unattached woman was that she knew what marriage was. She knew what she was missing. Husbands were fascinated and wives were nervous. I remember a neighbour who used to call her husband in from the front garden when I came out of the house,' says Clara.[20]

She did not want to get around the divorce ban, as many other people did, by obtaining a foreign divorce and hoping it would be recognised in Ireland. 'I wanted Irish recognition. I was Irish.

I felt strongly about that. I didn't want a hole-in-the-corner arrangement. I wanted to be recognised in Ireland.'

For years Clara fought for divorce with activists like Deputy Alan Shatter of Fine Gael and Mary Robinson. Mary had presented her own draft divorce Bill to the Labour parliamentary party in April 1980. When Labour in government with Fine Gael in 1981 agreed only to consider the divorce issue, Mary published the text of her own Bill in the Senate in a frustrated effort to push Labour to move on the issue. Labour's rural conservatives were as opposed to divorce as any Fianna Fáil deputy. Mary joined the parliamentary joint committee on marital breakdown in 1983, and she eventually managed, in 1985, to help produce a majority for a Bill removing the ban on divorce from the Constitution. She had worked hard on that Bill, which had to be put to the people in a referendum. Again, as with the abortion referendum, she went out to persuade the people to vote for tolerance. They didn't, turning divorce down by 63 per cent after an anti-divorce campaign which painted a lurid picture of abandoned wives, abandoned first families, with no proper inheritance or pension entitlements. The government's failure to iron out convincingly all the legal implications of a change in the marriage law told in the end. 'It was badly prepared,' Mary says.

She had long ago learned never to leave anything to political chance and at the time of the divorce campaign, she was exploring the legal as well as the political avenue to changing the law – it often yielded better results. She fought for the right to divorce before the European Court of Human Rights.

The Johnston case, in which she represented Roy Johnston, was in fact about the rights of unmarried families. Roy Johnston and his partner, Janice Williams, were claiming that their rights under the Convention had been violated because they couldn't marry in Ireland – Roy having been married before. But the court did not find for them on the divorce question.[21] 'I think the court went slightly political in not wanting to require, from Strasbourg, that Ireland amend its Constitution on the divorce issue.'

At the time of the first divorce vote there were 40,346 Irish people whose marriages had broken down. That figure had risen to 88,433 in the ten long years before the country voted for change in November 1995.[22]

For Clara Clark it had been a lifetime. The final irony came in 1997 just after the divorce laws finally came on stream. 'After campaigning for twenty-four years for divorce, in June of 1997 I was widowed.' Her first husband died of cancer and Clara finally remarried in Kildare Street Registry Office with no need, after all, of the divorce courts. The outcome of the successful divorce referendum was formally signed into law by President Mary Robinson. How did she feel on that day? She grins broadly. 'I held my emotions in check.'

11

TAKING THE BATTLE TO EUROPE

'One of the women couldn't be in the photograph. Her parents told her if she went public, she couldn't come home for Christmas.' Senator David Norris describes the first official reception for the Irish Gay and Lesbian community in Áras an Uachtaráin. They were welcome in the country's first official residence, even if they weren't welcome at home.

It was a brave move for the gays and for the President – after all, gay sexual activity was still a crime. Such a visit would have been unthinkable in the convent-like Áras of Mary's staid predecessors.

'People felt it was the final act of acceptance,' says Norris, 'being welcomed into the Irish family at last. A lot of people had felt the need to hide the fact that their sons or daughters were gay, and this gave them courage.'

The final act of acceptance would actually come one year later when Mary Robinson as President signed into law the act which de-criminalised homosexual relations.[1] It was she herself and David Norris who had forced this change. After a ten-year battle through the Irish High Court, the Supreme Court and finally the European Court of Human Rights, they had left the Irish government nowhere else to hide. Gay-rights champion Norris, with Robinson representing him, produced a European Court ruling which said that the Irish laws against homosexuality violated Norris's rights to privacy.[2] The government had to act.

Norris, who is now a senator and Joyce scholar, was a Trinity lecturer in English when he began his case in the late seventies. Ireland then was no place for gays. Proscribed by the law,[3] condemned by the Church, they found it almost impossible to raise the subject of gay rights because when they did, the male political establishment collapsed into giggles. The fear and embarrassment that homosexuality aroused among most Irish men made it difficult for them to address the principle involved. What you can't bear to talk about, you can't deal with.

David Norris, remembers the reaction in the Dáil chamber when the left-wing deputy, the late Dr Noel Browne, addressed the issue in the seventies. 'He was laughed out of the house for his trouble. Gerry Collins was Minister for Justice at the time. I just remember nervous laughter in the house.'

Many Irish gays left, choosing a sort of sexual exile in Britain or in the US. Those of us who worked in broadcasting remember colleagues who disappeared abroad. We'd meet them in TV studios or editing rooms in London or New York and they would ask eagerly about Ireland. We didn't ask when they were coming home. We knew they'd chosen freedom for themselves and protection for their families. Parents could accept that their child was gay, but living with the daily reality of it in Ireland was another matter.

Ger Philpott, director of the organisation Aidswise in the early nineties, now a film-maker, remembers coming across a gay friend from Cork in an Edinburgh nightclub. 'He was ten years older than I was and he'd left Cork years earlier because he just couldn't live there. He was now HIV-positive and there were tears in his eyes because he would have given anything to come home. But he had to stay away because he couldn't hurt his family.'[4]

The law against homosexuals was not used very often, but David Norris still remembers flats being raided, and people being brought to court. 'People in the District Court (Irish local courts) were held up to ridicule. The judges would humiliate someone by making him describe intimate details in a public court-house – it was meant to be entertaining.'

In 1977, Norris, then a lecturer in English at Trinity, decided to challenge the constitutionality of the 1861 Offences Against the Person Act which outlawed homosexual practice. Donal Barrington, and later Garrett Cooney, was his senior counsel and Mary Robinson his junior. It wasn't likely to do her any political good. 'There were no votes in it,' she said. 'There was a lot of sniggering. It was a very sniggery time for that issue.'

She had known David from Trinity, and realised one night when they were on a pub crawl together that he was gay. They got on well, but David knew that Mary didn't always appreciate his more flamboyant outbursts. Sometimes he got giddy, he said, whereas Mary would take matters quite seriously. 'She didn't so much rebuke you as gaze at you with a disdainful look in her eye as if to say "I wish you hadn't said that."'

Mary had to prepare an affidavit for the judicial review. 'I asked David to write down for me what it was like, as a boy, as a teenager. And he hand-wrote me one of the most moving accounts, and tears came to my eyes as I read of the hurt and the pain . . . the raw pain is what I remember.' They lost their case in the High Court on 10 October 1980, in front of Mr Justice McWilliams, but they had a series of star witnesses – Cambridge professors, US psychiatrists, Catholic theologians, Protestant bishops – who kept the case on the front pages every day. 'At least we broke the conspiracy of silence,' says David. They were turned down mainly on the basis that the Irish Constitution was that of a Christian country and that homosexual practices undermined marriage which was protected by the Constitution.[5] The Supreme Court found against them, too, on 22 April 1983. But of the five judges led by Mr Justice Tom O'Higgins, two dissented – Mr Justice Niall McCarthy and Mr Justice Seamus Henchy. Those 'two wonderful dissenting judgments', as Mary calls them, showed that there was a body of domestic legal opinion which believed that David Norris had a case. This, and the fact that Norris had exhausted all domestic remedies as the European Court of Human Rights requires, meant he could now approach Strasbourg.

Mary remembers how 'nervously engaged' David was in the European court. All the lawyers were preoccupied, and David was sitting on his own, but Nick Robinson went and sat beside him. The eminent Irish judge, the late Mr Justice Brian Walsh, was on the bench that day and Mary remembers that he suddenly began to giggle. 'And we learned afterwards that the judge sitting beside Brian had said: "Is that David's friend?" – meaning Nick! And it was typical of Nick that he sat beside David that day while the rest of us were up on our podiums.' It was an emotional day. 'I remember at the end of the court hearing, when we knew we were going to succeed, that David had tears in the eyes. He's normally so articulate but that day the words didn't quite come.'

The European Court found that Norris's rights had been breached under the privacy provisions of Article 8 of the Convention. It would take five years for an Irish government to change the law and then it was done quickly and decently, as Mary Robinson acknowledges, by a woman Minister for Justice, Maire Geoghegan-Quinn.

Mary's success in using both the Council of Europe's Convention on Human Rights and the treaties of the European Union helped convert many on the liberal left to the European idea. Europe was turning out to be a force for equality and progress. Feminists, pluralists, socialists who had fought losing battles for years, saw that the European route could actually change things.

There is often understandable confusion in the public mind between the bodies set up by the Council of Europe – the Commission and Court of Human Rights which interpret the European Convention on Human Rights on the one hand – and, on the other hand, the court of the European Union, the Court of Justice. But there is a direct connection. The EU's Court of Justice considers itself bound to interpret EU law so as to conform with the Convention on Human Rights and therefore any domestic court interpreting or applying EU law must take the Convention and its human rights requirements into account.[6] And, since Ireland is a signatory to the Convention, it is politically obliged to comply with its provisions.

Mary had spotted the potential here very early on. She was an enthusiastic European and had always criticised the Irish begging-bowl approach to the European Union. Membership was about much more than grants and subsidies, she argued. And she set about ensuring that if Ireland had signed up for the whole European idea, it would find it had also signed up for European ideas of tolerance, privacy and freedom.

Even before Ireland joined the then EEC, Mary was familiar with its treaties. She did her Harvard thesis in 1968 on the Rome Treaty. Before Ireland joined in 1972, she became a member of the EEC's Vedel committee looking into the challenges posed to the community's institutions by enlargement. From early on, she was a member of the Irish Council for the European Movement. She understood, as almost no one else did, the extent to which Ireland was now subject to European law; argued for the setting up of an Oireachtas Committee on Secondary European Legislation; and was then one of its most active members. As Reid Professor of Law at Trinity, as well as lecturing in criminal and constitutional law, she had voluntarily taken on the teaching of European Community Law, probably then the only such course in the country. In the late eighties she set up, with her husband Nick, the Irish Centre for European Law in Trinity, College Dublin, which was linked to the Law School in Trinity, and had an independent board chaired by Mr Justice Tom O'Higgins, then the Irish judge on the European Court of Justice in Luxembourg. A few years earlier, she had joined the Board of the International Commission of Jurists in Geneva which specialises in human rights. She was also on the advisory council of an international human rights lawyers' organisation called INTERRIGHTS and a co-founder, with British human rights barrister, Anthony Lester QC (now Liberal Democrat peer, Lord Lester of Herne Hill), of a network of European lawyers called Euro-Avocats. In the year before becoming President, she joined Lester's chambers in London and expanded her international legal career.

Crucially, both she and Lester had had a formative experience in Harvard. There they came to understand the extent to which federal law can influence state law. It wasn't a perfect model for what was developing in Europe, but it was as good a working example as there was. 'We both had an American legal background, we both saw Europe through Bill of Rights and federal spectacles, really,' says Lord Lester.

'It became quite natural for each of us in our own country to look for trans-national remedies when we couldn't manage to obtain justice for our clients in our own system. Both of us were cosmopolitan, internationally-minded people.'[7]

Mary accepts that few Irish lawyers in the early seventies would have seen the law as an instrument of social change at any level. 'I saw in the US a federal system working, conflict of laws working,' she says. 'I suddenly understood the potential of the international level influencing the national level.'

Again and again, she brought the Irish state before the European Court of Justice and the European Court of Human Rights. She challenged almost every illiberal law on the statute book: the laws on homosexuality, on illegitimacy, on abortion information, on contraception information, on divorce, on adoption, on the treatment of women. But if Mary was to choose the European case she is most proud of, it would probably be the Airey case establishing the right to civil legal aid in the Republic.

Mrs Josie Airey couldn't afford a solicitor to represent her in procuring a legal separation from her husband. She claimed that since Ireland had no civil legal aid scheme, she was being denied her constitutional rights of access to the courts, and her family life was not being respected. When she wrote a letter to the Commission of Human Rights in Strasbourg complaining about this, the Commission provided her with legal aid to put her case before them and she retained as her legal team Mary Robinson, instructed by solicitor Brendan Walsh. The Irish state's argument was that the lack of civil legal aid in Ireland did not mean that Mrs Airey was being denied access to the Irish courts since she could always represent herself. But the European Court of Human Rights found this argument unrealistic and in 1979[8] ruled that the Irish state had violated her right of effective access to the courts and had not respected her family life.

As a result, the Irish government had to introduce a form of civil legal aid – a restricted scheme, not the proper legislative scheme

Mary wanted – but at least the vital principle had been established, and in 1997 a legislative scheme was finally introduced.

'The Airey case was the most ground-breaking case I took as a legal practitioner. When the Commission found in my favour, I got a letter from Tommy Conolly [a well-known senior counsel], who was a God of constitutional law and someone I greatly admired. "Dear Mary, Congratulations on a really remarkable result." And I almost broke into tears because he had understood. I can't tell you how important that recognition was. There were so few who even understood what the issue was. But Tommy knew. It was establishing a right to civil legal aid and it was one of the first successful Irish cases before the court.'

Mary's constant reference to the European Convention on Human Rights didn't go down too well with Irish judges, even the more liberal ones. Because Ireland has a written Constitution, she would always have to go first through the Irish High Court and the Supreme Court, testing if she had a domestic remedy under the Constitution. 'And on that route I began to argue Convention issues. And Tom Finlay [High Court and Supreme Court Judge, later Chief Justice] was adamant – and Brian Walsh didn't want to hear. The Constitution predominated!'

Mary suggested that the Convention could influence the interpretation of the Constitution. She recalls the judicial horror: 'Our Constitution! Influenced by interpretation! It's for God and the people to interpret!' She would argue Convention issues again and again before Irish courts which were utterly unreceptive. In the David Norris case, Chief Justice Tom O'Higgins told her in the Supreme Court that, 'the Convention . . . does not and cannot form part of our domestic law nor affect in any way questions which arise thereunder'.[9] Legally speaking, of course, it was true that the Convention was not part of Irish law. When Mary brought a case to the European Court of Human Rights, and the court found that rights guaranteed under the Convention had been breached, that was not a legally enforceable decision. What the decision did create was a moral and political obligation on the Irish state to comply with the Convention. The Irish government might drag its feet on European Court decisions, but in the end it always changed the law in deference to Strasbourg.

Some flavour of the judicial resentment of Strasbourg's influence is caught in recent remarks by former High Court judge, Mr Justice Rory O'Hanlon, a pro-life activist, who castigated the government for giving in to Strasbourg. He picked out two of Mary's most famous cases in front of the European Court – the homosexuality case and the abortion information case. 'Any Irish government worth its salt would have refused to give effect to this judgment, or to the earlier judgment in the Norris case, and taken a stand on the principle that the sovereignty of the Irish people in matters as fundamental as the moral law must remain unimpaired regardless of the consequences internationally.'[10]

If the judges were suspicious of her European activities, many of her fellow barristers were decidedly huffy at the publicity she got. It was quite noticeable at the time that Mary was one of the few lawyers who constantly took pathbreaking constitutional and European cases. There were others – Donal Barrington, now a Supreme Court judge; Susan Denham, now on the Supreme Court; and Gerry Durcan. But early on, Mary was one of a small group who saw the law as an instrument for social change. She describes her colleagues in her early days at the Bar as, 'very conservative, very set in their ways, protocol and precedent oriented, political in a Fianna Fáil and Fine Gael and even Labour way ... I felt much happier being an outsider.' But even as time moved on and a new set of more liberal young lawyers came on stream, they were still dealing with a system which conditioned barristers to be cautious and conservative.

'Everything conditions one,' she says. 'Look at the schooling. If you're at the Bar, you have to support yourself from other earnings for years. It's a difficult world to enter unless you come from a comfortable background. Anthony Lester's chambers in London start barristers at a reasonable economic rate.' Lord Lester argues that the lack of a chamber system in Ireland reinforces conservatism because the radical lawyer is isolated. 'Having this extremely fragmented, isolated system means that it was harder for Mary to build up a corps of like-minded people.' The eminent Irish criminal lawyer, Patrick MacEntee SC, who has for decades represented a liberal tradition, argues that the real problem has been the lack of a proper civil legal aid system. 'Civil legal aid would have given us a tradition of radical lawyers.'

It therefore suited the authorities not to provide such a system, he says. 'To make a living as a civil lawyer or in social welfare or family law, you had to do so many cases and there are so many unserved needs.'[11]

The Criminal Bar, too, was badly paid and barristers, under the taxi-rank rules, simply had to take whatever came up. One wasn't allowed to pick and choose. 'Mary had the advantage of being an academic, of not having the rough and tumble of ordinary practice. She had more time to look at the long term, to do the reading, and when she got the bit between her teeth she saw it through,' MacEntee says. Mary says she chose quite deliberately to subsidise her legal practice by teaching. The priority, as always, was freedom of action.

'I always had this need to be independent and to accelerate the process as a barrister by paying my own way and not getting caught in the taxi system. Paddy's quite right. The teaching was the learning. I had access to academic conferences, to the literature. I had the time because I had the income.'

MacEntee has no doubt about the scale of her achievement. 'She explored the potential of the European Court of Human Rights before anybody else did. She made an enormous contribution in opening our system to the practical application of European human rights law.'

By the end of the 1980s, Mary Robinson had won every liberal campaign medal there was. A new generation was living comfortably within the freer society she had helped introduce; the older generation had begun to accept that the sky, after all, wouldn't fall. Ger Philpott had, like so many of his gay friends, emigrated. He was living in San Francisco in 1990.

'And there and then, when I heard Mary Robinson had been elected President – there and then I decided to come home.'

12

THE CANDIDATE

It should have been the great reconciliation. Despite her break with the party, Dick Spring was asking her to be Labour's nominee for the presidency. 'But I had a feeling that once I'd made it clear I wouldn't rejoin the Labour party, Dick was almost sorry that he'd asked.'

It would affect their relationship during the campaign and well beyond. Even when the party came back to accept her terms, she felt Spring's disinterest. He wanted a party resource. She wanted independence.

'I know that John Rogers was totally enthusiastic, as was Ruairi Quinn. I never really felt that Dick Spring was completely enthusiastic once it wasn't a Labour ticket. For quite a long time, he wasn't really involved in the campaign and it was only when the momentum built up a great deal that he became fully involved.'

Spring had done something more important. He was the man who first saw the political space and played into it. He hadn't been capped for Ireland without knowing that you use the whole rugby pitch. The presidency was an under-used and undefended political corner. Spring was determined to move in on it. First, he was going to make Fianna Fáil fight for the presidency. Their nominee had almost always held it and they still behaved as though it was theirs by right.[1] People hadn't been allowed to elect a President for seventeen years. If necessary, he announced in January 1990, he would run himself.

He had his friend, John Rogers, draw up some notes about an expanded role for the presidency. Ruairi Quinn's assistant, Denise Rogers, threw in one decisive name in the discussion about candidates, and Spring authorised John Rogers to approach Mary Robinson on St Valentine's Day.

After the first shock, Mary's initial reaction was to say no. But Nick, who has always been ambitious for her, persuaded her to come out to lunch and talk about it. She looked at the Constitution. She saw what a narrow space the office had. She saw how important that narrow space could be. But this woman had left politics and the Senate the year before, had started a new international legal career. It didn't make sense to turn back.

And yet it made perfect sense. All her life Mary Robinson had been ahead of her time. Politically she'd paid the price. Now Ireland was starting to grow up along the more modern, tolerant lines she had worked for. There were growing pains – the two bitter referenda on abortion and divorce showed that. But in a country struggling towards maturity, Mary Robinson didn't look out of step any more. Her time, in a way, had caught up with her.

Life had left its mark, too. She had brought up three children. She had suffered the death of her elder brother Aubrey, from cancer. She had looked after Nan Coyne, her own nanny, her children's nanny, had lovingly nursed her, bathed her, cared for her when Nan, too, was dying of cancer. By the age of forty-four, Mary was more than an eminent human rights lawyer. She was a mature woman whose own experience helped her understand other people's.

She was also a woman for the big stage, the big picture – the petty dealing of party politics had defeated her. This was a job which could make sense of twenty hard years in public life. She knew she could do it superbly, if she could win it. And she knew she could win it.

Dick Spring did what nobody else could do for her – he got her nominated.[2] Independents were effectively excluded from presidential elections because the nomination required twenty members of the Oireachtas.[3] So if Mary wanted to be nominated, she needed Labour. Spring jumped the gun by declaring publicly that Mary Robinson was the party's nominee, and then promptly had to draw back when supporters of veteran left-winger, Dr Noel Browne, insisted that their two names be put to a vote.

It was, to quote Bride Rosney, 'a mess'. Mary was furious that the public announcement of her candidacy had been sidetracked into an internal party row. But on 26 April the Administrative Council of the party voted four to one for Robinson. It affected her relationship with former Senate colleague, Michael D. Higgins. 'I had an ambiguous relationship with Michael D. During the presidential campaign Michael D. was not helpful because he had backed Noel Browne. We never quite resolved that. We got on quite well but . . . there was always a but.'

As a constitutional lawyer, Mary knew the limitations of the presidency. But she also knew that it had become in the public's eye a tired office, under-used and associated particularly with retired politicians of the Fianna Fáil party. She wanted to make it independent and active, fully representative of all the people of the nation. 'I was very much of the view that by standing as an Independent I was interested in the office as a resource, as a way of gathering in a sense of Irishness and linking with a much wider extended Irish family, so the independence was utterly crucial to that. I would not be politically aligned.'

Spring now accepts she was right not to rejoin Labour. 'It was the smartest thing she ever did. At the time, I was keeping my eye on the main chance and the main chance was trying to rebuild the Labour party. In restrospect, it was the correct action for her to take and gave her a far broader brush to work with than had she become the Labour party candidate. I don't mind admitting when I'm wrong.'[4] He was also wrong about her chances of winning. Beating Fine Gael into third place would have done him nicely. After all, Spring was at the time in the process of outshining the Fine Gael leader, Alan Dukes, making himself the real opposition leader by scoring point after point off the increasingly beleaguered Taoiseach, Charles J. Haughey. 'From day one, I would say that we started out with the hope that this would be the biggest vote that the Labour party ever got – which probably meant we would come second,' said Spring.

That wasn't how Mary saw it. That wasn't how Bride Rosney saw it. Mary wanted to win. 'She was the most professional politician I ever worked with,' says Eoghan Harris. 'I've worked with a lot of tough people but she was ruthless. You have to be ruthless.'[5]

When Harris arrived as an adviser to Mary's campaign in April 1991, she had already made a single-minded commitment. Despite being the main breadwinner, she had given up her job to start a full-time six-month campaign. She had postponed all other career plans and, most unusually for Mary, she would soon decide to open the door on her closely guarded private life – if earnest of intent was required, this was it. Harris admired Mary because of her stand against the Anglo-Irish Agreement. After a turbulent career as a producer at RTE, he was leaving the organisation, equally hated and admired for his zealous pursuit of those whom he suspected of being too liberal in their attitude to the Provisional Republican movement. He had produced a famous poster and television publicity campaign which helped Workers' party leader Proinsias de Rossa win a seat in the European Parliament.

Now he'd left the Workers' party, advising them to take the more social democratic road which, as the Democratic Left party, many of them did. He wanted a career as a media adviser and in a long letter to Mary in April, outlined the campaign road she should take.

Much of what he told her reflected Mary's – and Nick's and Bride Rosney's – instinctive view that she would do better if not heavily tagged as the liberal-left candidate. The liberal left had nowhere else to go. She needed to win the Fine Gael vote and, if possible, detach some women Fianna Fáil voters. She needed to draw on the many other campaign medals she'd won – not to drown under the weight of divorce and abortion controversies, what Harris called the 'distortion' issue.

In a visit to the Robinsons' home in Sandford Road, in Dublin, he outlined a strategy. The campaign should start early with small communities around the country. Munster, with the prosperity brought by EU agricultural subsidies, had a new middle-class, ready to be more adventurous. The campaign should be aimed at a mythical Munster voter called Carmel Murphy, 'a bank manager's wife, Cork bourgeoisie, Jack Lynch voter, progressive but Catholic in the Cork sense. She says. "I'd vote for Mary Robinson but for her position on abortion."' Mary should use the John Fitzgerald Kennedy explanation – that even though he was a Catholic he would represent people of all views as US President. She should also declare early on that everyone knew her views on the abortion amendment and divorce, but that as President she would represent the views of the Irish people.

'Repeat that every chance you get for a whole week and you will never have to say it again,' said Harris.[6]

Everyone respected her, he said – her job now was to appear more feminine, vulnerable, to let people like her. When she visited deprived groups, she should visit those who were fighting back – people liked positive, caring stories. She needed to appear, not in the *Irish Times*, but in the *Sunday Independent*, in the *Sunday Press*, in the tabloids. And she needed constantly to surprise people, to keep ahead of the posse, to keep ahead of the press. Harris's advice made perfect sense, particularly to Mary's close confidante, Bride Rosney, who fought off any political tag that might limit Mary's appeal. But it did mean distancing herself from old friends, and left some bruised feelings in its wake. Early in the campaign, Mary invited about fifty women to her house in Ranelagh. The veteran warriors of a dozen liberal and feminist campaigns gathered to give her advice. 'We were all singularly and spectacularly useless,' recalls Nell McCafferty.

Also present were Mary Maher, Mary Cummins, and Mary Holland of the *Irish Times*, Dr Máire Woods, Anne O'Donnell and Máirín de Burca. They went away and came back the following week, as Nell remembers, with not very much to offer. 'Weren't we ever useless in the women's movement! We weren't ready for straight politics.'

What was suggested that night was that Anne O'Donnell of the Rape Crisis Centre should become Mary's public relations officer.

Anne had led the campaign against the abortion amendment. Anne was offered the job. Then she was dropped. She remembers the phone call she got from Mary Robinson, removing her. 'She said there were Labour party people who had moved in and said that I would be a liability because of my profile as a feminist, which would damage her campaign,' says Anne. Mary wouldn't tell her who precisely had objected. 'She just said her major focus was on winning the campaign. I said, well, then, your whole focus of running as a woman with independent views is a sham. You are not a person of independent views if you are letting other people run your campaign for you.'[7] Anne had been working to make the Rape Crisis Centre respectable and ordinary and she felt Mary's action had demonised the centre, and the philosophy attached to feminism. She decided to keep quiet about the incident because she didn't want to damage Mary's campaign.

'Mary did that a bit roughly,' says Máirín de Burca. 'I rang her to ask if she knew how hurtful it had been to Anne. But that is the steel in Mary's backbone. She wouldn't give in and she wouldn't meet us. She said there was no point in meeting.'[8] Mary had decided not to proceed with Anne's appointment after she had talked to Bride Rosney.

'When she told me, I said, "Fair enough, you've done it. But I think you're crazy,"' says Bride. 'I said Anne O'Donnell smacks of abortion. I'm not saying that's what Anne O'Donnell is, but that's what the public perception will be. People carry baggage.'

Mary accepts that she could have handled it better. 'I wanted somebody whom the press would see as neutral. Anne, very much out of conviction, would inevitably project a certain image and people would remember what she was associated with, and it would be more difficult to broaden the range and perceptions of what I was hoping to project as a presidential candidate, and stand for as President if elected.'

Mary insists she did not distance herself from liberal feminists to get herself elected. 'What I was doing was being tough and strategic which I needed to be. And I had a very clear track record which I never in the slightest compromised on. I took a case to Strasbourg, the Well Woman case (on abortion information), and argued it during the campaign. I don't think that's well remembered!'

When Mary did choose a campaign co-ordinator, she chose a professional from the public relations world, Brenda O'Hanlon. O'Hanlon, now an author and journalist, was then with Wilson Hartnell Public Relations. She had no political affiliations. She knew about publicity and she knew about style. Mary didn't have to be told to change the way she looked, says O'Hanlon – Mary herself asked for help. O'Hanlon recruited Catherine Donnelly, then working with McConnell's advertising agency, who would be one of the key figures in a group of PR and advertising executives helping out voluntarily on Mary's campaign. Donnelly suggested Alan Bruton of Reds to do Mary's hair and, to advise on clothes, Cecily McMenamin of Private Lives in Brown Thomas's store.[9]

This was a new world for Mary. When a clothes-conscious acquaintance heard she was running for the presidency, she asked Mary patronisingly: 'Oh, but have you got the wardrobe?' Mary thought of a large piece of furniture with mirrors and wondered why you'd need one of those to run for election. Cecily McMenamin, however, knew all about wardrobes and knew that Mary's wouldn't do. 'It consisted of black suits and white blouses and black shoes. There was nothing else really except for some Ib Jorgensen evening wear chosen by Nick.'[10]

Cecily did lists of her good and bad points. 'Her assets were that she had a super figure – size ten, lovely long legs, a nice long neck, and a lovely Irish face. Her disadvantages were the colour of her skin – she was almost too pale – and almost too thin in terms of some of the designer clothes.

'I suggested that jackets were most important. I wanted to get her out of the white shirts. She was better covered rather than uncovered, so I chose polos, black or navy. We put her into short skirts because of her lovely legs.' On a small budget, Cecily suggested that she buy some Michelina Stacpoole knits which wouldn't crease, and some jackets – red, camel – to wear over the dark polo, skirt and tights. Her hair was cut and softly permed to show off her face. 'You never had to think of hair-dos,' says Mary, 'when you wore a wig in court.' But now it was time to drop the dowdy lawyer image. Donnelly warned against going overboard. 'We have Katherine Hepburn,' she said in a memo to the campaign committee in June. 'Why try to turn her into Joan Collins?' The woman who emerged from this process was lively, leggy and, most important of all, she wanted to please. Perhaps for the first time in her political life, Mary Robinson felt the need to make people like her.

She started to smile – and she has a brilliant smile. Pre-1990 photographs of Mary were usually grave. But during the election campaign and beyond, her face lit up, opened up. It changed the public perception of her completely.

Early in the campaign, she arrived at an accountants' luncheon with her brother Adrian and asked to be allowed to make her pitch. A fellow speaker that day, well used to Mary's cool, businesslike style, remembers with astonishment how she charmed the audience, how she told stories against herself which made them laugh, how they liked her because she desperately wanted them to. Something had changed. 'Until she stood for the presidency, in her public career there was always a reserve and a reluctance to allow her warmth to show through, which meant that people totally misunderstood her,' says Garret FitzGerald. 'It always bothered me. With most people there is a reasonable relationship between their public and private persona. In her case there was a difference. She had a real difficulty in her public form. That's why she was such a bad election canvasser. She must have made a conscious physical decision early in the presidential campaign to change. I thought she hadn't a hope of winning, because of her personality.'

Mary had no difficulty with changing the way she looked. Opening up, making herself vulnerable to people was harder. 'But if you were going to be chosen by the people to represent them, they had to know much more about you, to get the emotional side of you. They had to have a sense of your family. I resisted for a while because I wanted to keep those spaces, that privacy. The voters had to know the rounded person. The first indication of a willingness to go along with that was the first newspaper photo of my family. We discussed it in the family – it meant that we were going to be more public.'

One of the first family photos appeared in *Hello* magazine. It was a publicity coup organised by Brenda O'Hanlon. Mary and Nick had never heard of *Hello* magazine, but Ireland's premier television and radio broadcaster, Gay Byrne, had, and he was just as important. 'Gay Byrne had ignored us until she appeared in *Hello* magazine,' says Bride.

Gay was impressed. 'Talk about Mary Robinson, wow!' he said on his morning radio show. 'All over *Hello* magazine, all over it. Pictures of Mary at home, in the kitchen, with husband Nick, with the rest of the family, and what a big transformation in Mary's image, the clothes, it certainly won't do her any harm, looking extremely smart, like the new hair-do – long time coming and it looks very good. Looks a lovely house, garden, dog, family, all of that, and the skirt up above the knee, if you don't mind, above the knee for Mary Robinson, our Presidential candidate.'[11] It was a coup, he pronounced. And so it was. It would be read in every hairdresser's salon and doctor's surgery in the country. It associated Mary with success, with winning. But for all its strategic sense, this wasn't a shop-bought campaign. It was home-made, a patchwork of votes stitched together over six long months.

Very often, in the early days, there would be only herself and Nick, travelling to small country places. People didn't know her down the country, but they were ready to talk and she was ready to listen. They needed somebody to listen. It was an early lesson for the presidency.

There was another vital lesson, one Bill Clinton would understand two years later in the US: use the local press and radio. They're kinder to you and closer to the voters. 'You can talk directly to people,' says Mary. 'I was interviewed by so many journalists in the first few months for local papers and radio, and at the end of the interview the journalist would say, "You know, you'd make a great President but you haven't a hope," but I got yards of local exposure. And I think it made a huge difference quietly.'

Mary's campaign was launched on 1 May in Limerick on as broad a platform as she could have wished. The late Jim Kemmy, the former Democratic Socialist TD who had just rejoined the

Labour party, made sure that women's groups and environmental groups were there as well as Labour and the Workers' party. 'It was the first formal event of the campaign and Jim was politically generous – the Workers' party was included, which wasn't always the case,' says Mary. Kemmy was generous with his advice, too. A former stonemason, he had a keen interest in the arts, but a fine disregard for his own appearance. That didn't stop him advising Mary. 'Listen, Mary,' he said that day to the severely-dressed lawyer sitting beside him in the Pike Inn in Limerick, 'You're going to have to tidy yourself up.' Looking at the well-worn suit and tousled hair which were Jim's own trademarks, the accompanying Labour advisers tried to keep a straight face. So did Mary.

Over those early months she visited local clubs and community groups in places like Kilmallock and the Allihies in Munster; Gorey, Bettystown and Laytown in Leinster, Donegal and Letterkenny in the North; and Innishboffin, Inishturk, and Clare Island off the west coast. They told her about living at the edge – on the periphery of Europe, at the margin of their own society, on the sidelines where real community effort and endeavour exist unnoticed and unsung. She retold their stories throughout her campaign. They remembered that.

Mary always had around her the small group of people she trusted. As well as Nick, they included her friends Bride Rosney and Peter MacMenamin, both community school teachers deeply involved in the Teachers' Union of Ireland.

Brenda O'Hanlon worked part-time for many months and then left behind for ever a career in public relations to work full-time, from the end of August, as Mary's campaign co-ordinator. There was Ann Lane, Mary's secretary for almost twenty years. Eoghan Harris was kept out of sight for fear of objections from Labour and the Workers' party. His sharp analysis was presented in the names of Nick, Bride and Peter MacMenamin.

'Eoghan was a very significant catalyst and influencer. He prompted a lot of thinking and reaction to what he proposed. He was an extraordinarily clear, arrogantly explicit explainer of what should be done,' says Mary. 'But he was one of many and I think he didn't know how many he was one of!' she says. 'Eoghan thought he ran the whole thing, while Eoghan played a crucial role throughout the campaign which I deeply appreciated, we also had a whole team of significant representatives of PR and advertising companies.'

Like Eoghan they were all voluntary and they included some of the brightest operators in their particular fields: Catherine Donnelly of McConnell's advertising agency; Sheila Gahan, Brenda's colleague from Wilson Hartnell Public Relations; Dolores McCarthy of Ark Advertising and Brian Dunnion of Saatchi and Saatchi. Catherine Donnelly came up with a constant stream of slogans and headlines for publicity and for fund-raising: 'Put your hand in your pocket for a President who isn't in anybody's'; 'Above politics not above people', and, with reference to the presidential residence in Phoenix Park: 'Your voice in the park', 'A woman's place is in the park' and 'Put your woman in the park'. 'A President for all the people' and 'A President with a purpose' were the campaign slogans adopted. Many of this close group operated from Mary's elegant house in Sandford Park in Ranelagh. The larger campaign committee which met in Merrion Square included Ruairi Quinn TD who was Labour's Director of Elections; Ray Kavanagh, Labour party Secretary; John Rogers, and Fergus Finlay, then Labour's press officer, later Dick Spring's adviser. Anne Byrne, who would later be Minister Brendan Howlin's programme manager in the Department of the Environment, and Ita McAuliffe, joined the campaign staff on behalf of Labour. Accountants Greg Sparks, Kieran Corrigan and Niall Greene of GPA were on the official fund-raising committee.

The campaign was a miracle of free labour. In the end it would cost £200,000 as opposed to about two million pounds spent by Fianna Fáil. Businessman Cartan Finnegan and retired businessmen, Kevin Burke and John Gogan, mounted an eight-week mail and telephone fund-raising campaign along with unlikely bedfellows such as veteran socialist Nora O'Neill. The Bourke family used their legal and medical contacts to solicit funds. Others organised lunches, cocktail parties, brunches. Apart from the money raised, it pushed Mary's candidacy among powerful professional women. Angela Douglas, dressed with her team of twenty in Mary Robinson sweat-shirts, ran the publicity at race meetings, football matches and pop concerts, handing out leaflets and buttons. It looked like a well-resourced campaign, but the public didn't know that these were always the same twenty people dressed in the same twenty sweat-shirts carefully laundered between events. Eoghan Harris produced three political party broadcasts memorable for their sheer power, sophistication and economy – he did them all for five thousand pounds. Only in one of them did Mary actually speak. The messages came through music and image. The Irish song *Tabhair dom do láimh* ('Give me your hand') ran over Mary's outstretched hand of friendship; *Nessun Dorma* from Puccini's *Turandot*, the World Cup anthem, did double duty for World Cup soccer fans and opera-lovers – all the music running over slow-motion images of Mary with labourers and shoppers and office-workers. There was even a loving close-up of Mary rubbing her sore feet. Ruairi Quinn says the hairs stood up on the back of his neck as he saw the rough-cuts. By the time autumn came, Mary had been five months in the race on her own – no other candidate had yet been declared. The press was talking about what Fianna Fáil would do, what Fine Gael would do and what Mary Robinson was already doing. She was the focus, not the party who had nominated her. It would cause constant and understandable tensions within the campaign.

Bride Rosney, Aubrey's godmother, still working as principal of Rosmini Community School in Dublin, clashed constantly with Labour. Her main objection was to Labour's lack of ambition – they assumed Brian Lenihan of Fianna Fáil would be elected President. 'At one point I blew my gasket at a meeting when Ruairi Quinn said: "Think of the great speech you can make, Dick, when Mary gets 28 per cent of the vote!" 28 per cent of the vote! I couldn't cope with that! I locked the visors. I turned on everybody. "I'm not in this to be second." It was the Labour party's aim to come second, to beat Fine Gael into second place,' says Rosney.

The tensions show right through in the minutes of campaign meetings. In July, Bride expressed concern that Dick Spring had been quoted in the papers speculating about a by-election in Dublin West, Brian Lenihan's constituency – assuming thereby that Brian Lenihan would win the presidential race.

In August Peter MacMenamin complained about a quote from Fergus Finlay in the newspapers: 'I am not going to predict we will win, but we will frighten a lot of people.' In future, it was agreed, it would always be maintained that the campaign was winnable.

Labour were also determined to thwart the Robinsons' determination to broaden the scope of the campaign by getting the Workers' party involved on the campaign committee. They managed to keep Eamon Gilmore [a Worker's party TD] off the committee until October, as Ruairi Quinn readily admits. Quinn considered that the Workers' party's Stalinist associations were a real minus, with democracy breaking out all over Eastern Europe. The Robinsons found Gilmore and the WP to be hardworking and helpful.

Labour felt they were getting a raw deal. Labour workers were slow to come out and work for Mary, says Ruairi Quinn. It didn't help when she insisted she wasn't the Labour candidate – she was independent. At meetings, Labour complained that the party wasn't mentioned in articles or in fund-raising advertisements. Worker's party TD Pat Rabbitte remembers sitting with Dick Spring in Val's Bar in Ballyhaunis listening to Mary on North West Radio. She was being challenged as to whether she had any real understanding of rural life or farming matters. 'You'd think,' said Dick, looking gloomily into his hot whiskey, 'that she'd mention that most of Labour's deputies come from rural Ireland.'

One wet Sunday in Sligo, Dick realised she could win. He had joined the campaign bus tour for the last crucial three weeks. They'd had an astonishing send-off from Ballina, Mary's home town, and now they were standing outside Sligo Rovers' soccer pitch. As a sportsman, Dick knew the golden rule of canvassing: don't bother the people on their way to a match. 'But people were coming over from the turnstiles to shake Mary Robinson's hand. And I said to Fergus Finlay on the way back to Dublin, there's something happening here. I've seen politicians jeered at outside stadiums and ignored because people are going to watch their team play soccer and they don't want to be bothered with electioneering. But here were people going out of their way to shake Mary Robinson's hand!'

The other parties had finally declared. Brian Lenihan, widely liked and admired for his brave fight against a liver disease, would stand for Fianna Fáil. Lenihan was a legend in Irish politics. More than anything, he loved the political game, told the very best Irish political anecdotes, and often undersold his own considerable abilities by playing loyal lieutenant, first to former Taoiseach Jack Lynch, and now to Charles Haughey. A generous man who had friends in every political party, he would be a formidable candidate. Looking at the odds, two frontbench members of the biggest opposition party, Mary Flaherty and Jim Mitchell of Fine Gael, suggested that the party's best bet now was to back the strongest challenger, Mary Robinson.

Fine Gael leader, Alan Dukes, felt it was a pity Fine Gael hadn't approached Mary before Labour did. He decided the party should have its own candidate, and eventually persuaded Austin Currie TD, the veteran Northern Ireland civil rights activist, to go forward.

Polls early in the summer had shown that Mary would pull Fine Gael votes, particularly if their candidate was not Garret FitzGerald. An Irish Marketing Surveys poll conducted for Independent Newspapers in the first week of October showed Mary well ahead of Fine Gael: she had 33 per cent, with Austin Currie at a worrying 16 per cent, but Brian Lenihan was still safely ahead at 51 per cent.

Then came the Lenihan tapes débâcle. In an *Irish Times* series of articles published in September 1990, a research student, Jim Duffy, claimed that phone calls had been made to President Hillery by Charles Haughey and, at his insistence, by Brian Lenihan on 27 January 1982, eight years earlier, in an attempt to stop the President granting the then Taoiseach, Garret FitzGerald, a dissolution of the Dáil to hold a general election. The idea was that Mr Haughey would have an opportunity to try to form an alternative Fianna Fáil administration with the help of Independents, and without an election. Charged with this by Garret FitzGerald on a RTE television programme, *Questions and Answers*, on 22 October 1990, Lenihan denied it. But on Thursday 25 October, the *Irish Times* called a press conference and played the tape of an interview that Jim Duffy had had with Lenihan, where he said he *had* made a phone call to the President. On television that night, Brian Lenihan turned face to camera and claimed that 'on mature recollection' what he had said on the tape was wrong.

The whole episode left a major question mark over a popular politician. The liberal, market-oriented Progressive Democrats, in coalition with Fianna Fáil, decided that they could no longer support him in cabinet. On 31 October Charles Haughey sacked the man whose friend he claimed to be. The *Sunday Tribune*, in a memorable cover page the following Sunday, remarked: 'Some friend!'[12]

The public reacted sharply. A post 'tape' poll in the IMS/Independent Newspaper series, conducted between 27 and 29 October, showed Mary's support rising to 52 per cent and Brian's falling to 31 per cent, with Currie almost unchanged at 17 per cent.

Some in Mary's camp were elated at Brian's problems. But Nick said to Mary: 'You're the one in trouble.' It was true. Fianna Fáil would rally solidly to Brian Lenihan. With less than two weeks to the end of the campaign (polling day was 7 November 1990), Mary had a fight on her hands. She had made mistakes under the pressure of the campaign, some of which she particularly regretted. One was a statement put out in her name to the newspapers challenging Brian Lenihan to a head-to-head television debate. It was inspired by Eoghan Harris in an effort to catch tabloid headlines and make her noticed among the working-class male voters who, the polls showed, were not responding to her. It said that unlike Georgie Porgie, when the girls came out to play, Brian Lenihan ran away. It also referred to Lenihan as 'an ageing movie queen'.[13]

'It was just not my style. I knew at the time it was mean,' she says. 'I remember how outraged Nick was about that Brian Lenihan remark and I said to him, "I'm afraid I did clear it: Eoghan ran it by me and I said okay, and I didn't think any more about it at the time!" Nick was slating about it and said, "You should never do that" and I said, "Yeah, I know. It's done." That incident really stayed with me for a long time, particularly when Brian started to get into hot water.'

The Labour party were annoyed about the remark, too, and they were even more annoyed when Mary took Harris's last-minute advice to attack Lenihan in their first television debate on RTE's *Today Tonight* television programme.[14] It was a departure from her 'above politics' stance and she looked uncomfortable even as she did it. It taught her a sharp lesson. 'In stressful circumstances, the last person you speak to can have an undue influence,' she says. 'I am very conscious now of needing time to weigh up advice.'

However, Harris served her well in other ways in those last days, not only with the television set-piece broadcasts. He prepared Nick for a vital *Late Late Show* appearance with candidates and spouses, encouraging him to tell an anecdote about the traditional piper Seamus Ennis, which softened Nick's upper-class image.

Nick was a hit, which mattered that night because an exhausted Mary had started to make mistakes. On a *Today Tonight* programme, she denied she had ever said she would nationalise the banks and had to clarify it the next day. Fianna Fáil made much of the socialist connection right up to the end of the campaign, claiming that her election would affect jobs by sending out 'a negative signal' to the business and investment community.[15] When in a bullish *Hot Press* magazine interview she was asked if she would perform the opening of what would have then been an illegal contraceptive stall in a Virgin megastore, she said yes.[16] She later denied that she had meant to say yes, explaining that she had a habit of saying yes, meaning she had understood the question and was processing it – but to most normal people yes means yes. The controversy that followed again raised Mary's liberal record on the contraception and abortion information issue, with a Fianna Fáil TD, John Browne of Wexford, finally asking if she would use Áras an Uachtaráin, the President's official residence, as an abortion referral clinic.[17] The more conservative women voters were uneasy.

Then, with less than a week to go, Fianna Fáil made her a gift. It was a busy Saturday and Bertie Ahern was canvassing Shop Street in Galway. 'This rather attractive girl caught my eye. Next thing, she came over and launched into me. I didn't know why I was being attacked. It was only after I got ate about six more times, all by women up Shop Street, that I turned around and said what's all this about?'[18]

At the same time Charlie McCreevy, the Fianna Fáil Minister was canvassing a North Kildare housing estate. It was about 1 p.m. and from all the houses came the sound of *Rodney Rice's Saturday View* radio programme. By 1.30, Charlie and his canvassers were getting a cold reception. 'We'd never vote for Brian Lenihan – not after what your man said on the radio this afternoon,' the housewives told him.

What 'your man' – Environment Minister, Padraig Flynn – had said on the radio was that Mary Robinson had 'a new-found interest in the family'. He added: 'None of us who knew Mary Robinson well in previous incarnations ever heard her claiming to be the great wife and mother.'[19] Flynn would later write to Mary to apologise.

Women all over the country were outraged. 'I got far more hammering over that than I did about the bloody tapes,' says Bertie Ahern ruefully. After the tapes débâcle, 'we had worked so hard to get back up and we could have made it,' he says. 'We had the support of every nationalist, Republican and Fianna Fáiler in the country and were probably on 46 per cent but that remark just clobbered us.' But he doesn't detract from Mary's own achievement. 'She was a fair six months out in rural Ireland picking up the Ballymagash vote,' he says (Ballymagash is an imaginary rural location). 'In areas where previously Labour would get ten votes, she was getting ninety.' It was women who were voting for her. 'And it was herself going out to those country centres pulling in that vote. I'll give her full credit. That vote was earned.'

The result, when it came, would change the fortunes of the three main party leaders. For Dick Spring, it was the wave which would help sweep him to Labour's greatest ever victory in 1992.

For Fine Gael leader, Alan Dukes, it was the end. A motion of no confidence in him as leader was put down that very day and the rumours spread when neither he nor the Fine Gael candidate appeared on the platform for the declaration of the count. Dukes says it was all stage-managed perfectly by his opponents. Currie, who wanted to be there, had been told he wasn't needed at the count. Dukes himself remembers: 'I was half way there in the car when I got the message that this motion had been put down and I had no alternative but to turn back and decide what to do about it.' Dukes alleges that his opponents had timed everything deliberately to ensure that neither Fine Gael's candidate nor the party leader would be there for the declaration.[20]

For Taoiseach and Fianna Fáil leader, Charlie Haughey, it was the beginning of the end. He had dumped Fianna Fáil's beloved Brian Lenihan.

'I was almost the only member of the cabinet who refused to ask Brian to resign as Minister for Defence,' says Albert Reynolds, the man who would later challenge and replace Haughey as party leader and Taoiseach. Haughey should have stood up to the PDs and refused to sack Lenihan, says Reynolds. 'I felt terrible in the Dáil that day,' he says. 'It contributed to the later feeling that Haughey had to go.'[21]

Mary was in the basement at home, according to her brother Adrian, 'slumped in the middle of a couch, absolutely comatose. She didn't know her own name.' She wasn't stunned by what she had done – she had known it was possible for months. She was much more stunned by what she was going to have to do.

Ruairí Quinn, Labour Director of Elections, was besieged at the count. 'There was a media scrum and I said: "She's going to be here shortly. She'll be coming through that gate. You'll all get a chance to interview her, but RTE will go first. And lads, a bit of respect! We're talking about the President." And it was at that particular moment the penny dropped. It still resonates, I can still feel it.'

Mary's victory speech that night was sharp and simple. Harris had helped her write it and it hit all the right buttons. They cheered when she said: 'I don't know whether to dance or sing so I have done both!' They cheered when she talked of her ad hoc band taking on 'the might, money and merciless onslaught of the greatest political party on this island. And we beat them'. They even cheered when she said she was, as President-elect, bidding her supporters farewell. But they cheered loudest of all when she spoke of the women of Ireland, 'Mná na hÉireann who, instead of rocking the cradle, rocked the system.'

Women contacted her afterwards to tell her that for the first time they had voted differently from their husbands. 'I ignored him.' Even: 'I lied to him.' Polling stations reported women coming in on their own, refusing to talk to canvassers, their minds made up. This time, the head of state would have a woman's face.

Mary stood on the platform, the centre of attention and yet, as so often in her life, she felt she was outside it all. 'It was almost as though I was observing myself and the whole scene with awe. I was up somewhere saying this can't be happening. I was very conscious of Nick, my father and Aubrey, and also of Brian Lenihan and of his dignity.' She remembered the 'ageing movie queen' remark and regretted it even more. Brian congratulated her graciously. 'I remember his character and his dignity on the day, whereas Haughey had been so ungenerous.'

The Taoiseach, whose usual sense of ceremony was positively rococo, kept it brief on this occasion.

'Congratulations,' said Charlie. 'Your car and driver are outside.'

13

NEW BROOM

December 1990 was a miserable month. The Áras was a neglected place, with damp basements and a morgue-like atmosphere. 'People literally crept along the corridors whispering,' says Mary. 'It unnerved us and it unnerved our young.' Her attempt to change the staff would expose her to public anger and small private humiliations. The salted icing on the presidential Christmas cake was a sample.

Mary knew the battle was only beginning. To the public it seemed as though it was already won. International press interest in Ireland's first woman President was unprecedented, helped by the fact that Sky Television had given the campaign wide coverage in its round-the-clock bulletins. In the three weeks leading up to her inauguration, she did interviews for CBS and ABC in the United States, for Australian, German, Spanish, Norwegian and French television, for ITN and the BBC; for *Time* magazine, the *Chicago Tribune*, the *Toronto Star* and for French, Scandinavian, German, British and Argentine newspapers. She was so busy that it was only when she came out on the steps of her own house on the morning of her inauguration, 3 December 1990, that she realised how life would change. 'I saw all the neighbours and all of Aubrey's friends lined up.' It struck her then that she was leaving her home for ever.

The civil service didn't know what to expect. Cabinet secretary

Dermot Nally approached her hesitantly to say it had always been customary to use the presidential Rolls-Royce on inauguration day. 'And I said "Very much so, I'm in favour of using the Rolls." And we both laughed. Obviously he was thinking: Socialist Will Not Want Rolls.'

That morning she wore jewellery made by one of Nick's Waterhouse ancestors for his wife: a gold collar and matching earrings. It was given to her by Nick's Aunt Phyllis in trust for Tessa. It reflected the formal feel of the day: Mary's own purple moire Louise Kennedy jacket over black; the Rolls; the morning suits worn by the men. Charles Haughey had assumed, too, that Mary would want informal dress and was surprised when she did not.

She would always choose to maintain the formality of the office. It suited her own sense of the presidency and it reassured people who were afraid of change, while allowing her, in fact, to make substantial change. But her special list of invited guests to the inauguration showed just how much the focus of the presidency would actually change. Women dominated the list, a counterbalance to the heavily male list of government guests. They included the wives of former Presidents Hillery and Childers who, extraordinarily, were not invited by the government, just as Nick would not be invited to the next inauguration. They included the heads of the Council for the Status of Women and the Women's Political Association, Frances Fitzgerald and Frances Gardiner respectively. Representatives of organisations helping the homeless were there – Sister Stanislaus Kennedy of Focus Point and Eithne FitzGerald of the National Campaign for the Homeless. They included the country's leading women trade unionists – Patricia O'Donovan from the Irish Congress of Trades Unions and Inez McCormack then of the National Union of Public Employees in Belfast. Mary invited environmentalists, representatives of the disabled, of students and of young people. From Northern Ireland she brought the Ombudsman, Maurice Hayes; the then Alliance leader, John Alderdice; SDLP leader John Hume, and Ulster Unionist party MP Ken Magennis, the first Unionist ever to be invited or to accept an invitation to the inauguration of an Irish President. She also invited Gordon Wilson, the Enniskillen man whose daughter Marie had been killed in the IRA's notorious Remembrance Day bombing of 1986.

She took her oath of office with great solemnity. She would repeat it to herself over the next few months as she tried to break through the barricades that hemmed her in: 'Mo lándhícheall a dhéanamh', to do her best to maintain the Constitution and serve the people. She signed her oath with the quill originally used by de Valera – it was Charles Haughey's and he had lent it to her. Her speech, written with help from philosopher Richard Kearney, and quoting from the poetry of Eavan Boland and Seamus Heaney, spoke of a presidency extending not only to Ireland's four provinces but also to a Fifth Province. This Fifth Province, she said, included the seventy million people of Irish descent around the world, and the often forgotten community groups who were providing real local democracy. She dedicated herself to Irish language and culture, to contributing to the promotion of human rights internationally, to extending the hand of friendship to both communities in Northern Ireland and encouraging mutual understanding between all the different communities sharing the island, to finding a voice for women.

The speech finished with an invitation which this shy woman would probably have been unable to deliver even one year earlier. It showed how far she come out of her lawyer's shell and how conscious she was that waiting out there was a ready response. 'May it be a presidency where I the President can sing to you, citizens of Ireland, the joyous refrain of the fourteenth-century poet as recalled by W.B. Yeats: "I am of Ireland . . . come dance with me in Ireland".'[1]

Her family took her at her word. 'Adrian had hired a limousine which stretched from here to town,' says Henry. 'We had a bottle of gin and we laughed the whole way to the Áras.' At lunch, they were surrounded by Fianna Fáil Ministers, not their natural political milieu. Adrian was fooling. 'I was sitting opposite Mary O'Rourke and Adrian was talking about how much better it was to leave brown hens out to feed and to keep white hens for battery, and Mary O'Rourke's eyes were glazing over, and Dick

Spring who was sitting near us warned, "Stop it, Bourkes, stop it, Bourkes".'

Mary's father was sitting beside Taoiseach Charles Haughey. He talked horses with Charlie. 'And I told him how very good Mary and Nick had been to me, that I had done a lot of travelling with them over the last twenty years since Tessa died. Whenever they went on holidays, whether they went to America, Spain, they always took me. I said, "I'm going to miss this now." Charlie turned to me with the hooded eyes and said, "Sure, what's to stop you now? Can't you take a young one and go off yourself?" I nearly fell off the chair laughing.'

That afternoon, when the official guests had gone, family and friends took over. 'We went mad,' says Dr Bourke. 'All the children were romping around. Garret and Joan FitzGerald arrived with all their grandchildren.'

'It was marvellous,' remembers Garret. 'There were children all around the house. Outside the sitting-room, a little boy said, "Come and see the Rolls-Royce." So he brought me up the stairs, down a corridor, out the back door and there it was. So I sat with eleven children pretending to drive the Rolls-Royce.'

At the lunch that day, said Mary, Charles Haughey had been critical of the staffing. 'He had in fact encouraged me – "You'll need to reorganise things around here." It was also said by the civil servants at the time.'

The whole house had an air of neglect. It needed dusting and cleaning. There were twenty-nine bluebottles on a windowsill of Mary's prepared bedroom on the day of the inauguration. The service was overbearing. A guest who came to lunch on the second or third day of the presidency remembers an array of cutlery which would do justice to a state banquet, and a staff member standing behind each chair – and that was in response to Mary's request for soup and sandwiches. 'The food, the style of catering was over-elaborate,' she says. 'We kept simplifying it. People literally crept along the corridors and did not speak. It was a strange atmosphere. When I went up to see Paddy Hillery, he was extremely warm and supportive and remained that way. But his unhappiness with living in the Áras was patent. The unhappiness seemed to pervade the Áras itself.'

Nobody had cherished the institution for a long time. Dr Hillery had reluctantly but loyally agreed to serve a second term. He had scrupulously observed his constitutional duties and had refused to take phone-calls from, it was reported, his former party colleagues during apparent efforts to head off the February 1982 election. His previous relationship with Charles Haughey had been cool. They had both served in cabinet under Taoiseach Jack Lynch until Haughey was dismissed in 1970 and subsequently tried and acquitted on charges of conspiracy to import arms.[2]

Once Charles Haughey became Taoiseach again in 1987, the President was not high on his list of priorities. The house fell further into disrepair. Almost two-thirds of Dr Hillery's small allowance of £15,000 went to feed the Áras staff. Eventually the Office of Public Works were persuaded to pick up the meals bill, but no attempt was made to improve the presidential allowance until Dr Hillery was within two months of leaving office. On the day of Mary's inauguration, the Bourke brothers noticed that Haughey's cabinet stayed conspicuously away from the former President.

Many of the existing staff were elderly, a number of them lived in, and there was a convent–like atmosphere in the house. 'I wanted to have a happy Áras, inviting, welcoming and reassuring to people. Those who came from the inner city or the country would get a cup of tea, have fun. I honestly believed the place couldn't be turned around without a new team.'

Mary confirmed with the Taoiseach's department that it was possible to redeploy the existing staff employed by the Office of Public Works, and have new staff recruited. 'I indicated that this was what I wanted to happen. As soon as I did, all hell broke loose.' There were wholesale leaks to the media that President Robinson was getting rid of long-standing members of staff at the Áras.

'In other words I was being shafted. I didn't see it coming. It was a particularly difficult and grim experience. I remember ringing

Mr Haughey and saying: "What's happening? I thought we were all working to the same agenda." "Oh, no, it's all right, don't worry," he said. "It's my job as Taoiseach to protect the presidency."'

The headlines were damaging and they first appeared two days before Christmas 1990. 'President sacks elderly staff' was the legend under the *Sunday Press*'s Christmas greetings to its readers, 'Áras shake-up dismays staff' was the *Irish Independent*'s front-page story on Christmas Eve. The President who said she would stand for the poor and the helpless, for other women, was now accused of sacking poor helpless women at Christmas. RTE's satirical programme *Scrap Saturday* did a take-off of the television series, *Upstairs, Downstairs*. They labelled her 'Lady Robinson' and picked up on her campaign slogan. 'I am a President with a purpose,' it mocked. 'My purpose is to sack anyone old and useless.'[3] 'Master' Aubrey was portrayed as complaining that his shoes hadn't been cleaned properly. When one of Mary's staff mentioned to the programme's star, the late Dermot Morgan, that this was unfair, Aubrey was left out of the programme in future.

Mary had been assured by the Taoiseach's office that the Áras workers would be found other jobs, but their official employer, the Office of Public Works, was obviously in no hurry to do that. Somebody was enjoying Mary's discomfiture.

Kevin O'Driscoll, now National Secretary of the Health and Welfare Division of the union IMPACT, was then the official representing one of the workers. 'They were vulnerable people – six of the eight were women. One was a former contemplative nun,' he said. 'Another women in her early sixties had worked in the Áras for eighteen years.' Many of them had no homes to go to, they had to be booked into hotels for Christmas. 'These weren't pictures on the wall to be replaced. These were people,' says O'Driscoll.[4]

He feels that Mary Robinson, a President he admired, would have been better advised to take a few months to sort things out and ensure that alternative jobs had been found. 'There is no point in talking about human rights in general if you don't apply them to the people you are dealing with as individuals.' Kevin O'Driscoll says his row was with the employers, not with Mary, but that he had to use publicity to make them respond. He threatened a picket on Áras an Uachtaráin unless the row was sorted and he gave interviews in front of the gates of the Áras to this effect. On the eve of his threatened strike, the affair was settled. All the workers were found other jobs or they were compensated.

Kevin did his job as a union official but, he says, after a while he realised that the situation was being manipulated. Some people wanted this row to go on.

'There was no great political will to sort it out. I was given a run for my money because the press coverage suited some people just fine.' He remembers officials from OPW and the Department of Finance saying it suited certain people in government not to sort it out. Kevin O'Driscoll still feels that he and the Áras could have worked together if only they had contacted him, even indirectly. Mary had Labour party connections, Bride had trade union connections.

Mary says the whole incident shows how trapped and isolated she was. She couldn't have used political connections – the presidency must be above politics.

And she couldn't speak out to explain herself. 'You had no public voice except through the Taoiseach's office at the time'. Although she met with senior civil servants from the Office of Public Works on December 5, 1990, and although there were contacts subsequently between her office and the OPW, it was made clear to her that protocol required her to leave the real negotiation of staff changes to the Taoiseach's office. 'I couldn't even talk with total directness to anybody from the Office of Public Works according to the protocol then.'

She knew, too, she could have handled it better. 'My inexperience of working in a government department of any kind made me much less aware of the implications,' she says. 'I remember being terribly distraught about the whole thing and almost disorientated by how naive I had been. I had simply been green and I had been shafted.'

Her friend Sister Stanislaus Kennedy of Focus Point reassured her, saying she, too, set about change when first put in charge of social services in Kilkenny. 'It mattered immensely to me, because I had begun to feel miserable about what I had done. I felt destabilised since I was not in a position to account for myself because the Taoiseach was doing that on my behalf, and he was shafting me as he did it.'

But the changes were vital and they worked. 'The staff taken on here were taken off the unemployment register. They were delighted to get the jobs, delighted as we were to make it warm and welcoming. Rosaleen McBride and Tina Weir stayed on as cooks and blossomed. There was laughing and singing in the kitchen and people talking along the corridors in a normal tone of voice. That took a couple of weeks. It's hard to recall now how institutionalised, sad, demoralised and frightened people were. Maybe they were frightened of the new broom.' It was one of the cooks who discovered that the Christmas cake made for the new President had more salt than sugar in the icing. The cook was distraught but life moved on.

When Mary opened the house up to the public as never before, they saw it as the warm place she wanted it to be. 'People wrote. They thanked the guards at the gate, the staff, they loved the house. Making that happen was one of my earliest objectives and it looked very unlikely that first December and early January.'

These months were doubly difficult for Mary because she'd left behind all her old allies. Labour were still glowing from her victory, but she had to make it clear that they no longer had any political claim on her.

There had been some outstanding issues from the campaign – not least the campaign debt of about £80,000. She agreed as President-elect to attend a dinner and art auction in the Burlington Hotel which raised the bulk of the money. But there was still about £30,000 outstanding and though the issue was raised at meetings during the campaign, it had never been made clear who would take final responsibility. Ruairi Quinn felt she could have done more to help with the debt. Mary rejects this vigorously. 'I would be personally hurt by any implication that we didn't pull our weight on the money front,' she says. 'The debts we had incurred as a family as a result of our both having ceased to be working professionally over a period were of horrendous proportions. And it had been made very clear that the way in which the campaign would be run would be that the responsibilities would be taken by the various component parts. And there was never any suggestion, and there couldn't be, that we would be made liable. As far as Nick and myself were concerned we went the extra mile and five miles further in every direction.' There were many contributions to Labour for the campaign which she knew nothing about, she said, like the £15,000 given to Ruairi Quinn by Ben Dunne of the Dunne's Stores family, which Labour later revealed to the McCracken Tribunal investigating payments to politicians, without telling Mary about it.[5] On a visit to London as President in 1997 she heard about it from a media source and was shocked. The Workers' party and the Green party had spent money on the campaign and never approached her for help, she said, but despite their role in getting her elected, it wasn't they, but the Labour party, who gained.

Labour expected that they would get special recognition for their role, that she would be grateful. 'She was outrageous,' says Labour Leader, Ruairi Quinn. 'On the fourteenth of February, the anniversary of the day John Rogers came to her house, she invited all of us on the campaign committee, with our partners, up to the Áras and we had drinks and stood around for a chat and a thank you very much and a framed drawing of the Four Courts. And that was it. And that was the cause of a lot of anger among a lot of Labour people.

'She was reserved. She wasn't the sort of person you go for a pint with. She also had a sense, which I respected, of the dignity of the office. But that didn't mean she couldn't invite gurriers like us up to the Áras. It upset some people. To a certain extent it upset me because the perception among my mother and a lot of other people was that we were invited up there every second week-end.'[6]

But Quinn got on well with the President and remembers personal kindnesses, such as the letter Mary wrote to Ruairi's new wife Liz when she heard Liz was pregnant. Mary, as President, was everything Labour could have hoped for. She was scrupulously independent, she was popular, she was successful. The benefit of being associated with that was something that

Dick Spring didn't appreciate and use to full advantage, Quinn says.

'Dick has a long memory and he neither forgives nor forgets. That has to do with his personality. My attitude would have been to bask in the glory. What did it matter? As Tánaiste and Labour Leader, he could have basked in it more fully than he did.'

For Mary it was fundamental to distance herself from former supporters. 'When I said immediately afterwards in my acceptance speech that I would have to say goodbye to them, that was very deliberately saying from the very beginning that I intended to be President for all the people, to be very fair about it.'

After her party for campaign workers, she had rejected pressure to have groups of constituency workers up to the Áras. 'The majority of those I was coming in contact with were proud of the independence of it, proud that they had delivered a President who was doing what was intended.

'I think that Dick Spring never quite saw that contribution to the checks and balances within our whole system as being as important a contribution as others like Ruairi did. I don't think he even quite acknowledged or saw that the Labour party did, in fact, greatly benefit later, in the 1992 election.'

Mary had, as she promised, broken free of her political connections, but she was now prisoner of the politician who resented her most. In the staffing row, Charles Haughey had enjoyed sweet revenge. It was a sharp lesson for Mary, worth learning early. 'It was iron in the soul time . . . Now we know how vulnerable we are.' She had to find a way to speak out, to explain herself, and she reckoned that Charles Haughey would do everything in his power to stop her. She had to trust that the Constitution would let her find her voice. And if Mary Robinson knew anything, she knew the Constitution.

14

REGARDING MR HAUGHEY

The Gulf War was at its height early in 1991 when Bride Rosney opened what she called her Scud Missiles file. It documented the incoming fire from the Taoiseach's office to the Áras. This was a war that both sides would fight to the brink. It began with the Áras staff and it would end decisively with the Dalai Lama.

As with all wars, it was fought over territory. Charles Haughey saw himself as the real President of Ireland, a François Mitterrand figure, a Napoleon. He lived like an emperor, with his Gandon-designed mansion and estate, his island off the Kerry coast. He, and he alone, would represent the Irish people politically and symbolically. President Hillery had not interfered with Haughey's ambitions any more than Brian Lenihan would have. Haughey's whole attitude to the presidency and anything connected to it was dismissive. 'He described the Áras to me more than once as a "dog of a house",' says Mary. It was the presidential Taoiseach wanting to demote this rival office, she says. 'And that included the house and the surrounds.'

Haughey had reason to be uneasy. After only weeks in office, Mary was seen as a world player. In early January, she was approached to act as a mediator in the Gulf crisis by a group of Anglican bishops – the presiding Bishop of the Episcopal Church of the USA, Edmond Browning, made contact through Michael Hare Duke, Bishop of St Andrews in the UK, and Archbishop Donal

Caird of Dublin.[1] The initiative was abandoned when it became clear that the time for mediation had passed, but it indicated the sort of role that Mary could play internationally. Mr Haughey had other plans for her.

In this war there would be set battles and there would also be ambushes. Invitations to Mary to open conferences or new enterprises would mysteriously be withdrawn. The organisers would find sudden problems put in their way.

In March Mary was asked to open the Bundoran Waterworld, a £2 million leisure development. In April the government was asked to approve the invitation and in May a letter arrived from the organisers to the Áras regretting that the invitation was being rescinded, as the company now recognised that the performance of the official opening was the function of the local Urban District Council.[2]

An invitation to open the annual conference of Women into Technology in the European Community in connection with NETWORK, the Irish businesswomen's organisation, in Dublin Castle on 2 May, was withdrawn when the organisers were told they would lose the venue unless a government Minister performed the opening.[3] In September the President had agreed to launch the European Week of Information on Cancer, but she solved an embarrassing situation for the organisers by withdrawing when it was indicated that the Minister for Health would like to undertake the launch.[4] These, however, were skirmishes. Mary's biggest problem was finding a way to speak out independently and responsibly as President. To do that she had to deal not only with Charles Haughey's ego, but with a whole series of traditions which had attached themselves to the presidency, including a traditional interpretation of the constitutional constraints.

She remembers a particularly sharp exchange she had with the then editor of the *Sunday Tribune*, Vincent Browne, on 1 November 1990, towards the end of her election campaign. Browne had accused her of misleading people, of promising an active, outspoken presidency which it would be impossible for her to deliver within the limits laid down for her in the Constitution. He challenged particularly her claim in a speech on 28 September

1990, that 'the President of Ireland is free to speak out on issues of concern to citizens of our country'. He asked: 'Is there not a legitimate worry on the part of the electorate that if you are elected President you will get into a constitutional confrontation with the government of the day?'

'No,' said Mary, insisting that as a constitutional lawyer, she had repeatedly pointed to the constitutional framework within which the President must operate.[5] But Browne's questions rankled because they reflected a generally held view. 'He was encapsulating the orthodoxy of the time,' she says.

The orthodox view was that the President was a total prisoner of government, that she had almost no power to do or say anything without the permission of the government; that the only major exceptions were the President's absolute discretion to refuse a dissolution of the Dáil where a Taoiseach had lost majority support; and her right, after consulting the Council of State, to refer a Bill to the Supreme Court to test its constitutionality. All the other powers and functions, including the power to address the Oireachtas on matters of national importance, or similarly to address a message to the nation were covered by Article 13. 11: 'No power or function conferred on the President by law shall be exercisable or performable by him save only on the advice of the Government.'

All that seems fairly comprehensive, except that it refers only to powers and functions conferred on the President by law. It doesn't mention day-to-day speeches and media interviews. It doesn't mention the President's right to go wherever she likes within Ireland, or to invite whomever she likes to the Áras. It was in these unexplored areas that Mary hoped to give a voice to the Presidency, one which would not be in conflict with the government, but which would be identifiably her own. The Constitution grounded her – she couldn't leave Ireland without the government's permission. But she didn't have to accept the role of silent prisoner in the Park.

Before the inauguration in December 1990, before the conventions could close in on her, she said plenty just in case. 'I was on record as having said, as President-elect, an enormous amount. That was deliberate, so that my voice as President-elect would be heard.' She did interviews for almost every Irish radio and television programme, and every newspaper. She did endless international interviews. She repeated her determination to speak for the weak and the marginalised, to give a voice to women, to stretch out a hand of friendship across the border.

She flagged her priorities by attending Aids benefits, travellers, projects, a party for Cherish, the single parents' organisation. She met cross-border groups such as the Irish Countrywomen's Association and their Northern Irish counterpart and, significantly, she met a group from the Protestant Shankill Road in Belfast. She laid down markers: this was the sort of thing she meant by having an active, outspoken presidency.

But once she had taken her oath, she stayed quiet. 'I still remember spending a miserable month of December saying, "How am I going to work this out?" At a function for Threshold (the housing charity), I said nothing because I was still unsure of whether I could speak out. I simply said: "I'm delighted to be here. I'm supportive of what you are doing."' She went straight back to the Áras and said to Bride Rosney: 'We must plan a whole series of places I can be while I work out what I can say.'

One such place was particularly newsworthy. It was rare for a President to visit prisons but quite usual for a President to go to mass. Mary by-passed the red tape by attending mass in the Women's Prison in Mountjoy on 6 January, traditionally known in Ireland as the Women's Christmas. She also attended fund-raising events for the Rape Crisis Centre and for Third World development agencies. At least she could indicate by her presence what she thought was important, even if she still said nothing.

There was great government resistance even to letting her chose where she would go. Invitations channelled through the Taoiseach's office would arrive on her desk with the observation 'not appropriate for President' scribbled on the margin. These attitudes were ingrained not only within the Taoiseach's office but in her own secretariat.

Her secretary, inherited from President Hillery, was an Irish speaker, and of the old school. The first thing Mícheál Ó hÓdhráin said to her was: 'Beidh tú ag labhairt as Gaeilge?'[6] Mary said: 'I'll labhair as Gaeilge (I'll speak Irish) as much as I can. I'll have to get my Irish back.'

And then the secretary went on determinedly: 'But you *will* sign yourself Máire Mhic Róibín?'

'And I said, "No. I've always signed myself Mary Robinson. I'll keep my signature."'

'And he said pointedly, "We'll come back to that, Uachtarán (President)."'

'And I remember thinking, no, we won't really come back to that.' Mary decided at that moment that she needed a new secretary.

She chose Peter Ryan. He had been seconded to the Áras from the Taoiseach's office two years earlier when Mr Ó hÓdhráin was ill. His views were conventional but Mary had found him loyal and helpful during the staffing row. Mr Haughey suggested other candidates but Mary was wary of a spy in the camp. 'I preferred to have Peter whom I found to be straight, up-front, open, coping with a difficult situation in a very honourable way. I think I did have some concerns about having somebody else from the Taoiseach's office at that time: I mean, there was much more a sense of them and us at that stage than developed later.'

So she had Peter whom she trusted and she had Bride. When she asked Haughey before the inauguration about having a personal adviser, he told her expansively that she didn't need one, that all the resources of his office and the civil service were at her disposal. 'Bride who?' he asked as he agreed reluctantly to Rosney's appointment. He should have remembered Wood Quay. Trench warfare was Bride's forte.

One of the earliest spats arose out of Mary's St Patrick's Day message. Bord Fáilte, the Irish Tourist Board, had suggested to a US company called World Television Network that they do a promotional package from Ireland on the national day, 17 March. There was great US interest in the new President and Bord Fáilte helped set up an interview through Bride, who had family connections in the hotel and tourism business. Martin Dully, successful former head of Aer Rianta, the Irish airports authority, and then head of Bord Fáilte, remembers what came next.

'They put it out on TV stations across the States as part of a syndicated message. Nothing much happened until messages of congratulations came back to the Foreign Affairs Department about the excellent St Patrick's Day message seen across the US. The reports found their way to the Taoiseach's office. The Taoiseach saw them and got upset, maybe because he felt he should have been the man to deliver the message.'[7]

When Mr Haughey asked who had organised the interview, Bord Fáilte said guardedly that they had, and that they were not unhappy with the outcome. 'The Taoiseach got agitated,' says Martin Dully who was summoned to Mr Haughey's office. 'I was called in and a man called P.J. Mara (then Government Press Secretary) met me at the door wringing his hands. He said: "The Boss is in terrible form. You're going to be bawled out. He's upset."

'I wasn't very graciously received. I was told there was a protocol for accessing the Park – through the Taoiseach's office – and that Bord Fáilte, a state agency, had no right to approach the Park directly for anything. What could I do but try not to apologise for what all the evidence showed had been a successful campaign? His language was unparliamentary but then that was no different from his language in certain other crises. That was his style,' concludes Dully.

Mary began quietly to give interviews – she gave ninety-two in that first year alone – and more and more to ignore the scribbled warnings from the Taoiseach's office: 'not important enough to merit the attention of the President'.

The flavour of the combat comes through in an interview request from a Ms Kelleher of the *Los Angeles Times* forwarded from the Taoiseach's office with the advice that 'the Taoiseach remains of the view and advises that the President should decline to be interviewed by Ms Kelleher essentially because of their respective positions and because it would be difficult to see how the President could avoid being embroiled in matters of government policy in discussing the subjects listed by the reporter.'[8]

Mrs Robinson's response was that the Taoiseach's views were noted and that particular care would be taken to avoid questions encroaching on government policy. She indicated that the journalist had been asked to submit questions in advance and was arriving very shortly, so it would be inappropriate to decline at that stage as it could give rise to adverse comment.

Mr Haughey was particularly upset when Mary did a major interview for Denis Tuohy of the Thames Television *This Week* programme. It wasn't clear that he could prevent her doing interviews but he did use his power to stop her travelling abroad to give speeches. When the BBC asked her to deliver the annual Dimbleby television lecture, he pounced. She couldn't go. Reason? It was 'not appropriate'. The fact that former President Hillery had delivered a lecture at the University of Europe in Fiesole outside Florence didn't weigh with Mr Haughey. 'At the time I felt that Haughey was quite determined that I'd already had enough outings. That I'd been pushing out the frontiers. It wasn't just that it would be inappropriate for me to do it, but also that he didn't want me to have the profile of doing it.'

Mr Haughey, it seems, was determined to put a stop to this presidential gallop. In his view, apparently, the Constitution gave government a veto over any interview or speech Mary wanted to give. Mary's view was that the Constitution made reference only to the powers and function invested in her by law – the relevant powers in this instance being her power to address the houses of the Oireachtas (parliament) or address a message to the nation. The Constitution said nothing about government vetos over interviews or other speeches. Mr Haughey arrived to do battle in the Áras in the early summer, armed with senior counsel's opinion. Mary, senior counsel and constitutional expert, was ready for him. 'It was a case of taking on someone in her own area of strength, and he almost immediately regretted it,' she says, laughing.

'We had quite a discussion and I really enjoyed myself. This was my territory. When at one stage I said, "That's one lawyer's opinion," Haughey responded in an exasperated but humorous way. "I suppose you can get any opinion you like out of a lawyer if you pay them."

'When we began to debate and discuss, it didn't work very well. He said at one stage, "We'll come back to the Constitution," and I said, "Any time, Taoiseach. I would be delighted." But we never did, and I think that was the end of any overt attempt to rein me in.'

There was, however, one last dramatic confrontation. It took place behind the scenes and the full story never became public. Yet this was probably the defining moment of Mary's presidency. She knew that if she did not stand her ground, she could never be the President she had promised to be.

This final, decisive showdown with Charles Haughey arose over the Dalai Lama. All her life, Mary had greatly admired the Tibetan leader. He had personally written to thank her when she forced a debate in the Senate in January 1989 condemning Chinese violation of human rights in Tibet.[9] It was one of her last political interventions as a senator and she was trying to bring to public attention an issue on which the Irish had been peculiarly silent. 'This is particularly strange because much of what has happened to Tibet should evoke deep chords in the Irish people. The suppression of a whole people so that their independent, religious, social and cultural ethos is denied and that they are subjected to the humiliation of being colonised and indeed substantially being planted upon to such an extent that the Tibetan people have become a minority in their own country, should evoke an immediate response from us.'

When the Tibetan leader visited Ireland in 1991, Mary Robinson made it clear that she wished to invite him to pay a courtesy call to Áras an Uachtaráin. Immediately, she came up against official resistance, so she compromised, arranging instead to meet him on 22 March at a special exhibition of Oriental Art at the Chester Beatty Museum in Ballsbridge in Dublin. 'And then I was written to in a very subtle way – not told "you can't meet him" but suggesting that "it wouldn't be helpful".' Mary replied firmly, stating that she would go ahead with her plans.

'After I had responded, there was a further letter to say it would be considered very unhelpful by the government. This again was Haughey's doing.'

This second letter was, in effect, the throwing down of a gauntlet. It arrived only hours before Mary was due to meet the Dalai Lama, and once again it did not state why the government did not want the meeting to take place. She remembers sitting in her official study in the Áras when her secretary, Peter Ryan, came in to deliver it. He was white-faced. Like any experienced civil servant, he would have known that the whole affair was now sailing into very dangerous waters.

Mary was torn. She came from a human rights background. She had publicly espoused the cause of the Tibetan people. She had a profound respect for the Dalai Lama. And yet, by meeting him against the express wishes of the government, was she going to put at risk some element of state policy? She sat down with Peter Ryan to talk through the implications of the meeting. China had the world's biggest market in population terms and didn't easily offer access to those who criticised its human rights record. The Chinese watched out for any show of public support for the Dalai Lama and were quick to show their disapproval. They might issue an official complaint about Mary's action, or an Irish company in line for a major contract in China might find it had been put in jeopardy.

'The worst we could come up with was loss of a financial contract. I remember how pale and tense Peter Ryan was. I remember the load of responsibility I felt. I said: "If there is a price to be paid for this meeting, then I have got to pay it, whatever it is."' She was due to leave for the meeting in half an hour. She checked through the final details with Peter Ryan. Then they looked at one another, knowing an irrevocable step had been taken, and they both said: 'Well, there it is.'

'We almost shook hands, as if it was before the battle. And I went into my private study.' Mary sat there, gathering her thoughts, knowing that she might have launched herself and the presidency into a whole-scale constitutional crisis. She was prepared for the worst, and then the internal phone rang. It was Peter Ryan. His voice had completely changed. 'It's all over,' he said. 'It's finished.' She could hardly believe it. Charles Haughey had backed off totally. The crisis was over. Relieved and exhausted, Mary set out for the exhibition.

'I met the Dalai Lama and he clearly knew more, he knew what a struggle it had been and that I had aged several years just from the responsibility. But it was a price I knew I had to pay and, just like that, it was gone. I had stood my ground. It was a power-play that hadn't worked.'

It was only as she arrived at the Chester Beatty Library that Mary realised that two cabinet Ministers, Bertie Ahern and Mary O'Rourke, would attend as well. Mrs O'Rourke says she had asked at cabinet some time earlier whether she could go, but Bertie Ahern, now Taoiseach, says he went because Mary went. 'If she wasn't going I might have said, well, maybe . . . but it didn't seem to me to be right that the President should go and here were the administration staying away and that certainly fortified my mind to go.' So not only had Mary recognised the Dalai Lama, she had ensured that a senior government Minister had done so too.

It was the event that finally stamped her authority on the presidency. She still remembers it in vivid and painful detail, but the words etched on her memory will be Peter Ryan's, as he rang through with news of the Taoiseach's withdrawal. As ever with Haughey, there were echoes of Napoleon.

'It's all over,' said Peter. 'It's finished. The Taoiseach has gone to his island.'

15

OPEN HOUSE

In the drawing-room of Áras an Uachtaráin there is a gilded pink chaise-longue. Traditionally, this has been the President's chair when receiving visitors – no one else sits there. Indeed, there is depression at one end where it has borne the weight of six generations of Presidents. The presidential secretary knew things had changed when he came in one day to find Mary Robinson and three traveller women happily ensconced on it. The chaise-longue, like everything else to do with the presidency, was no longer to be an under-used resource.

In Ireland travellers were regularly thrown out of shops, pubs, hotels. Mary wanted them to feel at home in the Áras – like that group of traveller women from Clondalkin. 'They brought me some vividly-coloured artificial flowers, part of a project they were doing.' One of the women spotted a huge antique bowl on a table in the drawing-room and deposited the flowers in it with a flourish. 'And I said, "Don't they look great!" I was so pleased that she felt confident enough to do that.'

Mary had promised to open up the Áras. It was one of a number of promises she had made in her inauguration speech and she set about keeping each one of them. As the years went on it would become clear that she was ticking off those inauguration pledges one by one. No one would ever be able to wave that speech at her and claim she hadn't delivered.

There was a strategy from day one. She would open up the presidency, incrementally, step by step, so as not to create a rift with existing institutions, but she would start where she could – out on the ground in direct contact with the people, and symbolically most important of all, in her own home, in the Áras.

She made a strategic decision about her entertainment budget. It would not be spent on dozens of grand state dinners. It would be spent on tea and cakes for the ten thousand citizens who flocked to visit the Áras every year.

Though she had an official dinner, including spouses and partners, for each new government, in general she entertained the powerless, not the powerful, and she wasn't universally admired for it. But Mary was sending out a message. The sharper it was, the better it would be understood.

She was given £100,000 for entertainment; it would rise to £120,000 by the time she left office. It wasn't as generous as the £250,000 now allowed,[1] but a lot more than the £15,000 allowed President Hillery. It was Charles Haughey who had increased the allowance from October 1990, looking forward, perhaps, to the election of his friend Brian Lenihan, but Mary would be the first to admit that an increased allowance gave her much greater scope than had ever been possible for President Hillery.[2]

People wrote to her in droves and she asked them up to tea. Chris McCarthy from St Teresa's Gardens' Flats was part of a literacy group in the Mercy Family Centre in the Coombe in inner-city Dublin. They wrote to congratulate Mary on her election. 'We told her that for the first time ever we voted. We never voted before. We all marched up from here and we voted for her because she was a woman. We all voted that day. And because we did that, we felt that we had got her elected.'[3]

They wanted her to visit their centre. 'She wrote back and said she'd be delighted, but why didn't we come up there first?'

So they did and Mary spent an hour showing them around. One of the group had borrowed a pair of shoes which were too small for her. When she collapsed into a chair, Mary sympathised.

'She said, why don't you take the shoes off? You'll be more comfortable.' So the visitor did.

'She spoke to us about life in St Teresa's Gardens,' says Chris, 'And I said it was really nice to be there in the Áras but I have to go back and live in the shit I'm coming from. I have to go back to reality from here. I felt comfortable challenging her because she listened to people. When we went to shake hands with her she said to me that it was her son's birthday. And I said it was my son's birthday too. And she said, "Imagine them all running around here." And I said you have more room that I have in my flat. Why don't I bring 'em all up here to play!'

When Mary came to the Centre a few years later to open a playground, she remembered them all, says Chris, and what they'd said. 'There were lots of official people there but she wanted to be with the women.'

She kept her promise, too, about stretching hands of friendship across the border. In her first year Margaret McLaughlin and Rose Fellowes and Councillor Jim Rodgers from the Shankill Community Project came down to meet her. They were part of a North–South project to send teenagers from both communities and from both sides of the border to a seven-week residential course in Denmark.

The Shankill is the heart of Loyalist Belfast but nobody there had any qualms about going to meet the head of state of the Republic who was a Catholic. 'One of the big fears Unionists have about the South is the influence of the Catholic Church. One of the things about her was that when she went against the Church she showed us up here that she wasn't that sort of person. We were aware that her husband was a Protestant but that didn't matter. We felt she could genuinely help us with our problems,' says Jim. 'She put her money where her mouth was when she quit over the Anglo-Irish agreement. That says a lot for a person.'[4]

'She changed my view of the South,' says Margaret. 'I had nothing much good to say about the South except when things were cheaper there and we'd go down to shop. But I see the South in a different way because of her personally. She wasn't threatening.'[5]

'It was a real hand of friendship,' says Rose. 'The welcome we got! She greeted each person individually. She knew all about us, she knew about our area. She knew all about the kids who came from Wexford, but she took a particular interest in the kids from our area.'[6]

'She had proved she was genuine even before she was elected President,' says Margaret. 'All she had tried to do about the divorce laws, about women's issues.'

'She broke down barriers between Northern Ireland and the Republic. She let us realise that people in the south didn't have horns,' said Jim. 'And behind the smile she was a tough woman. I said to myself, here's a real tough individual who's dedicated to seeing this through.'

The youngsters still talked about that visit, said Margaret. They'd never been anywhere like the Áras before.

'It was the equivalent to us of going to Buckingham Palace to meet the Queen,' says Jim.

Jim Rodgers claims he was the first Ulster Unionist politician to meet Mary in the Áras. He wasn't the last. And others from more hard-line traditions came – one of Ian Paisley's Democratic Unionist party members insisted on having his picture taken in the Áras with the President. A group from the suburb of Shankill in Dublin and the Shankill in Belfast came and they included former loyalist paramilitary, now Progressive Unionist party member, Billy Hutchinson and his young son. Mary pointed out to them that the Áras represented part of their tradition, too. It had always housed the Crown's representative in Ireland, it had been the Vice-regal Lodge. Unionists were always tickled by that.

In fact, initially Northern Protestants were often more at home visiting the new Head of State than were Northern Republicans. Republicans weren't just suspicious of Mary. They were suspicious of everybody. They felt betrayed by their compatriots in the Republic and oppressed by the majority in the North. The ongoing violence had made them a pariah community.

In February 1991 the first group came down as part of a women's network linking the Falls Road and Shankill. They had just suffered government cutbacks to both centres and they realised they had more in common than they thought. They had a press release prepared. It said: 'We are not a reconciliation group. We are a women's network.' When asked why they were so adamant they said: 'Because we're fed up with being supported as a reconciliation group but not as a women's group. In other words, they won't support us for what we're really about. They'll only fund us if we are a reconciliation group.' Neither side wanted to be sanitised, cleaned up. The West Belfast women in particular wanted to be valued for their loyalty to their own tradition as much as because they were involved in cross-community activity. Throughout her Presidency, one group a week came down, cross-community and cross-border groups. That first group represented eight different women's centres. 'They came down by train. For them at that time it was an enormous adventure, a leap in the dark. They were dressed up to the nines. And they were intimidated and excited at the same time but they relaxed as time went on. How much I learned every time I had a group like that! It was my privilege to listen to their real concerns and have the time to do it,' Mary said, 'because those women had come down from Belfast to talk to a President and when they left they were recharged and I could see it.' They continued to maintain that they were not reconciliation groups. 'But I think they recognised themselves that they were part of a very advanced reconciliation . . . They didn't want to be homogenised, they wanted to maintain the difference and find strength in that difference, respect the difference.'

When a group of 200 from the same women's network came one beautiful summer's day, Mary remembers the sun streaming in the windows of the Áras drawing-room 'and everyone sitting on the floor and the fags being smoked and the very real sense of solidarity. At one stage I left them and I remember looking down from upstairs to the garden and there was a wonderful interaction going on. I had a sense of dialogue expanding all the time. All I was doing was being in touch with it and giving it that recognition and oxygen of support and respect.'

Mary was conscious that the house should respect all traditions.

Once a symbol of British rule, it had had the mark of Catholic Ireland laid on with a sometimes heavy hand. In the fifties, a Sacred Heart lamp had burned in its magnificent hallway. When Mary arrived, the tradition had been to have the Christmas crib in the hallway, but Mary, conscious that she represented people of all religions and none, preferred to have it in the Áras chapel.

Irish names had been tagged to the magnificent rooms. The state reception room was called the Seomra Mór (Irish for big room). Mary dropped the name, joking that everyone would want to know where the Seomra Beag (the small room) was. The little yellow sitting-room where the sun streamed in from both sides kept its Irish name. It was quite properly called An Grianán, the sunny room.

Mary wanted to celebrate the house itself and all its extraordinary history, from the time it was built in the 1750s up to the present day. When she raised the possibility of a museum and a permanent exhibition first with the Office of Public Works, they were hesitant about any reference to the British period. They felt it more appropriate to celebrate the Áras as part of a free Ireland since 1922. Mary knew she was up against the same prejudice from which the house had long suffered. Not only had it been hated as the Vice-regal Lodge up to 1922, but it then housed the last symbol of empire, the much-resented governor-general. In 1937 the house had fallen into such bad repair and such disrepute that there was talk of demolishing it altogether. When Mary moved in there was still flooding in the basements. A museum in the basement would rehabilitate the house in more ways than one. So she insisted that the days of Vice-regal glory would be remembered too, and the OPW agreed, commissioning writer Kevin Casey to tell the rounded story. The video and film presentations celebrate the fact that it became the official residence of the viceroy in 1782, that with its balls and gatherings it became the centre of Dublin social life; that Queen Victoria liked it when she visited in 1842; that King Edward VII stayed there in 1907 and George V visited in 1910.

One of the exhibits, a map of central Dublin, highlights the streets which were called after the viceroys. For many Irish people those streets are as familiar as their own names: Talbot Street, Marlborough Street, Dorset Street, Fitzwilliam Square, Haddington Road, Herbert Road, Percy Place – but they'd rarely made the connection before with this unsung period of their own history.

Mary suggested that the families of all the former governors-general and Presidents be approached for memorabilia, and then she invited all the families to a first viewing of the museum: the grandson of Tim Healy was invited, as well as the grandson of Eoin McNeill, Michael McDowell TD. Sile de Valera, granddaughter of Eamon de Valera, attended, as did relations of the Childers and the Hillerys.

In opening up the presidency, Mary knew that above all she would have to open it up to women. For the first time, the first citizen was a woman. That had to involve some change in the male trappings.

As a woman, she did not feel at ease with the military rituals, though she knew they were part of the office. She worried that she wouldn't conduct the inspection of the guard of honour properly on her inauguration day and pored over the diagrams for hours.

'Coming down from the inauguration, we stopped for photographs at the bottom of the steps and then the butterflies came. Would I do this right? And I then inspected the guard of honour and came back to the right place and waited for the guard to be discharged. And afterwards I got a huge number of letters from people saying, "That was the moment we realised we had a woman President." She remembers being at President Mandela's inauguration and recalls the ceremony, the heat, the solemn oaths. 'But it was when the military planes flew over that there was a roar from the 100,000 people down below. It was the military handover that mattered. And I thought to myself, in a completely different context, how many people had said to me that it was when as a woman I inspected the guard of honour that it really made the difference to them.'

She took her job as Supreme Commander of the Armed Forces

very seriously. But at an early stage she broke with the tradition that presidential visits required a guard of honour 'because it would have curtailed what I wanted to do, which was to be in very small places if that was the right place as far as I was concerned.' Again this was officially resisted. It was a break with tradition, it was a break for freedom.

What was also resisted was her attempt to make the military trappings more relevant to women. How? By having women soldiers among her aides-de-camp. 'There was resistance on the army front because the rank for aide-de-camp was commandant, and there was no woman commandant. So I said, "I'll have a captain, thank you." The sergeants at the Áras were superb and I always insisted one was a woman. Occasionally, when ambassadors came up for presentation of credentials, it was an all-woman team. A woman captain would see them to the door and a woman sergeant would open the door – you'd sometimes have a woman government Minister, a woman captain, a woman sergeant and a woman President. It was sending out a very interesting message to some of my more chauvinist visitors.'

She also ran into opposition when she wanted policewomen. 'I had an official driver and two security people and I said one of them must be a woman. "Oh, but we wouldn't have a woman trained." And I said, "Train them," and that meant training in firearms and special driving.' There was a problem because these were regarded as perk jobs. Mary got one woman garda but waited and waited for the second she needed so that there was always one woman on duty. Then she heard that the woman had already completed her training. 'And I learned that she wasn't going to get here unless I specifically again asked: why hasn't this person come?'

Women noticed every small detail of the changes. Authority had a new face, a woman's face. They responded to it. Journalists who followed the President on her visits to local communities around the country noticed how, for a change, it was women who took charge of the ceremonies. Rituals mirror what is valued in a society. Many women looking into that mirror were seeing their own reflection for the very first time.

Very often it is women in any case who run the local community groups, the self-help groups, the local history project; it is women who knit the community together. And it was women who stood proudly at the front of the crowd to welcome her, women who led her into the local hall, women who fussed about the protocol of who should sit down first.

When she finished her speech in Cappamore, or Ardee, or Letterkenny, it was women who rose to their feet applauding. The men sat, a bit shy of all this exuberance. Mary knew it was important to celebrate and recognise the work that women did. But she felt the need to do more. As well as focusing attention on women, she could contribute intellectually to the debate on women's equality. She decided early in her presidency that she must adopt this twin-track approach to all the important issues on her agenda. She would use the symbolic presence of the presidency to give support, and then she would distil the information she had gathered to add new ideas, to help develop a clearer analysis. It helped provide the intellectual stimulation she needed after a busy legal career and it ensured that the presidency benefited from the full use of both her symbolic power and intellectual ability. Her first major contribution to a new definition of equality between men and women was in a lecture for the Allen Lane Foundation on 25 February 1992.[7]

Equality between the sexes was neither a woman's issue, a marginal issue, nor a threat to the traditional structures of a society, she argued, but because of all these flawed interpretations the approach to achieving equality had itself been flawed and remained ad hoc. 'We make legislative changes and appoint women in response to organised insistence and the pressure of public opinion. Therefore the accounting of progress is recorded less through deep and generous shifts in established thinking, and more by listing laws or doing a number count of the women in public positions. This ad hoc approach ensures that the issue of women's equality is starved of reflective thinking and careful planning. It is, of course, important that women participate more in all sectors of modern societies, but it is not sufficient. The elusive balance requires a more fundamental re-evaluation of the role, the worth and the contribution of all women to their society.'

The movement for women's equality had been a protest movement, she said, using rallies, pamphlets, test cases in the courts. All of these methods of protest had been devised by men of conscience, so that the freedoms gained by men had helped women. Men, in turn, could gain from the structures developed by women. In meeting women's groups and groups involving women, she had noticed distinctive organisational skills. 'I was trained in the law, one of the oldest of the organisational sciences. It is based on precedent, and one spokesperson interprets the issues on behalf of many. I think that is the way in which many of the established organs of our society work. From that background, it was fascinating for me to observe – even in a preliminary and unscientific way – a different style of doing things. Often everyone in a group spoke to me. Everyone was encouraged to have their say.' She wasn't claiming that this was a hard and fast difference between women's groups and community groups and the rest of society, but it indicated an improvisational response to contemporary challenges. Women, she said, 'are not so much dismissive of precedent as unable to afford the delay involved in considering it.'

She was struck, particularly with the women's groups she met in Northern Ireland, by the way in which women could value individuality and diversity. Women had shaped the voluntary effort world-wide by their 'fresh, problem-solving' approach, their readiness to by-pass bureaucracy. Just as they had enriched the voluntary sector, they could enrich the established structures of society. Women's rights were human rights, she said. 'In a society in which the rights and potential of women are constrained, no man can be truly free. He may have power, but he will not have freedom.'

Almost everywhere she went, she was keeping promises made in her campaign: 'I said I'd come back . . . I promised I'd be here and I am.'

She set out to support community and voluntary groups. Father Sean Healy of the Conference of Religious in Ireland remembers when she came to the launch of CORI's pilot scheme for part-time job opportunities in Portlaoise. For the people involved, it was a chance to get back into the experience of working and, operating as ever at two levels, Mary picked up from them ideas she was later to use in giving the Rede memorial lecture entitled 'Civil society: renewal at work' in Cambridge University on 2 December 1996. A man in Portlaoise, she informed her audience, told her that his work experience gave him something to talk about with his family at their evening meal. She went on to talk of the way work connected the worker and his or her family to society. She also questioned the definition of work and asked whether work is visible only when it is paid for. And she questioned the hierarchy of work: 'It is useful to evaluate this hierarchy, if only to remind ourselves that childcare is generally poorly paid while money care – financial services – is highly paid.' This hierarchy of values was reflected in the fact that growth in gross national product was the accepted measure of a society's progress, she said. New indicators of progress were required which would value activities like caring, voluntary and community work, currently not counted, and often done by women.

Groups like CORI were delighted to see Mary quoting their work to inform the intellectual debate, but her personal visits to their projects were invaluable. Her presence in Portlaoise resulted in the local newspaper headline 'Programme has Presidential approval'. 'That,' says Sean Healy, 'was the sort of publicity that raised the profile and gained respect for the voluntary and community sector. She gained respect for the work we were doing and a growth in government recognition. It's no accident that in 1996 the government formally recognised our sector as the fourth pillar in the negotiation of national agreements, along with the farmers, the unions and the government. Others pushed at that door as well but she played a big role by raising our profile.'[8]

Mary has been criticised, particularly by politicians, for her somewhat regal air. And it is true that, despite her determination to make the presidency more accessible to ordinary people, she always maintained its formality. Punctuality was almost a fetish. She would stop the car on the outskirts of a small town or village rather than commit the sin of arriving too early. The flag at the front of the car would be placed there at the last minute so that it would be fresh and undamaged when she entered the town. She dressed formally. She greeted people with a smile, but formally. She did not dispense with the trappings. This was quite deliberate. Ceremony and a slight sense of distance were an essential part of the office. 'I was conscious that Presidents have their style. I wanted to get out and around but to keep the ceremonial and dignity of the office, to reinforce the concept that this was being done by the President. In many ways it mattered more going into the inner city or going into a rural area, that you went with the flags flying and the outriders. You had to have that sense of the presidency, as well as being very accessible and listening and being in touch. But it was a President they wanted, not a community worker.' She had to affirm, as President, that what local communities were doing was worthwhile. 'You brought a sense of the office as well as the warmth of the person. People who always knew their work was worthwhile felt the President had confirmed that. I think there was a need to do it with the trappings of office.'

By the places she chose to visit – prisons, charities for the home-less, Aids groups, children's charities, travellers' and unemployed projects – she made it clear where her priorities lay. On five of the six occasions she went to Mountjoy Prison, it was she herself who asked to visit. The women – she visited the women's prison four times – were not at all fazed by the fact that this was a President, and that a President had never visited prisoners in Mountjoy before. 'We told them, "Now, you're not to hug her!"' says Mountjoy governor, John Lonergan. 'But every time the same thing happened. Prisoners hugged her. They called her Mary and they asked her about her clothes and her hair. Women with great Dublin accents: "That's a lovely coat you have. Where did you buy the coat?" In their eyes she was just another person. But she knew why she was coming in. She was using her office to reaffirm that prisoners are an integral part of society and that they will go out into society again. For the first time ever she gave society the message that prisoners are their responsibility. She felt strongly about the demonisation of prisons and prisoners. She was acknowledging that prisoners are victims, too.'[9]

There was no official resistance to Mary's first visits, but as time went on, says John Lonergan, there was increasing political resistance to her being photographed with prisoners.

'The last time she came, she was being filmed by Charlie Bird of RTE and I had awful hassle to have her filmed in the prison. They didn't want the images. It's political. They are afraid that it is a glamorisation of prison, that the public might see prisoners singing and laughing with the President and that the public would probably prefer to see prisoners suffering, that prisons are places where people should suffer.' Politicians had stopped having their photographs taken with prisoners, he said, on the basis that being soft on crime meant losing votes, and when Mary came to the Mountjoy production of *West Side Story*, John Lonergan fought 'a great personal battle with the Department (of Justice)' to have her photographed with the prisoners. But she *was* photographed with them, and the positive publicity, and the fact that she attended, he says, helped to ensure packed houses again for their drama in 1998. 'She conditioned important groups in society, like the media, to be more understanding and supportive. The media coverage in 1998 was totally positive.'

In case anyone had any doubts about her priorities, Mary copperfastened them officially in her appointments to the Council of State. This is the body which advises the President on her formal addresses to parliament or to the nation and which advises her before she refers a Bill to the Supreme Court to test its constitutionality. Mary immediately increased the number of women appointees.

She appointed Monica Barnes of Fine Gael; Professor Emer Colleran, the environmentalist; and Rosemary Smith of the Irish Farmers Association. She appointed a Northern Protestant for the very first time – Quentin Oliver, director of the Northern Ireland Council for Voluntary Action. She appointed Donal Toolan from Focus on Disability Group. And in appointing Dr T.K. Whitaker, former Secretary of the Department of Finance, governor of the Central Bank, and without doubt the outstanding public servant of his time, there was even a connection with prisoners. He had chaired the Whitaker report into the penal system.

As Mary's agenda became clearer and clearer, invitations started to roll in from people who would never have written to the President before. She was always happiest with the people at the edge, less happy with the glittering occasions. 'It was the ceremonial-type occasions, openings or state dinners that I probably felt most distanced in. They were what I felt least comfortable in attending.' That was probably because they were the people who least needed her, she said. She did the big occasions as respect for the office required. 'It wasn't as though I was grudging about undertaking the ceremonial or well-got occasions, but I preferred being on the other side of the divide.'

Chris McCarthy was on the other side of the divide. From an area with 80 per cent unemployment and all the problems associated with inner-city crime and drugs, Chris and her community had fought back. From local literacy and basic examination courses, Chris moved on to a Women's Studies' course in University College Dublin. She found the university intimidating at first but she hung on. She wrote a poem about it which, unbeknownst to her, her tutor sent to the President.

> Which way is in? The room has two doors
> I wonder if they'd notice if I crept in on all
> fours.
> I'm in the room now but I feel quite sick,
> I need to sit down and double quick.
>
> After some time I began to hear voices
> All of these women were discussing choices.
> So I sat up and took part in the session
> Lifting the lid off my oppression.
> So now I'm having the time of my life
> I'm not just a mother or somebody's wife.
> Today I celebrate being a woman
> And the courage it took to keep on coming.[10]

Just before Christmas, when the great and good were getting the President's mimeographed signature on their Christmas cards, Chris had a letter out of the blue. The President wrote to congratulate her on the poem, on her university course, and on all the work she had seen her do in the area – and to wish her and all in St Teresa's Gardens Flats a very happy Christmas.

Chris framed the letter and hung it on her wall.

16

HEALING WOUNDS

On 27 August 1979, an old man was bombed to death in his boat off the Sligo coast. The Provisional IRA chose him because he was Earl Mountbatten, uncle of Britain's Prince Philip and cousin to the Queen, who came every August to his west of Ireland holiday home at Mullaghmore. Killed along with him were his fourteen-year-old grandson Nicholas Knatchbull and a seventeen-year-old boatman, Paul Maxwell. Lord Mountbatten's daughter Lady Brabourne was injured, as was her husband, her son Timothy and the eighty-three-year-old dowager Lady Brabourne.

It was a particularly cowardly murder but its message was clear. No member of the Royal family, even the best disposed, like Mountbatten, could be safe in Ireland. It was striking at the very heart of the British nation. Over and above all the violence in Northern Ireland, this was an especially symbolic blow. If relations between Britain and Ireland were ever to be healed, they would have to be healed, too, at this symbolic level.

For Mary Robinson, better relations with the UK were vital for Northern Ireland, for the people of both islands, and for the beleaguered Irish community in Britain. She was determined to work for friendship at every level but she knew that only she could meet the Queen as an equal, head of state to head of state. Only the Irish President and the Queen could symbolise for both nations the new spirit of friendship. She decided to start with a simple visit to Britain – a straightforward matter, one would have thought, except that no Irish President had ever made an official visit to Britain. When she asked the government if she could accept an invitation to attend the opening of the European Bank for Reconstruction and Development, there was outrage.

'Who does she think she is! Presidents don't do this sort of thing and, secondly, it's Britain and Presidents don't go to Britain,' says Mary, laughing as she describes the official reaction. Mr Haughey's own reaction was even stronger. 'He didn't want me to go to the opening of something such as the European Bank for Reconstruction and Development in London because that would give me status.' He could veto any request by the President to leave the country. 'He kept me waiting and waiting until the bank was pressing me for a reply.'

There was no reluctance on the British side to welcome Irish Presidents. Mary's predecessor, Dr Hillery, had been invited to the wedding of Prince Charles and Princess Diana but was officially advised to decline. The long-standing Irish position, reflected in the Constitution, was that there was unfinished business between the two states over Northern Ireland and that precluded the normalisation of relations which official presidential visits would symbolise.[1]

In fact, relations at a political and trade level were already fairly normal. The Anglo-Irish Agreement had established new common ground on Northern Ireland. Irish and UK Ministers met almost daily on European Union business. Just as important, however, was the equalisation of living standards brought about by Ireland's increasing prosperity. The UK's sense that it was better than, and different from, the poor and backward Irish could no longer be sustained in face of vastly improved Irish education standards, the standardisation of urban and rural lifestyles, improved infrastructure – much of it subsidised by the EU. Irish per capita income actually outstripped Britain's in the 1990s.[2] There was a new sense among Irish and British people of sharing the same sort of lives, watching the same television programmes, having many of the same expectations of life.

Presidents, however, were retained in a time-warp. While government ministers trotted happily over and back to Britain and Northern Ireland, the head of state was expected to stay at home and radiate disapproval, an official nationalist skeleton which could be rattled whenever the British got too complacent.

The role of Britain's official non-friend was one Mary would not play. She argued that other heads of state had been invited to the bank opening and that she had been involved in selecting the logo for the bank with President Hável of the Czech Republic and others. But, from Mr Haughey's point of view, she would be rubbing shoulders with the great at a time when he, with the presidency of the European Union just behind him, was used to striding the European stage all by himself.

'Haughey was incredibly unenthusiastic,' she remembers. He reluctantly agreed to let her go so long as she didn't stray beyond the confines of the bank opening. Everything else was off limits. She accepted the constraints because she had now at least broken a taboo. The President would go to Britain.

Next time she upped the ante. She wanted to accept an invitation to make a speech in Cambridge. Once again, Haughey agreed, reluctantly. He knew Mary was going to Cambridge to receive an honorary degree. What he did not realise until the last minute, however, was that the University Chancellor was the Duke of Edinburgh who would join Mary and her family for breakfast. Almost unwittingly, Charles Haughey, the most defiantly nationalist Taoiseach of modern times, had sold the pass. Mary had driven a coach and four through tradition and not even Haughey could turn it back again.

She had done it simply by asking, by refusing to take no for an answer. There is no record of any major discussion among officials or Ministers about the policy implications of this crucial change in presidential behaviour. Neither the Department of Foreign Affairs, nor the Department of the Taoiseach can indicate whether key groups of policy advisers were consulted, or whether it was the subject of any internal report or analysis.

Officials fretted, and politicians bad-mouthed her, but she had caught them unawares, and by the time they tried to rein her in, she had established the vital precedent.

This was new ground for the British Royal family as well. Mary, Nick, their daughter Tessa, and her father, Dr Aubrey Bourke, met Prince Philip for breakfast. 'I remember feeling that the Duke of Edinburgh was quite uncomfortable with how to deal with an Irish President. Now, partly because I've never been fazed by royalty of any kind, least of all by the British Royal family, I felt entirely relaxed. But I remember seeing my young daughter as I have never seen her before, sitting ramrod straight with a sense of the formality of the occasion. I teased her about it afterwards and she was furious.

'The Duke spoke and he was warm; he welcomed me warmly. But he said something about "Eire" (a term normally used by Unionists which Irish people find most offensive) and all the Irish ears heard, of course.[3] And when he sat down, he turned to the Vice-Chancellor and said: "Well, that seemed to go okay, didn't it?"'

Mary's brother Henry was there, too, and says he realised the significance of the day during the formal procession before the degree ceremony. 'We had to walk through the town and as we approached the College with the Duke at the back whipping in, we looked up at the walls. And there at the second highest point was the Royal Standard and above it was our national flag. A head of state takes precedence even over the Duke of Edinburgh!'

The next time she met the Duke was in Warrington, near Liverpool. On 20 March 1993 the IRA had placed two bombs in litter-bins in a shopping precinct in Warrington. They injured fifty-six people and they killed two boys. Jonathan Ball was an only child, three years old. Tim Parry was twelve. He was badly injured and died a few days later in hospital. He had gone into town that day to buy a pair of football shorts. It was a Saturday. All over Ireland that day youngsters had gone into town to buy sneakers or football shorts. They probably supported the same football teams. Almost as never before, the Irish public identified with the grieving parents in Warrington. There was a new realisation that your average Irish family had more in common with their English counterparts than with any Republican.

There was a new anger against the IRA and a new determination to disassociate ordinary Irish people from Republican violence. Crowds milled on to Dublin's O'Connell Street to demonstrate their solidarity with those killed and injured in Warrington. President Robinson caught the public mood when she accepted an invitation to the memorial service on 7 April in St Elphin's Parish church in Warrington, to represent, as they put it in their letter to her, 'the true spirit of Ireland'. An Irish President had never expressed any public reaction to such an event before, let alone gone to the very scene of bombings in the name of Irish freedom. Mrs Robinson's presence was welcomed as 'a wonderful gesture of sympathy and healing' by the Catholic Archbishop of Liverpool, the late Derek Worlock, and she was applauded as she left the church.

'I remember two people that day,' says Colin Parry, father of Tim. 'Derek Warlock and Mary Robinson. They left their mark on me that day because of their sincerity and their humility.'[4]

Colin says it mattered enormously to him that she came. He remembered the huge crowd who gathered in Dublin to express their grief and shame. 'She captured that mood and she was the embodiment of the Irish nation. We knew that she took risks by what she did. We knew she was stepping outside that mould, leading from the front, and representing the Irish to the English nation, a real expression of regret.'

Colin says he still treasures the introduction she volunteered to write to his book *Tim – an Ordinary Boy*. She did some filming with Colin and Wendy Parry for a BBC *Panorama* special about Warrington and he remembers one particular moment in the grounds of Áras an Uachtaráin. 'We were walking back to the house and we came to a steep embankment. President Robinson and Wendy walked up the embankment as though it wasn't there, but I had leather shoes and I kept slipping back. On the fourth attempt she put out her hand and pulled me up. She didn't do it with symbolism in mind but I always saw it that way.'

When she came back to Warrington in October 1993 she

met Prince Charles. They were both there for the launch of the Warrington project, an attempt to build links between the various Irish and British communities hurt by the Northern Ireland Troubles, and the warmth between them, says Colin Parry, was obvious.

Every time Mary shook a royal hand, she was laying a ghost. Popular Irish interest in the British Royal family is huge, but it is accompanied by political hostility to the Crown as a symbol of Irish oppression. This never extended to Princess Anne. The Irish admire brave horsewomen and for years the Princess Royal had quietly turned up at equestrian and charity events in Ireland. Mary met her for the first time on a visit to Scotland in January 1993. The Princess was President of the Scottish Rugby Union and Mary was invited to lunch with her in the Club Room in Murrayfield. As Mary and Nick climbed up to the top of the stand, accompanied by the chairman of the club, a steward blocked their way. He held up his hands. 'No women allowed here,' he ordered. 'Back down there to gate nineteen.' The chairman said: 'What are you doing?' And the steward said: 'You're the one who makes the rules. I'm paid to implement them. No women in here. Back down to gate nineteen!'

The steward was waiting for the President of Ireland but no one had told him that the President of Ireland was a woman. Eventually, he was pushed aside by some solid rugby types and Mary went into the Club Room where the only other woman was Princess Anne. 'Tell me,' asked Mary, 'did you have any trouble getting in here today?'

'They'll know you the next time!' replied Anne.

When Mary went on Scottish television next day, the interviewer asked her what it was like to be the liberal woman president of a male-dominated society. 'Let me tell you a story,' said Mary gently, 'about male-dominated societies.'

When Mary had said publicly that she would welcome an opportunity to meet the Queen, the Irish government was distinctly nervous. When the Foreign Office indicated to the Irish Embassy that the Queen would like Mary to make a personal call, and when Mary indicated that she would be happy to accept, strict limits were put on the visit.

Charles Haughey would probably not have allowed her to go at all. Albert Reynold's government granted her permission in February 1993 to make a courtesy call 'on this occasion on the basis that it should be clearly understood that the courtesy call should not give rise to any question of a state visit which would require a return state visit by the Queen.'[5] At the time, as we now know, Reynolds was putting out secret feelers to the Republican movement in an effort to have them declare a ceasefire. He had to be careful of Republican sensitivities and nothing would be more sensitive than a state visit which seemed to accept Queen Elizabeth's right to call herself monarch of the United Kingdom and Northern Ireland.

So with the instruction that she could be friendly, but not that friendly, Mary set off for London and tea with the Queen. Her son William, then studying architecture in Glasgow, had come down to see her but decided to spend that day with his Robinson cousins in London. He arrived back unexpectedly at lunchtime. 'The cousins say that I should ... em ... could I come to Buckingham Palace?' he asked. So, quietly, Will came, too.

For Mary it was important that there be a photograph of this historic occasion – after all precedents are better set in public than in private. The palace officials were reluctant. The occasion would not be as newsworthy in Britain as in Ireland and, then, they had dignitaries in and out of the palace all the time. Bride had to push hard. 'They didn't want press inside the grounds at all. We had to fight for it.' They agreed eventually to a pool system which limited press numbers. Then the palace Press officer said to Bride: 'You'll have to keep control of your people. They can't be shouting questions.' So Bride agreed to talk to her people.

'Part of the significance of the visit to us was making it available to the media, to have the photo-call on the steps. It wasn't enough to have the cars going in. It would backfire if there wasn't a photo.'

Mary was wearing a fuschia pink suit by Ib Jorgensen which she would later donate to Madame Tussaud's for her own wax model.

The Queen, flanked by her corgis, had a relaxed tea party with Mary and Nick and then brought them down in the lift. She had never raised any objection to a photo-call. 'I was very conscious that she was aware of making this a very public occasion because of its significance for good relations on this island,' says Mary.

Outside, says Eric Luke of the *Irish Times*, the Irish photographers besieged one of the Queen's press assistants, pointing out that it was vital that the Queen turn towards them and give them time to get a proper picture. 'I shouldn't worry,' said the assistant gently. 'You know, the Queen's awfully good at this sort of thing.'

As Mary came out of the lift with the Queen, Bride and Peter Ryan and William were waiting and Mary introduced them. 'This is my son, William, who is studying architecture,' said Mary. 'Oh, and do you like modern architecture?' asked the Queen, whose family's views on modern architecture are well-known. 'Yes, some of it,' answered Will and then added diplomatically, 'but not all of it.'

'And then,' says Mary, 'we were moving towards the exit where the photographers and TV crews were. So we went and stood outside, initially the Queen and myself, then Nick behind us. No one was directing things. She was talking about where she had her garden parties and enduring the clickety-clicks and being relaxed about it, and meanwhile Bride and Peter Ryan had slipped out to where the cars were waiting. But Will, who lacked all the social skills but knew how to keep out of the eye of the cameras, had backed into where he had met the Queen. After two or three minutes of heavy photo-call, our car rolled up on cue and we shook hands with the Queen, thanked her and got into our car. Meanwhile poor old Will was still inside.'

The pictures of this historic meeting led every news bulletin and front page in Ireland and next time the two heads of state met in Buckingham Palace, courtesy had been promoted to friendship – the visit in June 1996 was official. This meant that Mary was the guest of the government but not of the monarch, thus avoiding a state visit with all its implications. The atmosphere was easier – this was Mary's fifteenth visit to Britain as President. But since on this official occasion she would have to be introduced publicly, the old problems arose. Her proper title is President of Ireland, but the British, because of Northern Ireland, had problems with that. They wanted to call her President of the Republic of Ireland, but the Irish objected to that. So the President solved the problem by suggesting she be called simply President Mary Robinson.

On the day, the British were gracious. John Major introduced her at a Number Ten lunch as the President of Ireland and the Buckingham Palace press passes stated 'for the visit of the President of Ireland'. Wars have been fought for less.

For many Irish people the true recognition of a new British–Irish entente came with that formal welcome to Buckingham Palace. Mary drove into the palace and was welcomed by the Queen and Prince Edward who walked her down to inspect the guard of honour. It was the Irish Guards, resplendent in their bearskins. 'That was the special moment,' says her brother Henry, 'when she stood to attention at Buckingham Palace and the Irish Guards played the anthem and the national colours flew.' For the group standing there – the Foreign Minister Dick Spring and his wife Kristi; Irish Ambassador Ted Barrington and his wife Clare; Bride Rosney and Peter Ryan, the anthem said it all.

'I remember thinking this is right,' says Bride. 'I've seen much the same happen to her in Poland, in Africa, in Japan and now it's happening in England and somehow it was England rather than Britain – the soldiers of the Crown saluting the Irish President by playing the Irish National Anthem.'

The talk at lunch was about horses, about the upcoming Royal Ascot meeting, about the Irish Derby, about Mary's hunting grandmother and race-horse-mad grandfather. The dark bay horses used by the Queen for ceremonial purposes in the Trooping of the Colour are Irish-bred. It emerged over lunch that she sends over to Ireland for them every year and is amazed that Ireland produces such a wealth of dark bays. But the talk ranged wider than horses. It covered the impact of the Afghan War on Muslims in the Middle East, how new ideas and new weapons had radicalised them. It covered politics in Europe.

It was Bride, sitting beside Prince Edward at lunch, who raised the subject of Lord Mountbatten. 'You couldn't not,' she says. 'I talked about the sense of shame people had at the time. The prince said that the death had impacted on the family in a very real way. They hadn't had a grandfather and he had been a grandfather figure.' Edward had just completed a documentary on Mountbatten. 'He felt someone in the family should do something about him.'

Mountbatten's death had deeply affected someone else, Prince Charles. The Prince had a difficult relationship with his own father and was very close to Lord Louis. It was as a result of the Mountbatten murder that the Royals were advised not to visit Ireland. Prince Charles had spoken again and again, whenever he met Irish people, of his wish to come to Ireland and of the insistence by his security advisers that he should not. He told Albert Reynolds so when he met him during the Edinburgh summit in 1993.

As Albert describes the conversation, he said to the Prince: 'Sure what's stoppin' ya? I'm not stoppin' ya! You're welcome to come hunting if you want to. Why is it your sister can come and I'm lucky if I get twelve hours' notice. She's in and out.'

The Prince replied: 'But I'm not allowed to do the things that Anne does.' And Albert told him: 'Well, I'm not stopping you. You'd better find out who is.'[6]

Charles's keen interest in Ireland may well have sprung from the Mountbatten connection but he also wanted to support better relations. Mary knew that when she met him. 'Charles was very keen to help.'

He understood the links she was trying to make between the two countries and between the two communities in Northern Ireland. He had made contacts though his own charity, the Prince's Trust, with young people and with business and community groups in Northern Ireland. 'We were both coming from similar perspectives, that the more you can have relevant links – doing business, being involved with young people, providing job opportunities, cultural links – the better. I think Prince Charles had, before he came to Ireland, a longing to come, a sense of closeness.' The Warrington project, which they both helped to launch in October 1993, encouraged exactly the sort of cross-community links they both worked for. She had met him too when she received an honorary degree at University College Cardiff where he was Chancellor. 'He told me a couple of times that he'd love to visit Ireland, and would that be possible.'

After the 1994 IRA ceasefire, it was possible. A delighted Charles visited in 1995 and announced to everyone he met that he 'never believed this day would come'. He came to lunch at the Áras. 'When he came to lunch he was full of more than just the pleasure of a visit. He, too, saw it as a hopeful normalisation of relations, something that mattered in a very real sense.' They talked about the history and the architecture of the house, and Mary kept it a relaxed occasion. 'He likes informality more than comes across on television. He likes to be at ease and relaxed.'

That wasn't how his security advisers saw it. There were some edgy meetings between the security people from the British Embassy, the Gardai, and the Áras Secretariat. The British wanted to saturate the Áras with security personnel. They wanted security people standing in the room where the President would have her private lunch with the Prince. The Áras said no. Then the British demanded to have security personnel standing outside the door of the room.

'And we said we didn't allow that for anybody and we were following standard protocol,' said Bride. The British reluctantly accepted Peter Ryan's compromise – that they could have one security person in the room across the corridor from the room where the President and Prince sat. Peter had quietly had his way. 'It was like watching Clonmel Christian Brothers School take on Old Etonians,' said Bride, 'and Clonmel CBS won.' There was one wobbly moment, when Peter Ryan insisted to the British: 'This compound is 100 per cent secure,' and turned to the Garda representative for confirmation. The Garda man agreed. 'This is a 100 per cent secure compound,' he reassured the British, 'and it will be even more so on the day.'

For Charles it was a visit that allowed him to lay some ghosts. When his official duties were over, he left for the west of Ireland on what amounted to a personal pilgrimage. He was joined at a fishing lodge in Delphi in Mayo by his Mountbatten cousins, their first time back in the area since the Mullaghmore bomb. Lady Brabourne had lost both her father, Lord Louis, and her son that day. She and Lord Brabourne had sold their local holiday retreat, Aasleagh Lodge, but made a point on that return trip of visiting the local people who used to work for them. Mrs Brigid Keane, their former cook, was astonished and delighted to see them. 'I never expected to see them again after what happened at Mullaghmore,' she said. Local publican, Irene Hastings, had been talking to the family on the morning of the fatal boat trip, and she was deeply moved to see the Brabournes back. 'The Prince coming has meant the healing can finally happen,' she said. 'Both their family and this community can be healed.'[7]

Mary knew how important that visit had been to the Prince by the welcome he gave her on her official visit the following year. After tea and a long chat in the Prince's apartment in St James's Palace, she and Nick went on to their formal engagement with him, a celebration of the achievements of young people on Prince's Trust projects, and it was then that Mary realised what a special guest she was. 'He had John Major as Prime Minister and Tony Blair and Paddy Ashdown on one side of the platform and we were on the other,' she said. 'When Prince Charles got up to speak he began by saying how much he welcomed the fact that it had been possible for me to be there. It was more than courtesy. It was genuine warmth and valuing of an identity of interests in a number of areas, in particular in relation to the involvement of young people and local communities.' He saw her as an ally, she says.

Mary always stresses that her visits to royalty were made in the interest of friendship, between Ireland and Britain, between North and South, between those of different traditions in the Republic and most of all between the Irish and British in Britain itself.

'I was trying to normalise relations, meaning not being fazed by royalty. The Queen was a head of state and I was a head of state – I always had that attitude and the fact that she was a Queen was simply their tradition. I've never had any sense of being fazed by royalty one way or another.'

But the visits mattered. She had respected the other tradition, just as she had by laying wreaths in Westminster Cathedral to the Irish who died in the First World War, by attending the memorial service in Dublin for the Irish dead of the two World Wars. Until then, no Irish President ever formally respected the memory of the 35,000 Irish who died in the First World War and the many thousands who died in the second. They were regarded as traitors by a political culture which was predominantly nationalist. Approaches to President Hillery had met an official wall – British Legion officers were told he had been advised not to attend.[8] The official reply to the Legion's invitation stated: 'It is not the practice of the Head of State to attend, or to be represented at, the memorial services for the armed forces of other countries.'[9]

Mary Robinson changed that for ever. She went to the service for the first time on 14 November 1993 and again in 1995. When Mary resigned in 1997, the new President continued the tradition. 'Mary Robinson has created a fact,' says Kevin Myers who has written extensively of the Irish regiments in the two wars. 'It would be unthinkable now for the Head of State not to participate in commemorating the dead of the two world wars.'

The resonances were greatest of all in Northern Ireland, says Myers. 'Unionists could always point to the neglect of this ceremonial and say, "You don't really care about us." They were able to say that the declared ecumenism of Irish nationalism was a sham and this proved it. She changed that.'[10]

Mary was conscious that events in Ireland in the years of her presidency had provided an opportunity, as perhaps never before, to find a more generous definition of identity for those living on the island of Ireland. Such a time had arisen for the poet, W.B. Yeats, at the beginning of the century when he spoke of Ireland being 'soft wax'. Such a moment had arisen again, she told an audience at the John Galway Foster lecture entitled 'Imaginative Possessions' in London, on 26 October 1995. The end of paramilitary violence, increased economic co-operation and contacts north and south, and a new emphasis on parity of esteem and the building up of local communities, had marked the moment. But it needed to be marked in more imaginative ways, she said. She pointed, as she would again and again, to the lessons in generosity and tolerance that Ireland could learn from its diaspora. 'After all, emigration is not just a chronicle of sorrow and regret. It is also a powerful story of contribution, of adaptation. The reality is that this great narrative of dispossession and belonging, which so often had its origins in sorrow and leave-taking, has become – with a certain amount of historic irony – one of the treasures of modern Irish society. In essence, our relation with the diaspora beyond our shores is one which can instruct our society in the values of diversity, tolerance and fair-mindedness. It is like a mirror reflecting back to us on the island. It encourages us to see that Irishness is not simply territorial. Therefore it can reach out to everyone on this island and show itself capable of honouring and listening to those whose sense of identity, and whose cultural values, may be more British than Irish.' She went on to quote Nobel Laureate, Seamus Heaney, a nationalist who grew up under British rule in Northern Ireland, on his experience of 'two-mindedness'. Heaney said:

'There is nothing extraordinary about the challenge to be in two minds. If, for example, there was something exacerbating, there was still nothing deleterious to my sense of Irishness in the fact that I grew up in the minority in Northern Ireland and was educated within the dominant British culture. My identity was emphasised rather than eroded by being maintained in such circumstances. The British dimension, in other words, while it is something that will be resisted by the minority if it is felt to be coercive, has nevertheless been a given of our history and even of our geography, one of the places where we all live, willy-nilly. It's in the language. And it's where the mind of many in the Republic lives also. So I would suggest that the majority in Northern Ireland should make a corresponding effort at two-mindedness, and start to conceive of themselves within – rather than beyond – the Irish element. Obviously, it will be extremely difficult for them to surmount their revulsion against all the violence that has been perpetrated in the name of Ireland, but everything and everybody would be helped were they to make their imagination press back against the pressure of reality and re-enter the whole country of Ireland imaginatively, if not constitutionally, through the northern point of the quincunx.'[11]

Mary returned to this theme of identity repeatedly as politicians in the north and south of Ireland, and in Britain, set out on the long and difficult path towards an inclusive political agreement. She herself had tried to enter imaginatively into the minds of Northern Unionists. She had resigned over the Anglo-Irish Agreement, she had remembered the world war dead – a huge issue with Unionists – and she had met the Queen. Her welcome in Northern Ireland was as warm as any southerner could expect.

She left her first trip to the North until 1992. Charlie Haughey was gone and Albert Reynolds was quite happy to trust her. 'She knew what she was at,' says Albert happily. 'As far as I was concerned, let her off!'

She met with ritual resistance. The Democratic Unionist party Mayor of Belfast refused to meet her on her first visit there. But her itinerary was carefully balanced. She met cross-community groups – the Women's Network who had come down to the Áras, the Women's European Platform and the Northern Ireland Equal Opportunities Commission. She would balance religious and political interests during the eighteen visits to the North, nine of which included Belfast, four took in Derry and she also visited Coalisland, Newry, Craigavon, Armagh, Omagh, Newcastle and Dungannon. Three visits to Fermanagh included the funerals of Gordon Wilson, whose daughter Marie had been killed in the 1987 Enniskillen Remembrance Day bomb, and the funeral of Gordon's son Peter.

Little by little, her visits across the border, her visits to Britain, were becoming normal. And, even among those who would pride themselves on flying the nationalist flag, even among traditional Fianna Fáilers, there was a new acceptance that all her missions of friendship, including those to the Royals, had a tangible result. 'I had no difficulty with her visit to the Queen,' says Taoiseach Bertie Ahern. 'If it was going the other way and the Queen had to come here, well, I think until there is a Northern Ireland settlement that's a difficulty. But her going to visit the Queen didn't remotely worry me. And the fact that she made so many visits – that was all positive. That terrible attitude here in the late seventies, the Brits Out campaign with slogans on the walls all over the place – that did immense damage to this country. And I have no doubt that she can take her fair share of credit for building that back up, and that was good, normalising, showing we don't all have horns here. Her appearing at those functions and meeting the dignitaries and going to Oxford and Cambridge and Manchester and all over the place, was all positive. And now the place is swamped with English tourists again and long may it last.'[12]

17

THE FORGOTTEN IRISH

'I suppose,' an official overheard the Queen say wryly as she looked back at all the Irish, 'I suppose they're going to have a céilí in there now.'[1] It had been an all-Ireland occasion in St James's Palace. The two heads of state, Mary and Queen Elizabeth, were both guests of honour at the celebration of the 150th anniversary of the Queen's Colleges in Ireland – Queen's University in Belfast and what are now the National Universities in Galway and Cork. Mary and the Queen came in together and went down opposite lines of the assembled staff and students shaking hands. It was a high-profile celebration of the two traditions in which the Irish President was given equal status with the Monarch. It was all reported that night on television.

In the Irish Embassy next day, Mary met representatives of the Irish community from all over Britain. 'They were full of having seen something on television about myself and the Queen,' says Mary. 'They said, "You have no idea how much good that will do, no idea!" It was extraordinary – the very people you thought would resent your being in Buckingham Palace, in St James's Palace, were the people who said "You have no idea how much good that will do."'

She had every idea how much good it would do. When Mary met the Queen she was doing it, most of all, for the Irish in Britain. Outside Northern Ireland, this was the community hit hardest by the Troubles. The religious and social prejudice which met the early immigrants was re-ignited by the Republican bombing campaigns in Britain and the killing of British soldiers in Northern Ireland. If you were Irish you kept your mouth shut, your head down, and nobody at home particularly cared.

After savage IRA bombs killed twenty-eight people in Guildford, Woolwich and Birmingham in 1974,[2] it was more difficult if you had an Irish accent to find a job, a flat-share. You didn't open an Irish newspaper on the tube. You didn't ask for an Irish whiskey.

But these were small irritations compared with the attacks on Irish communities and Irish centres around the country, and with the false convictions of ten people for the Guildford, Woolwich and Birmingham bombings, and the false convictions of the Maguire seven on explosives charges.

'A low profile was the name of the game for a while after the bombing,' says Pat O'Neill of the Irish Community Forum in Birmingham. 'The people you worked with didn't want to speak to you. Your neighbours didn't want to speak to you. It was a hard time for us in Birmingham. We had to be discreet for a long time. The scars are still there,' he says. 'Afterwards there was no singing in pubs. There were no rebel songs. You learned to be like that. You had to look after yourself. You had growing families.'[3]

Mary had made a point of meeting the emigrants on a trip to Britain during her election campaign, and reflected their view in her *Hot Press* interview that 'nobody gives a shit about them'. She had promised the emigrants in her inauguration speech that she would represent them, but Haughey wasn't going to make it easy. He refused her permission to visit the Irish community on her first visit to Britain. 'I was very angry,' she says. 'To me, to meet the Irish community in London was more important than meeting the Duke of Edinburgh or the Royal Family. Part of the reason that Haughey didn't want me to meet the Irish emigrants in London at all was fear of criticism of the government. A group of emigrants would be anything but polite about the government and I would be the recipient of it. I had gone during the election campaign and therefore I would be "putting them up to it".'

Haughey and his predecessors had good cause to feel sensitive about emigrants in the early 1990s. Irish governments have always accepted emigration as an answer to the unemployment problem, but the flight of young people during the recession of the eighties had reached crisis proportions. Between 1982 and 1990, net emigration figures reached a massive 207,000, equivalent to six per cent of the population.[4] Behind the statistics was the human cost. Parents on phone-in programmes across the country asked who was going to bring their children home. 'I spent my life rearing them. Now I spend my life on the phone to New York and Sydney and London. What was it all for?'

Many of them went to Britain, mostly to look for work but often, too, to escape Ireland's strictures against abortion, and against homosexuality, and to escape the social stigma which attached to AIDS. Once gone, they were forgotten by official Ireland. The failure of any Irish government to raise the issue of the wrongfully convicted Guildford Four and Birmingham Six is a sharp example. Nothing was done until investigative British television programmes, Yorkshire Television's *First Tuesday* and Granada's *World in Action*, had already fought and effectively won the battle. The Irish community had nobody to represent them. They had good reason to feel resentful.

'The odd politician would come,' says Pat O'Neill. 'Albert Reynolds would come, for instance, to the Longford Association but no one came from the government as such.'

'I would have to stress the parochial nature of previous politicians' visits,' says Michael Forde of the Irish World Heritage Centre in Manchester. Politicians would come with an eye to the effect in their own constituencies, their own vote at home. 'The Irish community didn't want that. They wanted a clear demonstration that the Irish abroad were part of the Irish nation, that they would be allowed access to government structures.'[5]

Mary, who had been one of the very few Irish politicians to question publicly the convictions in the Birmingham and Guildford cases, knew that this community had to be supported and recognised within their British context.

They needed their President to visit them. She reluctantly

agreed not to meet them on her first trip to Britain, 'because I felt it wasn't appropriate for the President to be in open confrontation with the government. You have to fight battles quietly behind the scenes.' But she made sure to meet the Irish community on her visit to Cambridge. 'And everywhere I ever went after that, I made sure to meet them.'

They backed her to the hilt in all her public gestures of friendship. They didn't scoff when she went to Buckingham Palace. It showed their British friends and colleagues that they had a head of state who cared about them and who met on equal terms with the Queen. It raised their value in British eyes. 'That's what they felt in incredibly strong terms and it showed how low the morale had been, how defensive over the years a lot of Irish people had been.' This new British–Irish friendship had to be made at head of state level, she says, because it was the President, more than any domestic government representative, who could represent the nation, and the emigrants as part of the nation. 'The Irish in Britain were the particular Irish that I had to be in touch with, whose identity and confidence I wanted to bolster. And meeting the Queen was an important element in that.'

In the nineties the Irish abroad had become more successful, more visibly proud of being Irish. 'You had almost an overdoing of the successful Irish in New York, but in Britain there was a tendency of those who had been successful to assimilate and downplay their Irishness, and that began to change a couple of years into the Presidency and very dramatically towards the end of it. There were a lot of reasons for that change, I think, but one of them was the building up of confidence and pride in Irish identity in a British context and recognition of the huge contribution the Irish had made to Britain,' she says.

People of Irish parentage make up 4.6 per cent, or 2.5 million of the British population, making them the largest migrant minority in Western Europe. Recent research indicates that despite their size, they have the poorest physical and mental health record of any ethnic group in Britain, are twice as likely as native-born British to be unemployed or in low-skill jobs, and are disproportionately likely to be in bad housing, or to be homeless. In the mid-eighties two out of every seven people who slept rough in London were Irish.[6]

The story of the Irish in Britain had been told by Dónall Mac Amhlaigh, by Patrick MacGill, but for all its humour and colour, it was very much a story of loss.[7] Mary wanted to change that. One day in February 1997, in Tameside outside Manchester, a string of small towns was transformed into a mass of green, white and gold. The President was coming to celebrate the Irish who had helped build Britain. 'We did a survey of Tameside which consists of seven or eight little towns such as Ashton-under-Lyme,' says Michael Forde. 'It turned out that 25 per cent of the people there had Irish connections going back to a time when they were building the railway tunnel through the Pennines from Manchester to Sheffield; building the great North of England canal network; building up the mills. The President thought it was vitally important to emphasise that the Irish had been part of the industrial revolution.'

She stressed the positive contribution Irish people had made to Britain, and through receptions and meetings she celebrated the nurses, the trades unionists, the people involved in civic life, in local government.

She wanted the Irish to hold their heads high and she wanted to help break the association in the public mind between the Irish community and IRA violence. Feelings ran so high in Birmingham after the horror of the 1974 bombings that the Irish there could not find any way of publicly expressing their own sympathy with the victims. When Mary came to Birmingham on 11 March 1996, she did it on their behalf. 'She walked from the Council House to lay the wreath at the Birmingham Bombing memorial in the Cathedral. It was an emotional moment for a lot of people – I was here when the bombing happened,' says Pat O'Neill.

Thousands of people lined the streets, he said. 'It was a very public gesture and it was the major point of the visit. And she went straight from the memorial to the Irish centre. It finally made it clear that we were not associated with violence. She was finally laying it to rest.'

Six days later, the Birmingham Irish had their first St Patrick's

Day parade since the 1974 bombings. For twenty-one years, the security advice had been against it. The Irish community knew that Mary's visit would make the difference, and it did. They asked the City Council to invite her, says Pat O'Neill, 'and we had no problem getting them to agree. She was so well-known. She was great and really good for us and I was so proud to see her meet the Queen.'

The violence, however, hadn't stopped. What happened twenty years earlier in Birmingham was still happening in Manchester. Manchester was home to one of the oldest and biggest Irish communities in the UK, and Mary had visited there in March to launch the Irish Festival. The bomb went off on 17 June 1996, injuring 200 people and damaging over 700 businesses, and immediately Mary asked if she could go back. 'I was so devastated by it and I was determined to go back as soon as possible.' She consulted Irish Ambassador Ted Barrington whose judgement she'd come to trust. 'Ted had to think about it. Was it going to open up old wounds? Once he recognised what I hoped to do – a fortnight to the day after the bombing – it seemed to him absolutely the right thing to do.' Mary was determined not to leave the field to the Provisional IRA. The bombing, she said in Manchester, was not done 'in the name of any Irishness that I represent as President.'[8] 'It was important for me as President of Ireland to go and share in the devastation, to meet some of the victims, to meet the security forces. It seemed important that I do it openly, showing an Irish caring side of that whole dimension of the violence rather than a guilt.'

For Michael Forde of the Irish Heritage Centre, the real proof that the Irish were now accepted came the actual day of the June 1996 bomb.

'The leader of the City Council, the chairperson of Arts and Leisure, came to the Irish World Heritage Centre to show solidarity and support with the Irish community that night. This had never happened before at official level, this public demonstration of support. This had a tremendous effect on the Irish community only hours after a bomb had gone off, that they came to the centre,' he says.

Mary's earlier visits had helped to create this new acceptance of the Irish community, says Forde, just as her visit after the bomb confirmed it. The Irish had been trying for years to establish an Irish Festival but they hadn't really got official backing and support. That changed once Mary agreed to come and open it officially. 'People of second or even fourth generation Irish extraction on the Council weren't displaying it publicly,' says Michael Forde. 'But with Mary Robinson coming to the centre they were invited to meet her and when she went to the town hall the councillors began to "come out" so to speak. A lot of people whose grandparents had been Irish but who never identified with Ireland saw her as an international figure, someone you could link into and want to to be part of.'

Official attitudes changed, he says. The Council paid for full-time co-ordinators for the Irish Festival, gave access to public buildings. The police came out in their full ceremonial gear on horseback to lead the St Patrick's Day Parade. The Council gave fourteen acres for the building of a new Irish centre celebrating an outward-looking Ireland, a move away from the social clubs where the embattled Irish banded together against a hostile world.

Sister Elizabeth Cahill noticed the change, too. She helps run Irish Community Care in Manchester, a voluntary organisation helping older Irish people, or the many who worked illegally on the 'lump' building system and have now lost touch with the social services, and with their own families. She had been trying for years to get a grant from Manchester Council. When she sat beside councillors at the official welcome for Mary they told her who to talk to on the Social Services Panel. 'We had a meeting and then we got the grant. Doors opened.'[9] Now she has six or seven workers and knows that her organisation is recognised as legitimate. 'I would put a lot of that down to the visit from Mary Robinson. Only in retrospect did I realise that it was a gift.'

The British liked Mary. When elected she was chosen as the *Guardian* newspaper Woman of the Year. Liberal newspapers like the *Independent* constantly pushed her as a future head of the UN.[10] A *New Statesman* columnist commenting in 1993 said: 'I find it almost painful to contemplate Mary Robinson. She is radical, literate, a woman and she's in power. Couldn't she be President of us as well?'[11] With that sort of endorsement abroad, Mary might reasonably have expected an interested audience when addressing the Irish Parliament, the Oireachtas, on 2 February 1995, on a matter of national importance, 'Cherishing the Diaspora'. She spoke of the sorrow of emigration but also of the lessons of contribution and adaptation that emigrants could teach the home country. 'Our relation with the diaspora beyond our shores is one which can instruct our society in the values of diversity, tolerance and fair-mindedness.' She spoke of the need to create fora in which emigrants could be heard by the home country. She said people needed to be educated for emigration and praised the agencies who worked for emigrants. She said Ireland needed to learn from the experience of its famine emigrants in order to support sustainable economic development in countries threatened by famine now. And she quoted Eavan Boland:

> Like oil lamps we put them out the back
> Of our houses, of our minds.

The parliamentarians didn't like it. 'I felt it as I was speaking. I felt there was a resistance. When I came out, Father Paul Byrne of the Episcopal Commission for Emigrants was delighted. I had put the emphasis where he wanted it. And I said I have rarely spoken to a less responsive audience.'

The lack of interest at home was in sharp contast to the overwhelming response from emigrants. 'I found it strange. The reaction, the letters from around the world and the way it's followed me since, made it clear that probably of all the speeches I made, it had more impact on those I was speaking for than anything else I did.'

But politicians don't like having their consciences pricked, particularly by somebody who doesn't have to deliver the political goods. Neither does parliament necessarily like to have the President drawing its attention to matters of national importance – even though the Constitution allows her so to do. The reaction from TDs and senators, she said, was always likely to be defensive: 'Their attitude was, "We'll decide on our priorities. We're the ones who will deal with political issues." It's never going to be a very comfortable situation.'

John Bruton, whom Mary describes as the most frank of all the Taoisigh she dealt with, did give her a gentle warning, she says. 'The first thing John Bruton said to me was, "Well, don't make your speech too long".' She remembers getting advice from a friend when she started her Presidency. '"Remember, when you speak as President, nobody remembers what you spoke about. They only remember if you spoke too long." Sometimes I spoke too long.'

In this case, she says, she also stuck too rigidly to the script which had been approved, as the Constitution requires, by government. 'It was a set speech which I didn't depart from and therefore probably harder to listen to than one which you depart from and soften with a bit of humour. I was very conscious that it was a formal part of the Constitution and in retrospect I should have been more laid back.'

'That, quite frankly,' says Taoiseach Bertie Ahern 'was a terribly boring speech and everyone in the Dáil nearly fell asleep.'[12] He agreed with the message she was bringing back from emigrants, but the speech was too long, he says.

Alan Dukes says she was caught by the constraints of the presidency. She couldn't stray into the area of policy.

'She had to be safe, so safe she had to be platitudinous, but if so why say it in the first place! It was awful, a dreadful spectacle of a very, very intelligent thinker and a very consequential person having to mouth a whole string of banalities – starting off, shaping up, and then having to pull all the punches.'[13]

Boredom can often be a front for guilt. Mary talked about creating a forum for dialogue with emigrants and all parties have, at some stage, promised some sort of parliamentary representation for emigrants. When it came into office, John Bruton's rainbow coalition government had promised to create three Senate seats for emigrants. The idea was to reduce the number of senators nominated by the Taoiseach. The new senators would be elected from constituencies in the US, in Britain and Europe, and in the rest of the world. The government left office without doing anything about it. Nothing has yet been done about it.

Mary spoke about preparing people for emigration. She had seen what Germany had done to prepare young emigrants and what Poland had done to maintain links with its large population overseas. But this was asking Irish parliamentarians officially to recognise that emigration existed and take some responsibility for it, and maybe risk getting blamed for it. Nobody wanted to do that.

Father Paul Byrne, writing in April 1995 in *The Furrow* magazine of his amazement at the hostile home reaction to Mary's speech, describes precisely the political attitude. 'If I set up pre-emigration advice centres in prominent sites, advertise their existence, encourage the would-be emigrant to use them, supply him or her with information and contacts for accommodation and jobs abroad, won't I be seen as some sort of Pied Piper enticing *your* child from home? And there are no votes from that mindset. It's time for a sea-change.'[14] Mary did, however, force the pace on other fronts. No longer was London the only focus of Irish interest in Britain. By visiting Cambridge, Edinburgh, Cardiff, Leeds, Salford, Warrington, Manchester, Coventry, Birmingham, York, Aberystwyth, Glasgow, as well as Iona and the Western Isles, she dragged press and political attention to the Irish communities there and away from its single focus on Westminster and the Court of St James's.

John Bruton says that Mary's visits to the British regions made his government remember that Britain wasn't a monolith, and that this was particularly important at a time of British devolution.

As a result, he had suggested to the Department of Foreign Affairs the opening of consulates in cities other than London and indeed in June 1998 the Fianna Fáil/PD government announced the establishment of consulates in Cardiff and Edinburgh.[15]

Her big achievement, however, was to make the Irish community in Britain visible, not just to the British, but to the Irish embassy. With the co-operation of the Irish Ambassador, Mary involved the embassy intimately in the affairs of the emigrant Irish.

Up to then, the embassy had been preoccupied with the political priorities of the home government. Emigrants didn't figure in that and the Irish community often complained that they were hardly ever invited to the elegant embassy building in Grosvenor Place. 'People in the Irish community used to say about the embassy, "Well, no one would look to them for anything,"' says Dr Mary Hickman, Director of the Irish Studies Programme at the University of North London. 'Throughout the eighties, they were highly selective in whom they admitted to the embassy. If you were a successful business person or journalist, that was okay. But if you made the mistake of dealing with social welfare issues, or if you had a point of view on Northern Ireland which did not coincide with Dublin's at the time, you were a pariah.'[16]

Dublin at the time was very suspicious of anyone who supported contacts with Sinn Féin. Huge control was exercised, says Dr Hickman, in relation to views on Northern Ireland, 'over all of us who didn't parrot the Dublin government view and who have been proved right – you've got to bring people in from the margins. I was never invited to the embassy until Joe Small [then Irish Ambassador] asked me in 1991, even though I'd been appointed head of Irish Studies four years earlier and every other dean of Irish Studies was invited. I was seen as community-oriented and I invited people over from Northern Ireland and gave a high profile to the equality agenda for the Irish and to the fight against racism.'

Mary Robinson contributed hugely to changing that attitude, says Dr Hickman. Her election promises to represent the diaspora, her constant visits, coincided with efforts by many Irish people in Britain to raise the profile of the Irish. Only then, she says, did the embassy begin to open up in a more balanced way. And only then, she claims, did the embassy fight back publicly against anti-Irishness in the media.

'Joe Small put out a statement to the media in November 1992 saying Robert Kilroy-Silk's comments in the *Daily Express* about Ireland being "a country peopled by peasants, priests and pixies" were racist, and Ted Barrington [Irish Ambassador] protested about the *EastEnders* episode which portrayed Ireland and Irish people in a bad light.' The embassy never took up cudgels so positively on Irish issues before Mary Robinson, she says.

For Mary it was important that her visits to the Irish diaspora be outward-looking, a way to establish links with other peoples and other countries, not simply a triumphalist celebration of Irishness. And it was important that her visits include all sorts of Irish people, not just those who were powerful and successful. Initially she didn't always succeed. On her first visit to Boston in October 1991, there were complaints that the many new young Irish immigrants, some of them illegal, had been shut out. The dinner at the Kennedy Library, hosted by Senator Edward Kennedy, was by invitation only, while the reception at the Park Plaza Hotel, sponsored by the Irish Cultural Center and other Irish-American organisations, cost $30 a ticket. Odette Harrington, who worked at the Irish Immigration Centre in Boston dealing with many of the undocumented Irish in the city, said none of the young Irish people could have afforded the entry price. Speaking to Kevin Cullen of the *Boston Globe*, she said: 'I think it's really unfair, considering that Mrs Robinson made such a point of reaching out to young people. If you look around, there are no young people for her to reach out to.'[17]

Radicals who agreed with Mrs Robinson's election agenda had been kept away from her while arch-conservatives had not, complained Harrington. Bride Rosney, on Mary's behalf, was quick to agree with the criticisms, and on subsequent visits to Boston, Mary was careful to insist on a balanced agenda. In 1996, she was guest of honour at the Irish Immigration Centre's own dinner, and here she felt utterly at home. The centre, under Director Lena Deevy, has struggled to make sure that the new Irish immigrants don't adopt the prejudices and anti-black attitudes found among some of the Boston-Irish, and has tried to encourage multicultural, not ghetto, values. 'Mrs Robinson said she felt at home with us because of our broad appeal as opposed to the stereotypical Irish-American organisation fronted up by successful men. Women are largely in the leadership of our organisation and we reach out to immigrants from all backgrounds.'[18]

At the dinner, Mary met a group of black Irish people from

Montserrat in the Caribbean, where Galway people had settled in the 1700s. They celebrate St Patrick's Day, and their flag displays the Union Jack and a lady with a harp, integrating their two traditions. The centre had helped them to get temporary visas when they were fleeing volcanic eruptions on their island.

This was the spirit of generosity Mary wanted to encourage, and she came back in 1997 to launch the famine memorial in Cambridge, near Boston, which the centre helped to sponsor. The bronze figures, by Derry sculptor Maurice Harron who made the Hands Across the Divide monument in Derry, were part of a multi-racial effort to commemorate the Great Hunger, 'short on Irish sentimentality' as the *Boston Globe* put it, 'and long on how the Irish experience validated other immigrant groups'.[19]

Mary was always wary when Irish events were used to nurse old wounds. The 150th anniversary of the Irish famine, she knew, had to be handled with particular sensitivity. Historians differ as to the number of people who died during the great famine of the 1840s. Traditionally, the figure of about one million deaths and an even larger number of emigrants was generally accepted.[20]

The causes proposed for the famine have been even more diverse and controversial, ranging from the hardline nationalist view that it was Britain's deliberate act of genocide against the Irish people, to the view that it was the result of the laissez-faire policies of Lord John Russell's 1846 Whig government. Still others argued that it was the result of an act of God. Mary was concerned lest a complex debate be reduced to an opportunity for nationalist propaganda, particularly in the United States.

'In a couple of cases there was an element of bashing Britain about it which worried me.' She mentioned Governor Pataki of New York's measure in making the study of the Irish famine mandatory, along with slavery and the Jewish Holocaust, as part of human rights courses in state schools. The governor described the famine as the result of a deliberate campaign by the British to deny the Irish people the food they needed to survive. Mary was worried that only one view of the famine would be given. 'If you have a particular school text giving one version which is explicitly close to the genocidal, then that would be very worrying.'

The commemoration of the famine was a necessary catharsis for the Irish. Anger and shame had made it almost impossible to confront the reality of what happened and begin to accept it. As a result there was a blanking out, too, of those who were scattered by the famine, the diaspora, and of their story. Mary knew that to accept and value the diaspora, Ireland had to face up to the famine. 'I was aware from the time I was elected that the commemoration of the famine would be an important opportunity to look again at a time which was so deeply humiliating and so devastating to us as a people that we had never been able to come to terms with it. And that we hadn't properly honoured and respected and valued the contribution and sense of survival of those who took to the coffin ships and then made a new life in desperate circumstances. These people passed on to their children a sense of pride in their roots and yet look at what those roots were! We hadn't really linked properly with all of that.'

She wanted the famine to be remembered in all its complexity, the way it was remembered in the Famine Museum at Strokestown House, in Co. Roscommon. Strokestown brings a human dimension to something almost too big to understand. It tries to tell at least one story of the famine from all sides, and as a result, goes beyond blame and accusation to the real tragedy.

The picture emerges of a desperate landlord, Major Denis Mahon, who inherited a run-down estate just as the famine took hold. He chartered two vessels to allow those tenants who could not pay their rent to emigrate to Quebec. When newspaper reports emerged of the dreadful conditions suffered on the ships, local feeling mounted against the Major. He was assassinated on 2 November 1847, returning from a meeting where he had tried to keep the local workhouse open for victims of the famine.[21] The museum captures the story of a man who was probably inadequate, rather than evil. It displays the letters of representation on behalf of starving tenants, the letters to Mahon from his steward warning him that he must make the estate pay. The museum shows, too, how the fatal blight attacked the potatoes, and makes the link for Irish people with today's famines in Africa and elsewhere. Mary liked this open approach, the emphasis on the local and the universal. She became a patron of the museum, which was privately owned, and she opened it in 1994. Her support was crucial, to the financial and official recognition of the museum, said curator Luke Dodd.

For Mary, again using the twin-track approach of focusing attention on an issue, and offering her own analysis, Ireland would truly have honoured the dead and the scattered in famine times only if it responded to world hunger today. On the island of Grosse Ile in Canada, where so many of the sick and starving Irish had landed and died in the famine years, she threw down a gauntlet. People could chose between being spectators or participants. 'If we are participants we engage with the past in terms of the present. If we are spectators then we close these people into a prison of statistics and memories from which they can never escape to challenge our conscience and compassion.' To do real justice to the famine dead, one should think about how best to supply ordinary commodities like food and water. 'It may be less glamorous than standing in a posture of grief and regret. But a careful and analytical study of just how little, for instance, has been done to distribute clean water to areas of large slum dwellings or refugee camps, is both vital and overdue. And if this seems too ordinary a detail, I think we should remember that the thousands who died here, whose dreams were extinguished, whose future was lost on this island, died because of the detail of the failure of one crop. There are such details all over the world now, particularly in Africa, which need our urgent attention.'[22]

All during the commemorations she was conscious of how the starving Irish had been received. Thousands of Irish had landed at Grosse Ile, sick from their confinement on the coffin ships. 'When I went to Grosse Ile and saw the white crosses on the mass graves, I thought of the Mayor of Montreal who had cared for the sick and himself caught the contagion and died. And I thought of the number of Irish orphans who were taken into Quebec families and, yet I didn't know about this until a few years earlier when I read about it. When I listened in the crypt of a church in New York to historians talking about the unfriendly reception the Irish got in 1846, '47, and '48 because they were bringing disease and poverty with them and how they were robbed, it was compelling.'

She remembered the Choctaw Indians of Oklahoma who, themselves evicted from their lands, had raised 173 dollars for the relief of Irish famine victims. As she said of them in a speech at the University of California at Berkeley in 1991: 'They chose not to sleep on our wound.'

Neither should the Irish choose to sleep on the wounds of the world's starving millions, she argued. As President, she was determined that remembering the famine would be a lesson in generosity. She says now: 'As President I could tell the story, I could shape the story to include the Irish diaspora, to analyse the profound implications of the famine both for us and for our scattered family, and to make the connection with modern famine hunger. We could give this generation of young Irish a sense that their Irishness was broad and diverse, that the Irish had had a difficult history where they had been on the margins for a long time and therefore, as a people, the Irish should link with those on the margins – that's my political agenda.'

But for most of the people she visited, it didn't really matter what her agenda was. The most important thing was that she had come among them. For older people who had had no link with Ireland for years, here, for a moment, was home. 'They'd be all right until they shook your hand and then the tears would come.' The emotion took her aback in Perth, in Auckland, in Montreal, in Buenos Aires, in Harare, in Brent. The only way she could properly respect that emotion was to try to convey a sense of it at home, to speak with true feeling of 'Cherishing the Diaspora'.

And the lukewarm reaction to that speech ('Diaspora?' sneered one senator. 'Do you take two with a glass of water?') wasn't the end of the story. For results, she can now look to the definition of the nation contained in the new Article 2 of the Constitution which for the first time recognises the diaspora in her very words: 'The Irish nation cherishes its special affinity with people of Irish ancestry living abroad who share its cultural identity and heritage.'

Almost every Irish person she met abroad knew she left a light burning for them in her kitchen window. It may have been dismissed as a cliché at home but the emigrants believed in it fervently as did the whole Robinson family. Once, in her early years in the Áras, a power failure threw the house into darkness, and ten-year-old Aubrey came racing into his parents' bedroom, distraught. 'What will we do, Mum?' he said. 'The light has gone out in the window.'

A BREACH IN THE WALL

Mary sat in the Culloden Hotel outside Belfast, her hair washed and ready for the hairdresser. She waited and waited but the hairdresser never came. Ulster had taken petty revenge on the woman who had dared the day before to shake hands with the Republican leader, Gerry Adams of Sinn Féin. The Irish President would face a full day of public appointments with a damp head of hair.

The fury that Mary's handshake aroused in the Unionist community is a measure of the credit she'd built up. Her sensitivity to Unionist feelings, her recognition of the World War dead, her visits to Warrington and to the Queen – all these had made her a sympathetic figure to Northern Protestants. They felt let down.

But West Belfast had been feeling let down and abandoned by governments north and south for many years. Indeed, so isolated had this mainly Republican community become that there was no official body with which Mary could liaise to organise her visit. With the continuing IRA campaign, the Northern Ireland Office regarded them as a terrorist community; the Anglo-Irish secretariat at Maryfield in Belfast had little to do with them; their Republican representatives were banned from the airwaves north and south; they regarded most state officers as alien and hostile and the RUC and army as the enemy. It is a measure of their total isolation that the liaison role for Mary's visit in June 1993 was played by one woman, feminist and trade unionist Inez McCormack. McCormack, who as a 'puzzled young Protestant' had joined the civil rights group, People's Democracy, in the late sixties, is regional secretary of UNISON, a public sector union representing many part-time women workers in West Belfast. She says she was regarded as a 'crypto-Provo', a sympathiser with the Provisional Republican Movement, by the then Tory regime for her stance on employment rights for Catholics and for signing the McBride Principles, which urged foreign investors to insist on a required quota of Catholic workers before backing firms in Northern Ireland. She warned Mary Robinson about this when Mary invited her to her presidential inauguration, only to be told that the President 'knows what she's at'.[1]

'I'm not a Republican, but people have a right to be,' says McCormack. In singling her out and trusting her 'Mary was giving me and the issues I stood for space. You can fight for so long but "diminishing" does have its effect and the affirmation of her trust for what I was doing, that was a healing I needed.'

Inez had helped organise Mary's first visit to the North, with Mary Clarke-Glass of the Northern Ireland's Equal Opportunities Commission. That visit took a whole year and eighty-three separate meetings to organise. There were worries about security, timing, balance, but eventually the authorities were satisfied and Mary had a carefully balanced visit in February 1992 with women's groups from all parts of Belfast. After that, the women from West Belfast asked Mary to meet their community – not in a centre city hotel but in West Belfast itself. It was going to be controversial for her to go, says Inez. 'But it would have been blatant for her not to have gone. She had been everywhere else and this was part of her stated agenda.' It would take another year to organise and would involve several visits by community representatives to the Áras.

Eileen Howell, Director of the Falls Community Council, was one of the women's network representatives who had regularly visited the Áras. Those visits marked perhaps the first recognition of her community, she said, the first time they were listened to by anyone representing official Ireland. Eileen came together with area groups representing well over a hundred organisations involved in community activities to help form an umbrella group which could invite the President to West Belfast. 'Once the Áras came back to say they were interested in coming, we said, "You will have to take the community as it comes. We aren't going to vet our community. We'll have Gerry Adams, Joe Hendron of the SDLP, the economic organisations." As community organisations we couldn't invite her in and snub the largest political organisation in our area.'[2]

Since 1991 Mary had worked long and hard to build up trust with women like Eileen Howell. 'I had the West Belfast Festival people come down to show me their plans at a time when they were very isolated and nobody was particularly interested in the vibrancy of what they were doing. And to be able to come and show me their draft brochures – it was an opportunity to support the strength of identity that they had built up. They were doubly isolated in Northern Ireland, in Belfast itself and also from the rest of the island,' she says.

She accepted the invitation only when it came from a broad range of community groups, including those representing the young, the elderly and the West Belfast Community Festival organisers. She knew, just as she would meet the moderate nationalist Social Democratic and Labour Party representative, Dr Joe Hendron, that she would also meet Gerry Adams.

'Their planning of it was very much to reflect the fact that it was the community groups that I would stop and speak to in the hall,' she said, 'but that I should then meet Joe Hendron, Gerry Adams and other local councillors in that community context. Most of that was all arranged before there was any reaction at a political level to the visit. I knew that was part of the planning.'

To Gerry Adams the visit was crucial. For years he'd been pushing Republicans to look at the political options and was involved, as were others, in secret talks about an IRA ceasefire. But as yet there was no public recognition of Republican efforts to move towards a political solution. He had helped found the West Belfast Festival in an effort to bring artists and musicians into the area, but as long as violence continued his community was still shunned. They had been given no sign that they would be welcomed and valued in a new settlement. The Irish President who had been to see the Queen, he said, hadn't yet come to visit 'this strange race, Northern nationalists'. She could start to break their isolation.

'There were people who thought it would be a good idea in terms of her broad presidential programme to outreach into marginalised, demonised communities in the North – but also to do so in terms of my presence. I mean, by and large, that's what the visit was about. And I have no doubt that she understood that.'[3]

But when the British understood that, they hit the roof. 'John Major wanted me to stop her,' says Albert Reynolds, the then Fianna Fáil Taoiseach. 'His opinion was that if I said no, she wouldn't go. I said I would certainly convey their feelings but I wouldn't issue any directions on it.' Albert says he let her know in a broad sense that he was trying to get the IRA campaign of violence stopped.

'She would have had a fair inkling from my discussions with her when I came back from London and I told her straight out of the pressure I was under and, knowing the pressure I was under, and knowing I was still not asking her not to go, she would have drawn the inference that I was in favour of her going.'

Albert Reynolds says it was another demonstration of hands across the border. 'It was another breaking down of barriers and certainly from a political point of view for a Fianna Fáil Taoiseach to be preventing a President from going to Belfast did not line up.'[4]

Mary agrees she had no problem with Albert. The problem was with Dick Spring, then Foreign Minister. The difference between Taoiseach and Tánaiste (deputy Prime Minister) may be explained by Reynolds's emphasis at the time on getting the Provos to call a ceasefire, and Spring's task, along with Northern Secretary Sir Patrick Mayhew, of keeping the Unionists involved in a political talks process. Spring expressed the British concerns and Mary talked at length to him about it. She explained that the relationship and trust had been built up over a long period of time. 'And I had to keep faith with that or not go at all. I actually remember saying to him, "I would rather not go at all if we can't do it the way we were planning it."

'At no point did Dick as Tánaiste say he didn't want me to go,' she says. 'Because if he had said that I wouldn't have gone. I have my own parameters. But he came close to it.'

It strained an already cool relationship. 'It wasn't easy. It wasn't a case of my saying I have all the wisdom, and I'm going anyway. I wasn't utterly confident. It was an agonising time.'

Mary agreed to reflect on Spring's concerns and as a result she told the West Belfast organisers that she would meet Adams only away from the cameras. They were to speak again before Mary made a final decision but, before they could, word leaked in Belfast that the visit was on. Spring had gone straight from the Áras to London for a meeting with the Prime Minister and the Northern Secretary and ran straight into a British storm where he ended up having to defend the President.

'It put pressure on a process at the time we could have done without. It caused strains between the two governments. We needed every inch of co-operation we could get from John Major without pressures like this being put on him,' says Dick Spring.

'I remember a long long session with John Major where I said, "Do you know this woman has a 94 per cent popularity rating?" And he said, "Not only that, Dick, but I know if she goes to meet Gerry Adams she'll have 124 per cent." So we all knew the politics of it.'[5] When he had visited Mary on his way to London, he said, he was acting on behalf of the government. 'Some people represent it as a solo flight by Dick Spring. But this was Dick Spring very much post-government discussion having the full support of the government on his way to London,' he says. 'There was a sense at the time that she knew what was coming down the line and she was going to be part of it.' Mary was determined to make history, he said at the time.[6]

Mary knew of the efforts for a Republican ceasefire. She had read the Hume–Adams document when John Hume had shown it to her in Derry the year before. She carefully did not ask herself whether she might be helping to bring about a ceasefire, she says.

'Yes, hopefully I was building up a sense of bringing West Belfast out of its isolation, helping local reconciliation, but I never wanted as President to be part of a political peace process because I felt that would be a step too far. And yet I recognised the importance of doing something different that might help indirectly.'

Mary had her doubts, right up to the last minute. Both Albert Reynolds and then Dick Spring went to the Áras the afternoon before her visit specifically to tell her of British and Unionist concerns. Bride met columnist Mary Holland of the *Irish Times* that night to check what media reaction would be. Assured that Holland, at least, thought it was a good idea, Mary and Nick flew north on 18 June. Official reaction was hostile and already there had been official indications that it would be 'difficult' to guarantee Mary's security.

The authorities insisted to Inez for a few days before the visit that they would have to send in a large security presence to West Belfast to protect the President, and one of their arguments against the visit was that this force would be put at risk. The argument went on up to the morning of the visit. 'That morning I made it extremely clear that a large security presence would be taken as a political act, that it would turn a community visit into a confrontational situation and that they would have to take responsibility for that,' says Inez McCormack.

When the local police chief turned up with over twenty officers, Inez negotiated a deal – only half a dozen officers would come into the Rupert Stanley Training College in the Whiterock Road to guard stairs and exits. This was hostile territory for the RUC men. 'The police were apprehensive and nervous, I was watching their faces. They were seeing the people that they would describe as the enemy but what they were actually watching was a bustling community festival.' At one stage during the visit, she says, one of the local women walked up to what she thought was the protocol officer from the Taoiseach's office and pulled at his sleeve and said happily: 'What do you think? Don't you think it's going well?' The RUC Special Branch man looked at her and said: 'I don't think you know who I am.'

The press, says Inez, were determined to get a picture of Mary with Gerry Adams. Knowing he would be expelled before Mary met all the community representatives, one photographer got up on stage during the welcoming concert and pushed between the two young musicians playing so that he could get a long-angled shot of the President with Gerry Adams standing three rows behind her at the back. The photographer was pulled off stage by the protocol officers from the Taoiseach's department. Because of Mary's promise to the Irish government that there would be no photographs of the handshake, local people had left their own cameras at home and had forgone their right to have their picture taken with the President. The photographer from the *Andersonstown News*, who was there wearing his community hat, had also turned down lucrative offers for a photograph. West Belfast was keeping its side of the bargain.

For the press, says Inez, it was all too ordinary, it wasn't Republican enough. She remembers how all the camera lights were turned off when the prestigious St Agnes Choral Society from West Belfast began to sing a selection from Gilbert and Sullivan. This was too tame. This wasn't what the news editors had ordered.

When Mary met Gerry Adams and others, after the cameras had gone, he simply said 'Céad Mile Fáilte.' He was off camera but Adams had no doubt this was a moment of history.

'The significance of that visit has not been given the recognition it deserves and the effect of the visit as the first breach in the wall of marginalisation has not been given the importance it deserves,' he says. 'But the key thing is that it was popular. And the fact that it was popular, that people applauded what Mary Robinson had done, made it possible, you could argue, made it *imperative* for others to take the political lesson from that.' It probably helped in getting Adams a visa to the US six months later despite fierce British opposition, he says. 'I suppose it empowered those who were lobbying for the visa from the state department. If Mary Robinson hadn't visited West Belfast we would still have got the visa, but it was probably a brick, a hole being knocked in the wall and from our point of view that was quite intentional in terms of seeking to break down this kind of condition,' says Adams.

It was a celebration of West Belfast life, so there was Irish music and dancing and an exhibition of crafts. Mary was presented with a bodhran by local man Eamon Maguire and Nick was given a walking stick. She laughed as she was invited out to the mountain by Terry Enright of the Black Mountain Action Group, father of young Terry Enright who was to be killed at a nightclub in 1997. She ended up overwhelmed with masses of flowers. 'It mattered greatly to West Belfast that they knew I'd had a hard time getting there,' she says. 'Part of the exhilaration in West Belfast was that I had kept faith with them, that I had come as I said I would.'

Eileen Howell knew it was a breakthrough and it had an immediate effect in terms of press coverage, in terms of artists coming to the next West Belfast Festival. 'And we had recognised that if we could break that mould once, then others wouldn't have problems coming in and talking to our community,' she said. 'It was a signal that this community, predominantly a Republican community, was saying we want to be involved. We want two-way contact.'

Next day, when Mary's hairdresser failed to turn up at the Culloden Hotel, she had no doubt that it was an act of political protest by those who disagreed with her visit. The important thing was the reaction from the RUC man who almost always accompanied her on her northern visits. He was sure she'd been deliberately humiliated and frantically set about organising a hairdresser before her press conference later that morning. With no rollers, no hairdryer, she could do nothing and had to go ahead and visit Coalisland with her hair untamed. Republican activist Bernadette McAliskey used the occasion to protest against sectarian killings of Catholics. 'And there was a very funny moment at Coalisland Heritage Centre where Bernadette McAliskey was demonstrating with two or three other protesters and delightfully she was heard to say as I arrived, "And she didn't even get her hair done to come and see us!"'

When Mary arrived at Balance House, the home of former New Zealand premier, John Balance, later that morning, a hairdresser was waiting and the damage was repaired before Mary faced the public and the press. It was an act of real kindness by the RUC man, over and above the call of duty, and Mary never forgot it to him. There weren't many other gestures of kindness on the rest of that visit, not from the normally ebullient Sir Patrick Mayhew who was coldly polite to her at a Law Society dinner the previous evening, not from the papers, British and some Irish, who angrily criticised her Adams handshake.

But there was a supporter waiting for her on the apron at Dublin Airport when she came home. 'That day, I was in Cork and I drove back specially and rang up and asked if it was all right for me to go out and meet her,' says Taoiseach Bertie Ahern, then Finance Minister. 'In my view she was right, and the best way for me to show solidarity was to go to the airport, be there, walk out with her to face the cameras, because I knew they were out to get her. And then to stay back and answer questions for her, and I did that. I totally supported her. I didn't just take the view that she had no alternative but to shake Gerry Adams's hand. I said she was dead right to do it! At the airport that morning every question was hostile. She said a few words and then I did a press conference, but it was hostile stuff.'[7] Bertie Ahern knew that the government was trying to build up confidence and trust in the Republican community and he thought Dick Spring was wrong to get into a public row with the President over such a visit.

'I thought it was a lot of nonsense. Here we were trying to move away from a situation. The nationalists in the North felt betrayed and let down that we didn't show any recognition of them and that's why they were calling us The Free State, and if you've noticed, that phrase is dropping out in the last few years. It's because we're not ignoring them. Mary did her piece in that respect and I think she was right.'

Other cabinet Ministers, including Dick Spring, didn't appreciate his intervention and let him know it. 'People were miffed about the fact that I went to the airport so publicly,' he says. 'They would have known that I was making a point, that I wasn't there by mistake.'

Mary appreciated Bertie Ahern's presence. From almost every other quarter but Fianna Fáil, it seemed, there was condemnation. The opposition parties criticised her. The British media criticised her and Independent Newspapers had a field day. In the *Sunday Independent* of 20 June, Eamon Dunphy called her 'a foolish prisoner of her own conceit' and called on her to resign. The editorial on the same day said: 'The people of the South do not want to shake hands with apologists for terror. It was a mistake.' 'For the first time she has let us down,' said columnist Shane Ross. 'Mistake' was the headline on the editorial in the *Irish Independent* the day before. But the real response was the opinion poll commissioned by the *Independent* itself the following week. Asked if they approved of her shaking hands with Adams, a massive 77 per cent said they did.[8]

In popular terms Mary had carried the day. Now the political powers, both British and Irish, were determined to rein her in. This was sensitive territory, as sensitive as was the territorial claim over Northern Ireland in Article 2 of the Constitution. Mary never asked for government permission to go to Northern Ireland. Permission was needed to leave the state, but did the state consist only of the twenty-six counties, as successive Attorneys-General had advised the government, or was the state the same as the national territory which, according to the Constitution, included Northern Ireland? The Constitution is vague on this point and Mary, constitutional expert that she is, left the question open. The government automatically granted her permission once they were informed she was going north, but Mary carefully never asked for it. Quite what the constitutional implications of this government practice would be if tested in a court of law are not clear. What is clear is that the government were afraid to stop her going to the North. Their best line of argument was to say that 'the British are concerned'. After the Gerry Adams handshake, the British were more than concerned.

The British Ambassador in Dublin at the time, David Blatherwick, made little secret of his anti-Republican views. A week before Mary's visit to West Belfast, he had called to see the secretary to the government, Frank Murray, to express his authorities' concern that they had not been notified earlier of the President's visit to West Belfast, and to warn that such short notice presented serious security problems. His authorities wanted to be involved at the planning stage of such visits in the future.[9]

At the end of June 1993, after the Adams meeting, the British got tougher. They now implied that Mary's security couldn't be guaranteed if she didn't meet the following demands:

- all visits were to be cleared in principle not less than a month in advance and a full outline programme was to be agreed at least three weeks in advance.
- there were to be no more than three visits a year.
- detailed planning on visits to Northern Ireland had to be followed up with the British–Irish secretariat in Maryfield in Belfast.

In the absence of agreement and adherence to these procedures, the British said, it would be difficult for the British government to give the support necessary for future visits in relation to security, transport and protocol.[10]

The Irish government made it clear to the Áras that they were anxious to make an agreement with the British and wanted to meet with Áras and British representatives as soon as possible to settle it.

Mary resisted the pressure. Yes, she would give notice and would consult about visits and so on, but no, she would agree to no limits as to the number of her visits, and, no, she would not cede control of guest lists. The British were not happy and neither was then Foreign Affairs Minister, Dick Spring. He made it clear subsequently. One had to be judicious about the number of visits one made as president, he said. 'There was a lot of good value initially in reaching out to both unionist and nationalist communities, but overall I would agree with people who said: "Too many visits."'[11]

Of the eighteen visits she made to Northern Ireland, West Belfast is the one which is remembered. She attended Catholic and Protestant events, cultural and community gatherings, she attended the funerals of Senator Gordon Wilson and of his son Peter. But it was only after the Adams handshake that major question-marks were raised by the British and Irish governments about the wisdom of her visits, that people like David Trimble called her 'meddling Mary' and claimed her visits were 'the physical embodiment of the aggressive territorial claim in the Irish Constitution.'[12]

As a result of the West Belfast visit, Belfast City Council passed a motion banning her from ever entering Belfast City Hall. She lost friends in the North, and even admirers like Fine Gael leader John Bruton have never forgiven her for that handshake. It could be said that the Good Friday agreement of 1998 will prove her right, prove that she helped bring the peace by making, as Gerry Adams put it, 'the first breach in the wall of marginalisation'.

Adams says: 'I didn't have a baldy notion at the time that a ceasefire was possible. But that visit created the conditions wherein the argument going on at the time for inclusiveness was certainly advanced. It didn't do Mary Robinson any harm. The place didn't fall. The world didn't fall. And a lot of politicians realised that the people of the island of a generally nationalist spirit thought it was a good thing.'

Inez McCormack has no doubt that the visit was crucial. 'What she did was important and the Good Friday agreement was part of that. It was about changing relationships, about people doing things which were uncomfortable,' she says. 'Her agenda was about making the invisible visible, about the politics of networking and inclusivity, and those are the politics of the settlement.'

19

COOL SPRING

In his four years as Foreign Minister, Dick Spring never once went to Áras an Uachtaráin for the presentation of ambassadors' credentials, or for the annual presentation of New Year's messages by the diplomatic corps. Other Foreign Ministers went regularly, but Spring wouldn't go because he would have to wear morning dress. He tried to have the dress code changed. 'But I was informed,' he says, 'that this was not the desire of She Who Must Be Obeyed.'[1]

The Labour leader didn't like pomp, and anyway he was a busy Minister with more important things to do. But the regular visits might have allowed a thaw in his chilly relationship with the President, might have eased a whole series of crises between them. Relations were at best correct, at worst, hostile. Behind it all, Mary still believes, was her decision to be an independent Presidential candidate and an independent President.

'I think on both sides, that there was a reserve towards each other,' she says. 'I think Dick is intelligent, resourceful, probably the most talented of his generation of politicians but really very political. And I didn't fit into his perception of what he wanted either from his nominating me or from what I was doing as President,' she says. 'I'm a huge admirer of Dick's abilities and work rate and values. But I wonder if he has to control in some way those whom he's really close to.' He felt, she says, that there should be a greater pay-back to the Labour party from the Presidency. 'I think that Ruairi Quinn saw it in the way I saw it, that it would be of enormous benefit to the Labour party and even more so if they didn't try to own it. I think that Ruairi had no difficulty with that approach and concept. I think Dick had.'

Feelings ran high in Spring's retinue after the Adams handshake – as one Labour aide put it: 'She shouldn't be given permission to go to Disneyland.'² But the next confrontation would be doubly sensitive because it was a clash of legal views.

Dick Spring, junior counsel, had at one stage been lectured in Trinity by Mary Robinson, senior counsel. The gap was never really bridged, nor forgiven. But the real essence of the Ford Foundation row was Mary's need to establish the independence of the Presidency, to ensure, for the sake of the office, that she would not surrender the small space allowed by the Constitution.

The invitation to Mary to co-chair a Ford Foundation–Yale University group looking at the future role of the United Nations was particularly attractive. As President, she took an active and informed interest in UN issues and she was sure that Albert Reynolds would have no objection.

'Part of my sense of disappointment was that I thought Albert himself had understood the non-executive nature of it. It was a Ford Foundation think-tank approach to the future of the UN, not a United Nations policy-making body.' In December 1993, the government refused her permission to accept the invitation, citing advice that it would be unconstitutional. Mary had to accept the refusal but not the basis for it. 'There was no way in my understanding of the Constitution that it was unconstitutional. I felt it was important to clarify that, not just for my own sake but that of the office, because that will guide any successor of mine as well.' She asked permission to obtain counsel's opinion – she consulted Frank Clarke, then chairman of the Bar Council, and her former colleague on many human rights cases, Gerry Durcan.

'I felt it was a service to the office to have a constitutional assessment. And I think it was. Because now there is a very detailed legal opinion (on the powers of the President under the Constitution) and there is also the opinion on the Ford Foundation issue which was separate. I kept it separate deliberately. One was a long-term present to my successors. The other was answering a particular issue. And the answer to the particular issue was that there wasn't a constitutional objection.'

In January 1994, Mary wrote to the government saying that she agreed with the advice of her two barristers and insisting that the matter be discussed again. There was consternation.

Albert Reynolds now claims that he never believed there was a constitutional problem. Dick Spring says that there was a breakdown in communications, and that the original refusal issued to the President was 'not accurately phrased'. Mary says she couldn't possibly have mis-understood the basis for the government's refusal i.e. that there were constitutional reasons why she should not co-chair the think-tank. 'It was in written form. I couldn't have misunderstood it.' Spring went to see the President first because the Taoiseach was in Mexico. She says he asked her not to force the issue and showed her a copy of a recent newspaper interview in which he had spoken of expanding the role of the President. Albert Reynolds says that when he came home from Mexico, the whole affair was heading for a showdown. 'I had to take the bit between my teeth,' says Albert Reynolds. 'A serious situation was developing between Foreign Affairs and the Áras over it. When I went to see her, Labour genuinely believed that there would be a constitutional head-to-head over it. They were concerned that there wouldn't be a way through. They were expecting the worst from my visit.'

There was never going to be a crisis once Albert backed off on the constitutional issue, which he did. He explained to the President that there were policy, not constitutional, difficulties about her co-chairing the Ford Foundation group. It was simply that the Department of Foreign Affairs were particularly worried that a body of proposals would emerge called the 'Robinson' proposals and that even at some future date, these might be at odds with government policy, causing embarrassment between the Presidency and the executive.

Mary had no real problem once the government dropped the

constitutional argument. 'When the alternative was adopted by the government, that they were concerned that there would be a Robinson advisory report, the Robinson report, I felt that that was fair enough. I think it's back to always respecting the limits. To press it at that stage might have been seen as personal vanity.'

So the matter, it seemed, was settled.

Then, on 17 February 1994 the whole affair leaked to the papers – the fact that Mary had taken independent legal advice, from whom, and what that advice was. Emily O'Reilly's exclusive article in the *Irish Press* also included the information that 'the Taoiseach and Tánaiste made personal pleas to her to back down' and, for Mary a telling detail, the information that the Tánaiste had shown her a copy of his recent interview where he spoke of expanding the role of the President.

Mary wrote immediately to Dick Spring. The letter, dated 17 February 1994, went as follows

Dear Tánaiste,

I was very concerned at the article by Emily O'Reilly in today's Irish Press about the recent Ford Foundation invitation and related developments and I have written to the Taoiseach to express that concern in view of the effect that this breach of confidentiality will have on relations between my office and the government. In addition I am writing to you personally because of references in the Irish Press article to matters that arose during our recent discussions. These matters were known only to both of us and it is a cause of great personal disappointment and regret that matters that were discussed on a confidential basis between us should now be reported in the media.

I value the good relations that exist between my office and the government and will do everything in my power to preserve them but leaks of this kind are inimical to that process.

Yours etc.

Mary's letter to Albert Reynolds expressed similar sentiments and asked that the matter be discussed at their next meeting, to which Albert in his reply readily agreed.

Dick Spring's response was somewhat different. It came at 3.50 p.m. that same day in the form of a telephone message left by Spring's private secretary, Niall Burgess, with Mary's private secretary, Peter Ryan, to be passed on. 'The innuendo in the letter I received from the President this morning is both untrue and unacceptable. I cannot allow the inference in that letter to go unanswered. It must be withdrawn.'

Mary replied by letter the next day, 18 February 1994.

Dear Tánaiste,

I have received your message following my letter to you in the aftermath of the article which appeared in the Irish Press yesterday.

The letter was intended to let you know of my distress over the appearance in the newspaper of reports of discussions that were private to both of us. If matters that are discussed in such an intimate and confidential setting later appear in the media by whatever process, it is difficult to see how relations between this office and government can be conducted in an atmosphere that facilitates the open exchange of views on issues that arise for discussion.

I have made no inference in my letter. I have simply presented the facts as they exist. I am anxious to preserve the good relations that have existed between both institutions but as you yourself appreciate they are increasingly being placed under strain by the disclosure of the most confidential dealings between them.

Yours etc.

Albert Reynolds says that Dick Spring rang him about the ongoing row. 'I said, "I can't be the arbitrator. You had a meeting between yourselves. I wasn't there. I know nothing." I wasn't,' says Reynolds shrewdly, 'going to get involved.' To this day, Dick Spring denies that he or any of his staff was responsible for the leak. So who was? 'I don't know, actually,' says Spring. 'If I say it wasn't from the government, it sounds as though I'm saying it's coming from them, from the Áras. The government had nothing to gain by its being in the paper. It was of no political interest to me one way or another that it would be in the public domain. We've had this out and I can only tell you the situation as I know it.'

Mary was sensitive about leaks in the papers. In the third year of her presidency, Bride Rosney had gone to Spain on a reconnaissance trip in preparation for Mary's state visit there in 1993. Bride was struck by the opulence of the proposed reception rooms and conscious that red was the dominant colour, and, recalling that Dick Spring's wife, Kristi, who would be with them on the visit, often wore red, she sent a letter to her through Dick's office in Foreign Affairs, suggesting that she wear any colour but red. 'It was a very friendly gesture,' says Mary. 'But as written about in the papers, it was as if a command had been issued:– "The President will be wearing X and Y so don't you dare!" I know Bride was hurt by it and she had to live with it afterwards because it became part of the lore. And the way in which it was reported was the complete reverse of what happened.'

'Some people said the Springs were peeved about that,' says Dick. 'But I had no problem. It was welcome advice.'

Indeed the Springs and the Robinsons worked well together on a number of state visits including to Spain, Poland and the United States. And it wasn't always easy, Mary says, for a Foreign Minister to take second place, as he must, to a head of state on these occasions and Dick Spring did it with grace and ease.

It was when, in his eyes, she interfered with his work, that the sparks flew, as they did in earnest over the Framework Document on Northern Ireland.

That document, launched by the two governments in Belfast in February 1995, was the culmination of years of work by Dick Spring and his department – and the Taoiseach's department. Its purpose was to bring about all-party talks on a suggested settlement and it had to take into account the calling of the Republican ceasefire the previous August. It contained phrases which had become associated with the nationalist argument for change.

Commenting on it in an interview she did with the *Irish Times* diplomatic correspondent while on a working visit to Japan in February 1995, Mary Robinson expressed concern about the 'genuine fears' of Unionists that the Framework Document would undermine their identity. She said: 'The fear is very genuine. The fear of the ground shifting, the fear of a takeover, is undermining a sense of identity. If someone tried to undermine our sense of identity, if someone said to us Ireland should rejoin the Commonwealth tomorrow, think of the ripples of fear that would produce . . . if someone said we should join a unit with Britain tomorrow!'[3]

'That was straying into the political arena,' says Dick Spring. 'The two governments had been working for years to put together what is understood to be a seminal work in relation to Northern Ireland and the President of one's country goes out and expresses disparaging views about it!' Asked if he was angry, he says evenly: 'There was a certain amount of annoyance.'

Mary now says she can understand Dick's annoyance. The interview in which she made her remarks was done in Japan at the end of a very successful state visit. 'When you're on a state visit you do many things you wouldn't do in an Irish context. You are speaking to promote Ireland, or about the economy, or Ireland in Europe. It's a broader gathering in of the business of the government and people you are representing abroad. So when Joe Carroll interviewed me I think I said more than I would have said had he interviewed me in Dublin,' she says. 'When you're on a state visit you speak on a broader front and give interviews on a broader front that you would at home. I said nothing I felt I shouldn't have said as President, but had I been back in Ireland, I'm not sure I would have said it.'

Spring doesn't accept that she had more scope to comment abroad. 'I don't think she had. The role is non-political. It's above politics.'

Mary says Dick should have come to her privately about it. Instead he indicated to over twenty journalists at an off-the-record luncheon that her comments on the Framework Document in Japan were beyond the bounds of acceptability. He actually made very little of the issue, but the press went to town.

That Saturday, 8 April 1995, as the Labour party Annual Conference got under way in Limerick, the headlines were dominated by Labour's rift with the President. Journalists had immediately phoned Bride who refused to make any official response to an off-the-record comment. In response to an *Irish Independent* journalist, she snapped: 'Put it on the record and there will be a reply on the record.' Next morning, to Bride's consternation, the *Irish Independent's* headline read: 'President calls on critics to go public' over a story which said: '. . . the Áras issued an implicit challenge. "Put it on the record and there will be a reply on the record."'[4]

'Off-the-record' as journalists define it, means that one can use the information given, but not identify the source. The source was described as a 'Labour Minister'. As there were only six Labour Ministers, this did narrow the field somewhat.

Eventually, Dick Spring was named. He felt betrayed by the press. 'From my point of view, it was the shabbiest thing any journalist could have done. They weren't five minutes back in Leinster House after the lunch than they were on to the Áras trying to stir it up.' So why didn't he tell Mary himself that he felt she had gone too far, instead of taking chances with an off-the-record comment to the press? 'I couldn't. How could I tell her? It wasn't that kind of relationship. If I made that point to her and she said that she was inclined to act differently, well, then you were into a crisis. It's very delicate.'

Spring's feeling that he couldn't talk to the President is not shared by most of the Taoisigh she dealt with. The relationship with Charles Haughey was extremely guarded, but neither Albert Reynolds, John Bruton nor Bertie Ahern have expressed the view that they felt constrained in discussing issues with her.

There was a lack of personal trust between Mary and Dick Spring and Mary felt it had even affected the handling and the controversial press coverage of her visit to South America in March 1995.

'It may have been a carry-over from the Joe Carroll interview', she says, claiming that there was no support from Foreign Affairs and from Dick in particular. That visit, which is dealt with in more detail later, was the low point in what had been up to then the almost universally positive coverage Mary received in the media. 'I'm not entirely blaming Foreign Affairs,' she says. 'I think there was a lack of support and I believe the cue in Foreign Affairs was taken from the fact that the Tánaiste (Dick Spring) was probably saying: "Well, it's about time she was criticised. She has walked on water."' Both Mary and Dick Spring are conscious that their personal relationship could have been better and that they are both to blame. With Mary there is a real sense of regret. Much is made by Labour people of the fact that Mary never entertained Dick and his family at the Áras.

'I don't know how often you should renew an invitation, but one was given and renewed and the occasion just didn't come about. It was particularly my aim to have Kristi and Dick and Dick's mother at the Áras. I knew the importance of that. I had a great regard for Dick's mother,' she says. 'She was a fine woman, a remarkable woman. I had good rapport with her during the election and at meetings afterwards. It seemed to me natural that the visit would happen. I did ask and renew the invitation,' she says. 'Maybe I should have invited them for specific dates.'

Dick was aware of Mary's admiration for his mother and says that because of his mother's illness they never got together at the Áras. Mrs Anna Spring died in 1997. 'So if I have one regret over the period it is that we never got that lunch date organised,' he says. 'Because it might well have been the proper denouement of the whole relationship, or the moving of it on to the next stage, but it didn't happen. And in fairness, Mary Robinson went to a lot of trouble to try to set it up.'

They were two tough people, they didn't compromise. Mary had drawn a line between herself and Labour during the campaign and the presidency. Spring would stay meticulously on his side of it. 'There wasn't any way of making that relationship warmer without straying into the political sphere,' he says. 'That's not just because of two stubborn people at the end of the day, but also because one had to be very careful of not crossing that line.'

Ironically, they played one of the most successful double acts in Irish political history. He got her nominated. Her popularity helped win him Labour's biggest ever election victory. She helped change public attitudes – he pushed through legal change. She focused public attention on the poor, the marginalised, on the third world – he helped in government to increase spending on social welfare and development aid. She won respect for liberalism – his government changed the law on divorce.

Between them, they completed a liberal agenda. Rivalry may even have forced them to try harder, and it certainly protected them from accusations of forming a cosy cartel. It could have been a great political conspiracy.

But it wasn't.

20

THE PRESS AND THE GRAND PLAN

'Journalists like to balance the books. In the end you always pay.' Eoghan Harris warned Bride Rosney about the press at the beginning of Mary's presidency. During the campaign the media loved Mary, the underdog candidate. Now they would turn on her unless she could manage somehow to remain the underdog.

She could do that, he said, by relentlessly running high-wire risks and making herself vulnerable. 'Out of every risk you get six months' peace. You have to keep journalists in hot pursuit. If you stop to draw breath, they'll catch you.'

All her life, Mary had run high-wire risks for the things she believed in. Like most radicals, she had the bruises to prove it. But now she would have to move with a sharp eye on the press. Her office was largely symbolic, but that could be used to advantage in the age of television images and icons. She couldn't say anything very controversial, but she could speak volumes by the places she chose to focus attention on, the people she chose to be photographed with. By constantly breaking new ground, keeping one step ahead of the press, she could keep them interested in *her* agenda, not *theirs*.

Mary's agenda came from her inauguration speech. She would work through the promises, one after another. Bride worked out the strategy. She was the one with the lists, the wall maps. She was a one-woman surveillance operation, both scout and listening post. On any given weekend, Bride would do a café trawl from Bewley's in Westmoreland Street to the Unicorn in Merrion Row. She was friendly with people in the arts, the trades unions, politics, journalism. She knew that solid information is the basis for any successful campaign. Between them, Mary and herself hit the ground running.

They were an interesting pair, both tough, both alienated from party politics – Mary through bitter experience, Bride through natural scepticism. She has no party political loyalty and has voted right across the spectrum. What she shares with Mary is a general left of centre belief in justice and tolerance. 'Our friendship is issues-based – it started on an issue, Wood Quay,' says Bride. These two women set goals and were determined to achieve them.

Bride was born in Cahirciveen, Co. Kerry, in 1949 and moved to Phibsboro in Dublin when she was four. Her father was a solicitor and Bride went to the Dominican Convent in Eccles Street, took a science degree in UCD, did graduate work in computer science in Trinity College Dublin, worked for the Department of Education's Curriculum Development Unit, and at the age of thirty-seven became the first woman principal of a boys' community school, Rosmini Community School in Drumcondra which educates the visually impaired. When Mary asked her to become presidential adviser, Bride laid down two conditions: 'I don't do church services and I don't do sporting events.'

At her goodbye party in Rosmini, one colleague told her: 'You have one big fault. If you think someone is a bloody idiot, you tell them they're bloody idiots.' Bride regarded that as a compliment. She is frank and confrontational and she likes people who stand up to her – it's often her way of working out her own position. Mary, on the other hand, is deliberate and reflective.

But this was always Mary's presidency, not Bride's. 'She is the visionary. I am not. I am a very practical person with down-to-earth skills. She needed her own person, separate from the system. We played good cop, bad cop. I am basically quite tough. I never minded making or implementing hard decisions,' she says.

Mary campaigning against the
amendment to ban abortion in the Irish
constitution, 1983

Mary Robinson, then a socialist, addressing
the Labour party conference, 1980

Mary campaigning to save the Viking site at Wood Quay, Dublin. September 1978

Left Before: Mary Robinson
with Labour leader Dick Spring,
on the day Labour nominated
her for the Presidency
Above After: official campaign
picture of new-look Mary
Robinson

Above The rocky road to the Presidency
– Mary gets a helping hand while
campaigning on Inishmore, the Aran
Islands, August 1990

Roses all the way: Mary arrives at the
election count centre with Labour
Director of Elections, Ruairi Quinn
(now party leader) on the left, Aoife
Breslin of Labour Youth on the right,
and behind, Nick Robinson with Pat
Rabbitte and Proinsias de Rossa of the
Workers' Party, now Democratic Left

Mary accepts victory in the Presidential election as, on the right, defeated candidate Brian Lenihan applauds bravely, and on the left, Taoiseach Charles Haughey and Labour leader, Dick Spring, with whom she would have future tensions, confer

Above right Inauguration day: President Mary Robinson with her seal of office. To the left, Nick Robinson and Taoiseach Charles Haughey and at her shoulder, former President, Dr. Patrick Hillery; to the right, Chief Justice Tom Finlay and Cathaoirleach (speaker) of the Dail, Sean Treacy and at her shoulder, former Taoisigh, Jack Lynch and Garret FitzGerald

Above middle Mary's family celebrate victory in Mayo: back row from left: Tessa Robinson, Fiona Kerins, Mark Bourke, James Bourke; front row: Catherine Bourke, Nick Robinson with son Aubrey, Mary Robinson, Dr. Aubrey Bourke, Ruth Bourke, Adrian Bourke

Bottom right Bourkes: back row: Henry, Aubrey, Oliver, Adrian; front row: Mary and father, Dr. Aubrey Bourke, early eighties

Left Robinsons at the Áras: back row from left: Nick and Andrew; front row: Peter, father Howard, and Michael

Presidential showdown: President Robinson meets the Dalai Lama despite Charles Haughey's determined efforts to stop her. It was the defining moment of her presidency, March 1991

Kathleen (Collie) Power greets her President at the presentation of child care certificates to the travelling community, Taylor's Hall, Dublin, January 1995

President Robinson welcomes all gay and lesbian groups on the island of Ireland to the Áras: 12 December 1992. Gay rights campaigner Senator David Norris is second from right, back row

Below Chris McCarthy welcoming President Mary Robinson to the Mercy Family Centre in Brown St. in Dublin's south inner city; Mary was the first person Chris and her friends ever voted for

Left President Robinson with Taoiseach Albert Reynolds – 'that gambler's look in his eye' – and at her shoulder, her loyal secretary, Peter Ryan

Mary and Nick in West Belfast
with Falls Rd. Community Centre
Director, Eileen Howell. Sinn Féin
president, Gerry Adams, is back
left, June 1993

Above right Prince Charles with
the President at Áras an
Uachtaráin, June 1995. His visit
healed wounds left by the murder
of Lord Mountbatten fifteen years
earlier

Right She always wanted to be a
writer: Mary Robinson with
authors John B. Keane and the late
Bryan McMahon at Listowel
Writers' Week

President Robinson meets
children in a feeding line in
Somalia, October 1992

Two presidents shaped by the civil rights movement – Bill Clinton with Mary Robinson on his triumphant visit to Ireland, December 1995

President Robinson, former anti-apartheid activist, with President Nelson Mandela on her state visit to South Africa, Capetown, 26 March, 1996

Below Mary and Nick Robinson with the Duke of Edinburgh (left) and British Prime Minister, John Major, at the memorial service for the two boys killed in the Warrington bombing, April 1993

Mary Robinson meets the Irish community in Manchester – the first Irish president to visit and represent the forgotten Irish diaspora

President Robinson and Councillor
Jim Rodgers (far left) the first unionist
politician to visit the Áras with a group
from the Protestant Shankill Rd.

Right Robinson with children at Irish
aid agency Trócaire's project in Rwanda

Below right President Robinson, soon to
be UN High Commissioner for
Human Rights, with UN Secretary
General Kofi Annan, New York, July
1997

Below Republican campaigner and
former MP, Bernadette McAliskey,
protests about sectarian murders and
criticises the President's hairdo

Making history: the Irish and British Heads of State meet for the first time, President Robinson and Queen Elizabeth at Buckingham Palace, May 1993

Nobel Laureate Seamus Heaney and Mary Robinson receive honorary degrees, Harvard 1998

No veil: President Robinson meets the Pope, March 1997

Time to go: Mary Robinson says goodbye to Áras an Uachtaráin, September 1997

Mary, Bride says, is vulnerable. 'She's fundamentally very shy. She's slightly vulnerable and in certain situations very vulnerable.'

Bride took on more than the necessary battles with the various bureaucracies, domestic and foreign. After the early lessons learned over the redeployment of the Áras staff, Bride took charge of handling the press. *Irish Times* editor Conor Brady says that his political staff contacted Bride in the same way that they would contact the government press secretary. 'There had never been a channel to the President before. Now, if there was a presidential issue brewing, there was an identifiable operational channel through which communication could be made.' Bride scotched rumours. She handled difficult issues Mary couldn't be seen to comment on directly. She pointed reporters in the direction of other interesting information. And, the most important factor for journalists, she was always available. She would always return calls. In as far as she could with the press, she ensured that Mary was never left unprotected. And she was close enough to speak for her. 'On 95 per cent of the decisions, I would know what she was going to say before she said it, and I would say very comfortably, "Well, the President says . . ." and if she wasn't around, I would give the decision. But the important thing is I knew the 5 per cent I couldn't second-guess, and I would never do it.'[1]

'She has a blunter approach than I do on a number of issues but I can't think of any fundamental issues on which we differ,' says Mary. 'And Bride has always told me what I didn't want to hear: "That was a terrible speech," or, "I thought you chaired that meeting terribly."'

Bride, says Mary, is a very quick thinker under pressure and has good instincts. 'She was the vital catalyst in making it happen, in letting me develop the presidency as a resource. It needed eyes and ears and a person who could make the ideas happen,' she says. 'Bride was my link with a huge wide world out there, and probably because she was so good at her job, it allowed me to keep my space and my privacy. If she hadn't been so effective at communicating on my behalf I would probably have done much more of it.'

Bride always watched the balance. She had a map on the wall in her office and used coloured pins to mark the places Mary had been to – that way she could watch out for neglected areas. She had a list of Six Things To Do During The Presidency. They included visiting all twenty-six counties of Ireland during Mary's first year and all thirty-two by the end of the presidency, the first presidential visit to Britain, the first presidential visit to Northern Ireland, a state visit to the US, and visiting all the inhabited islands off the Irish coast (which Mary didn't quite manage).

More important, however, were the issues Mary chose to highlight. 'There was a strategy from Day One,' says Bride. 'On the fourth of December 1990, her first engagement as President was with Threshold, the organisation for the homeless. On the twelfth of September 1997, her last engagement was with Focus Point, the charity for the homeless. The choice for the first and last events had to be symbolic. She had to be with the most vulnerable.'

In her first week she set the pattern. She attended mass in Ballymun, one of Dublin's deprived areas, and would thereafter make a point of going to mass in the poorer parishes. She attended functions for the Rape Crisis Centre and the special Olympics. She attended receptions for third-world agencies. She went on in January to visit the prisons, to attend peace services, a concert for the Sudan Famine Appeal, the anniversary dinner of the Women's Political Association, to receive groups from Northern Ireland.

She set a scorching pace. As well as private meetings, she had twenty-nine official engagements in January, sixty-four in February, seventy-three in March, ninety-two in March. She had as many as five official engagements a day. She was doing about six media interviews a month. As the time went on it was clear that she was concentrating more and more on social services and disadvantaged groups, women's groups, educational and youth groups, as well as on cultural events.

More and more, visits from groups north of the border appear in the Áras diary. Solidly throughout the diary for the seven years are visits to travellers' training centres, travellers' workshops and development groups, and visits by travellers' groups to the Áras, all signalled by her establishment, as President-elect, of the President's special award for design of traveller accommodation.

Every time she visited a socially disadvantaged group, or a charity, she attracted publicity for what they were doing. That made it easier for them to argue their case for funding. Workers in the caring professions in Ireland and Britain, and those who work for the third-world agencies, have all attested to that – she knew exactly what she was doing.

Whenever Mary gave a major press interview, Bride tried to insist that the journalists would first travel with the President for a day or two, so they could see clearly what her agenda was. She forced media attention on travellers, on the homeless, on the hungry of the third world, on prisons – often to the consternation of the authorities. And she was sometimes very deliberate in the way she did it. One visit which infuriated the government and local politicians was in 1995 when she went to see the residents of Gort, Co. Galway, who were once again devastated by flooding. They were looking for government aid to get back on their feet. 'Because it was a rural area with country roads, there hadn't been much focus of attention on it. And I was very conscious that it was not a subject that I could say anything publicly on.' She chose to go on the national day. 'I was aware that by going there on St Patrick's Day I would be bringing more attention to the area and of course,' she grins, 'that wasn't strictly my business . . . I was trying to find a way of doing it, and going to mass there on St Patrick's Day was the best I could come up with.' It gave her an opportunity to highlight the helicopter and rescue services and to meet the local families, but she knew she was straying into the political arena. 'I used to say I wanted to work right up to the line and Nick would say, "Yes and sometimes you peek over it".' She peeked over the line on that visit, she concedes, 'but it was only a peek.'

Government reaction, says Dick Spring, was: 'Well, that's grand, but *we* have to find the money to do something about the problem. She was right to do it, in a general way, but the bottom line was the pressure put on the politicians to find the money from scarce resources.' Exactly. Mary knew what she was at.

She sported symbols which, other than the shamrock, no other President had done. She wore International Women's Day mimosa when she met the Pope; the red International Aids Day symbol when President Clinton came to Dublin – she was the only VIP to do so. On her inauguration day, she wore the green ribbon for the Gulf War hostages held in Iraq. 'They asked me to wear it on the day so they wouldn't be forgotten. As Nick said towards the end of the presidency: "You know, historians will say that you supported the Sinn Féin 'Free the Prisoners' campaign".' The ribbons are the same.

To be effective, however, symbols need to be on public display and it took Mary some time to get used to the constant presence of cameras. She has a brilliant smile – photographers like Eric Luke of the *Irish Times* say it was difficult to take a bad picture of her. But the smile, she says, was sometimes a mask. 'That smile is a defence mechanism. I know it myself. That's why I'm almost always photographed smiling. It is a nervous thing.'

She hated having her photograph taken because she believed, as people do in many cultures, that each picture took away a bit of your soul. She really appreciated the photographers who understood and sympathised with what she was doing when she went to visit marginalised groups. 'More and more I tried to get them to focus instead on the people. Like photographer Derek Speirs who does a lot of work with the travellers – a great guy. There were a number of times when we were in an unspoken alliance and I appreciated that.'

She hated the politician's trick of posing for the camera and found it exploitative. Particularly in Africa, she tried to avoid the set-up picture, feeling that the starving people she was visiting deserved, at the very least, to keep what was left of their dignity. 'I got used to carrying on a conversation, trying not to pose for the camera if possible.'

At home she was distant, nodding the odd time to a reporter or photographer she knew, but rarely speaking to them. The strictest protocol was observed at the presentations of ambassadors' credentials. 'It was never as formal before she became President. Photographers would wait in the next room and we would shoot the ceremony, through the doorway, from the next room. She would never address you directly. But I had no problem with that; she was maintaining the dignity of the office,' says Eric Luke. 'But a lot of guys did have a problem. They felt she was stand-offish.'[2]

She was. While she was President-elect, she came in to RTE for a television interview and the interviewer who had dealt with her for years said: 'Mary, what am I supposed to call you?' 'Mrs Robinson or President Robinson,' came the stiff reply. 'I don't think Mary would be appropriate.' She was determined there would be respect for a woman President. In ways she felt that she had to be more orthodox in her style than other Presidents in order to reassure people who might be made uneasy by her radical agenda.

She also had to accept that her appearance, in which formerly she took no personal interest at all, mattered greatly. It was strategically important to look good if she was to focus attention on the causes she wanted to promote. It was courteous to dress well, even formally, for those people who invited her to their community project or their housing estate. The poorer they were, the more careful she was. After all, it was the President they wanted and the President had to look special. She always wore Irish clothes and Cecily McMenamin of Private Lives in Brown Thomas continued to advise her for a few years until, says Cecily, 'she now knew the uniform so she was okay on her own'. Cecily advised against trousers in public and Mary agreed. 'I wore trousers a lot of the time privately but clothes is a *boring* story at the best of times and I knew if I wore trousers I was inviting a story.'

She wore jackets to carry her right through the day. Cecily preferred her in long jackets. 'Short jackets were too Ivana Trump,' says Cecily.[3] She wore round necks with a torc or pearls, and stud earrings. She deliberately wore bright colours and her favourite was red – the brighter colours projected the sense that she was the President and made her stand out in a crowd. One bright yellow suit caused a soldier in her guard of honour to snigger: 'Here comes Big Bird.' She didn't mind. 'I wore that Big Bird outfit again to the Royal Dublin Society Horse Show which is about as public as you can get. No, I wasn't going to be intimidated!'

Cecily would go up to the Áras with a rail of Irish clothes – by Pat Crowley, Louise Kennedy and other Irish designers. Nick would sit in on these sessions, too, and he liked the elegance of the established couturiers. 'Pat and Louise were particularly aware of the practicalities, of the need to have clothes that would travel and the need to be able to mix and match,' says Mary. 'I was very grateful to Cecily for the very practical approach she would take in that way.'

She wore a Pat Crowley traffic-light-green dress and three-quarter length coat when she had lunch with the Queen. She wore a Louise Kennedy purple coat and purple silk moire jacket for her inauguration. She wore a simple navy-and-white spotted silk dress by Michael Mortell on visits to India and Africa.

Cecily was conscious that the semi-fitted cut of the newer designers didn't always show Mary's size ten figure off to the best advantage. But Mary insisted that she would wear a range of Irish designs. 'I was more interested in being fair to young designers,' says Mary, 'so I wore quite a lot of their clothes even though they weren't my absolute chosen favourites.'

Mary wore the same clothes again and again, partly to prove she wasn't being extravagant, but also because she liked them. 'There were favourite outfits which I called my comfort blankets . . . particularly for evening, I had three or four.' One of her cherished comfort blankets was a white Louise Kennedy long-sleeved jacket embroidered with black, worn with a long black skirt, and another was a Pat Crowley emerald-green flecked tweed suit.

She had a soft body-wave in her hair and kept it short, so people could see her face. When preparing with Irish ambassadors abroad for Mary's overseas visits, her secretary Ann Lane warned them that two things above all could foul up her day – the late arrival of breakfast or of the hairdresser.

Mary wore a hat on only two occasions – she borrowed one from her sister-in-law Ruth to wear to the funeral of King Olaf of Sweden, and once she wore a large-brimmed straw hat to the Irish Derby.

'The Derby glass trophy was in two parts, a long glass and a stopper, and just as I had picked it up to present it, I thought my hat was about to fall off, and then the trophy nearly fell and it was very dramatic trying to catch it,' she says. 'So I decided – no more hats.'

Nick liked her skirts short – she had good legs. But the conservative public wrote in droves to complain, and eventually Mary gave in.

'You are mainly photographed getting out of a car and if you're not careful, you are showing more leg than is proper. We joked about that, because Nick would have liked my skirts shorter; it was one of the few things he wasn't fuddy about. And Bride would say, "No! I'm not going to face a whole series of letters." I also liked the longer length myself, eventually. I just felt an ease of comfort in a longer skirt and I wear it now quite a bit in preference.'

The letter-writers wanted her to be ladylike, to wear gloves and a handbag. But Mary thought the gloves were old-fashioned and says the handbag prevented her from shaking hands. 'I always wanted to free myself up,' she says. 'In a crowded situation, you shook hands with both hands. If you really wanted to be in contact, it was either one hand or both hands!'

Mary saw clothes as a necessary nuisance and gave the shortest possible time to trying on and choosing them. Cecily was fastidious about the fit and insisted on minute alterations. There was a certain amount of tension with Bride, who was determined Mary wouldn't be turned into a clothes horse.

When journalists asked what Mary would be wearing, Bride would retort. "Tell me what the Taoiseach will be wearing first and then I'll tell you about the President." When she appeared on the list of the world's best dressed women at the end of her first year in office, the Áras made nothing of it. But Irish designers appreciated the showcase she gave to Irish fashion and so did the public. One day, watching her review a guard of honour in designer Louise Kennedy's home town of Thurles, Co. Tipperary, a big farmer in the crowd sang Mary's praises. 'And what's more,' he said as though adding the final flourish, 'she wears Tipperary clothes.'

Abroad, Mary got coverage never before given to an Irish President. She was what journalists love, a surprise, contradicting the prevailing view of Ireland as an old-fashioned, male-dominated, Catholic country. In a lengthy profile headed 'Symbol of the New Ireland', *Time* magazine said: 'President Mary Robinson has recharged the spirit of her fractious nation and helped make it part of a modern Europe.'[4] Anthony Lewis, the veteran liberal columnist for the *New York Times*, interviewing her in 1993 called her, 'one of the most remarkable heads of state in the world today'.[5] *Vanity Fair* in an extensive report headed 'Proud Mary' with photographs by Lord Snowdon said: 'She's a little bit of Hável and a little bit of Hepburn.' It continued: 'Robinson's activist Presidency has marked a moment of redefinition in the soul of Ireland', and claimed she was, 'inspiring a wave of grass-roots feminism that is challenging centuries of repression'.[6] In the UK the *Observer* called her 'the thinking man's Princess Di' – not an accolade she necessarily relished.[7] The London *Independent* said of her in 1996: 'Many believe that her abilities as a moralist place her in the same league as Nelson Mandela and the Czech Republic's Vaclav Hável.'[8] On visits to the US and abroad, she appeared on most of the major television news and interview shows.

But the home base was most important and here the *Irish Times* was her almost totally loyal supporter. She fitted the paper's liberal ethos, both as candidate and as President and though the paper was careful to be even-handed in its news coverage of the election, editor Conor Brady says that his columnists backed her as something new and different, even though they didn't believe she'd win. 'I remember expressions of astonishment, even of grief, that we had come out on the winning side!'

Victory was a strange taste after the disappointment of defeat on the abortion and divorce issues, he said. He knew there was a danger the paper would suspend its critical faculties and alerted his staff not to give her an easy passage. 'But it was difficult to find things wrong with the presidency, alert as we were.'[9]

Most journalists are politically left of centre and that was certainly the prevailing ethos not only in the *Irish Times* but in RTE, the state television service. Both gave Mary generous picture and editorial coverage. The *Irish Times* reprinted in full not only her two Oireachtas speeches, but many other major statements, and hardly a day passed without a photograph of the President in the paper. 'No conscious decision was taken to follow Mary Robinson because she was Our Person,' says Conor Brady. 'We covered these presidential encounters more for the sake of the communities she was visiting than for her, which is how she would have wanted it.'

RTE, the state television service, say she was an easy story to cover because she and Bride were so politically astute. 'One of the important things about her presidency was how political it was and how they understood the nuances of political life,' says Ed Mulhall, now RTE's Director of News, who edited and produced most of the news and documentary coverage of Mary's presidency. 'You always felt they were a few stages ahead of the political game. Visits were carefully planned. They were aware of media interest, of what was visual, accessible.' They made life easier for editors like himself by giving quick decisions and precise appointments. 'They were highly professional.'[10]

Mary's news management of her nomination to her UN post is a perfect example of how she used the media, says Ed Mulhall. Kofi Annan made the announcement at the UN and RTE carried it on the six o'clock news. When they asked Mary for a comment, she said she would be making it in a speech to the Irish Refugee Council the next day. 'So she choreographed the announcement to give publicity to the Refugee Council. The Council benefited from the attention and also gave her the right context in which to announce her future in the UN.'

People were interested in items about her, he said, she wasn't a turn-off. 'She gave attention to communities and people who had never been listened to before. The time she gave to people in small communities, and the follow-through and the links she made – all of that explains her popularity. It wasn't always an easy story to cover on television, but that was the success story of her presidency; it was micro, at that community level. That's why she was popular, not because of her visits to Clinton or the Queen, or to Adams.'

Ed Mulhall denies that RTE's coverage was fawning. 'We covered events as they happened pretty straight, and we included the criticism of things like her Oireachtas speeches or her visit to West Belfast.'

Journalism is about giving a balance, says Ed Mulhall, 'but it is also about telling it as it is. We weren't going to say she wasn't popular when she was popular. There is room for journalists who bring people down from their pedestals, for the Eamon Dunphys in the *Sunday Independent* who sit on the sidelines and say that maybe 90 per cent of the people are wrong. Yes, there's room for hecklers but not in straight journalism.'

Independent Newspapers had no particular loyalty either to Mary or her agenda. From the time of the election campaign, the *Sunday Independent*'s gossip columnist, Terry Keane, Official Pal of Charles Haughey, had referred to Mary caustically as Her Poloness. This tilt at Mary's new-style polo-neck jumpers was taken in good part by the Robinsons.

The *Independent* had long ago learned that attacking popular icons makes for good copy. The bigger the icon, the better the sales. With their anti-Republican, free-market view of the world, they weren't in any case likely to be sympathetic to Mary's presidential trips to the margins. It was very noticeable that they gave less picture coverage to Mary's engagements.

But it was the *Independent*'s columnists who mounted the real battle. Eamon Dunphy, along with most of the paper's commentators except for Ronan Fanning and John A. Murphy, attacked her visit to West Belfast in lurid terms. The woman who had resigned because Unionists weren't consulted over the Anglo-Irish Agreement was exposed as 'a fake', said Dunphy, 'a false prophet'. 'She has given comfort to terrorists.' Her diaspora speech was sneered at by Shane Ross and again by Dunphy who spoke of 'guff', 'vacuous rhetoric', 'conceit'. In order 'to capture the world's attention, she is stripping her office of dignity,' he said.[11]

Aengus Fanning, editor of the *Sunday Independent*, says he had nothing against the President personally, that he agreed with her focus on the poor, that he ran a popular paper and she had a popular approach. 'I don't agree with those who rubbish the touchy-feely stuff. She was expert at catering for that.'[12]

But what of his own columnists who were rubbishing the 'touchy-feely stuff', who sneered at it, who attacked her? 'I don't think that was unfair. It was needed as a counterbalance and it was formidably argued. And seeing the 99 per cent adulation, it was needed,' he said. 'Seven years of eulogy, that's not reality,' he says. 'The *Irish Times*, I don't think, ever published a critical sentence. And it was in order for RTE to have done one or two documentaries that were more acerbic. Sceptical questioning was needed and RTE didn't do that.'

His paper, he says, made no conscious decision to cut her out of photographic coverage because they didn't agree with her agenda. 'What we have to do on a Sunday newspaper is find stuff that creates a different context. We don't want predictable stuff. If counting the number of pictures of President Robinson is synonymous with deciding if we are a caring newspaper . . . !' Unlike the Cork-based *Examiner* newspaper and the local papers who gave generous coverage to the local communities she visited, Independent Newspapers were slow to cover such events. That was probably because they were politically hostile to what she was trying to do, she says, which was 'to highlight issues of injustice, the needs of vulnerable groups. If I was there now, I would be spending a good deal of time with people looking for asylum because it would be appropriate for the agenda I had set for my presidency.' She would have welcomed more constructive criticism, she says. 'But some of the coverage in the *Independent* was really beginning to worry me. I had to tackle it because they were targeting my credibility and my moral authority. And when I had an unequivocal case, I took them on.'

When Mary sued the *Independent*, it was over a story headlined 'Top Car for Top Lady'. The front-page splash claimed that the President had ordered a new 7301 BMW costing £70,000, rather than a cheaper car. The price tag was twice that of most Ministers' cars, the story said, adding that 'the President is understood to have turned down a choice from the normal range of Opels and Mercedes available to members of the cabinet'.[13] A letter published in the paper about a week later criticised Mary's extravagance at a time when so many Irish people were poor or unemployed.[14]

The truth, Mary says, is that she didn't even want to have her Alfa Romeo renewed, but when told that it had to be changed, asked for the same model again. It was the security authorities responsible for servicing the car, she says, who insisted on a higher performance car.

'The moral authority of the presidency was the only strength I had in drawing attention to certain issues and if that moral authority was attacked and undermined as the *Independent* were attempting to do, then I couldn't do my job so well.'

In a meeting with editor Vinnie Doyle and lawyers, the Áras asked simply for an apology. 'I was seriously worried about the way in which they were trying to undermine the moral authority of the office. I had to fight back on behalf of the office. They had an opportunity to put it right which they declined,' says Mary.

The case was settled out of court for what is understood to have been £70,000 plus costs. Mary took some pleasure in directing the *Independent*'s settlement to her favourite charities – travellers were high on the list – but she also donated money to a fund for the widows and widowers of journalists.

It wasn't Independent Newspapers, however, but the well-disposed *Irish Times* and RTE who were responsible for the lowest point in Mary's relationship with the media. It happened on her trip to South America in spring 1995, a trip which, judging from the media coverage, seemed to lurch from one embarrassment to another.

The South American project was ambitious and it should not have been difficult to predict the political dangers, the potential for damaging publicity. Mary's mission as President was to the poor and oppressed, just like the mission of Irish nuns and priests all over South America who had been radicalised by liberation theology. These religious were more radical and more committed than anyone Mary was likely to meet at home, and they would expect her to identify closely with their oppressed communities, not with the host governments of which they were often openly critical. It was going to be almost impossible to steer a middle course between her hosts and these articulate activists and, judging by the press coverage, Mary didn't succeed.

It was a packed agenda. It involved three state visits beween 19 March and 1 April to Argentina, Chile and Brazil. These were state visits, so the host country called the shots. Bride did not do her usual preparatory visit, so advance arrangements were left to ambassadors on the ground who would not, understandably, want any hassle with the host government.

The trip was out of Mary and Bride's politically sensitive hands and to add another difficulty, only in Argentina was there a resident Irish ambassador. It was obvious that things could go wrong and when they did, the press made much of it.

The President was roundly criticised for not meeting the poor, not seeing enough of the Irish community and, finally, for shaking the hand of Chile's notorious former dictator, General Pinochet.

The first problem arose in Argentina where an impending general election had made President Menem's government wary of any event which could provide an occasion for public criticism of the government. A seemingly innocent visit by the Irish President to a poor area outside Buenos Aires served by Irish Dominican nuns was ruled out by Menem. It might focus attention on the government's economic and social failures. Local people had prepared for the visit, even though the Áras had never given the final go ahead.

When it was made clear at a late stage that the visit would not now proceed, local Irish religious complained to reporters covering the trip that they had arranged for £1,300 worth of refreshments at the Dominican site and that the people in Barrio José in Moreno had made Irish flags and rehearsed a welcome. Sister Joan O'Shanahan, one of twenty-two nuns in the community, said: 'People were terribly disappointed. Imagine the embarrassment of telling them the President wasn't coming, after three meetings to prepare for it.'[15]

A group of twenty people from the community set out to meet the President in central Buenos Aires where she was laying a wreath at the memorial to the great hero of the Argentine Navy, Irish-Argentine Admiral Guillermo Brown. Their bus broke down in the mud, and they turned up after she had gone. *Irish Times* reporter Conor O'Clery says he happened to come across them, forlorn and miserable. When he heard their story, on their behalf he phoned Bride Rosney at the President's hotel, and she arranged for them to come to meet the President there.[16] But the media damage had been done. The nuns were interviewed on Irish radio. O'Clery's story in the *Irish Times* was headed: 'Argentine politics splits President and poor'.

Mary says that visit to San Moreno was the one thing she really wanted to do on the Argentine visit and it was difficult to push it because President Menem's son had just died and the visit had almost been cancelled. 'In retrospect we should possibly have insisted.'

However, it should have been easy to explain to the media why she had difficulty in pushing for the San Moreno visit, says Mary. 'And it would have been the press office of Foreign Affairs who would have explained it. That coloured the situation. I just felt we were unprotected in an area in which I hadn't needed protection before.'

Coverage of the President's visit to Chile was dominated by her handshake with former dictator General Pinochet. A human rights champion shaking hands with a dictator – this was the sort of publicity disaster that advance preparation could have avoided. On the pretext of giving her a handkerchief, Bride pulled Mary aside at the official state dinner to warn her that Pinochet was there. At the request of the Irish delgation, the Argentine authorities ordered the RTE camera crew to leave the reception room just before what the *Irish Times* called Mary's 'frigid' handshake with Pinochet.[17] 'We genuinely didn't know he would be there. We were absolutely amazed. Bride was flabbergasted,' says Mary. But the impression was allowed to get into the press that Mary did know the dictator would be there, she says – not enough was done to counteract that. 'It was easy to clarify and it wasn't clarified.'

The rot in the press coverage had set in. When Mary visited a poor parish outside Santiago, Chile, served by Irish nuns and priests – an absolute replica of the visit she was criticised for not making in Argentina – the headline in the *Irish Times* was grudging: 'President finally makes contact with the poor of Latin America.'[18] In Brazil, the negative media coverage had begun before she even got there. Brazil is served from the Irish embassy in Portugal and invitations to meet the President were sent out in European, not Brazilian, Portuguese. Almost immediately there was a nun on RTE morning radio explaining how offensive this was to the Brazilians.

The press then reported that Mary didn't visit the poor in Brazil. 'I didn't visit the favelas in Rio,' protests Mary, 'because I was asked by the local priest not to. Because if I had gone there, there would have had to be a police presence in advance, which would have been deadly for the people of the favelas. But at that stage it had become the press position that I was deliberately not including these visits as part of the state visit. In other words, I was having receptions in centre-city hotels to which poor priests had to travel into from the outskirts. Now, normally, through the press office and through Foreign Affairs, something like that doesn't get warped in the way it did.'

By the time Mary came home, speculation was widespread that the real purpose of her South American visit had been to gather support for a job at the UN, perhaps the upcoming job of Secretary-General, and that this was why she had allowed the host governments to set her agenda. 'We flew back through Paris and the Sunday newspapers were there, universally critical,' she says. 'It was strange to come back from three extremely interesting, stretching, valuable state visits to a feeding frenzy of criticism . . . The business end went well for the trade delegations accompanying us in Argentina and Chile. Politically in Chile and Brazil it went well, and links continued at a warmer level than before. I met some extraordinary priests and nuns whom it would do your heart good to meet.' She remembered a final meal in Rio with Irish missionaries and the people they served. They talked to her about the inequality they witnessed every day and gave examples of how the poor were abused – girls who came to work in the city were sterilised before employers would take them on. She listened to them and learned from them. She was very proud, she says, of the Irish missionaries.

'I don't have memories of things not working out well apart from the problems in Argentina, which is why I was really surprised at the press comment afterwards,' she says. 'But I'd had more than my share of press plaudits, so I'd be the last to complain about press coverage. There are cycles in press opinion, too.'

The suggestions that she was touting for a UN job was a constant jibe from the *Sunday Independent*. But now that suggestion was being made even by the loyal *Irish Times*. Mary had told *Irish Times* correspondent Conor O'Clery in South America that she was not qualified for the job of UN Secretary-General and was not looking at it, though she would welcome a woman in the job. 'The President's reply was suitably bashful. No one would take it as a denial,' said the *Irish Times* in a tart editorial, four days after her return, asking if she was indeed seeking to replace Boutros Boutros-Ghali.[19] 'Those who say she is, claim to discern careful calculation in her international schedule, spreading her visits strategically in order to secure international support when the time comes.' Everybody would benefit if she were to play such an international role, said the paper, which then went on to list the reasons why she shouldn't seek a second term: the increasing tensions with the government over her diaspora speech, her Framework Document comments, her visit to Gort. 'And the South American tour has been characterised by a sequence of sour moments and rather transparent attempts at buck-passing as one embarrassment succeeded another. Sympathisers of the President speak with concern of attempts to cramp her style and her vision of the office. Others in contact with her activities speak of her sense of restlessness and claim to recognise a growing tendency to hauteur and stiffness about her.' Lessons, said the paper darkly, needed to be learned.

Mary dismisses the UN rumours. 'It seems strange to have to repeat this so often but I always would have resisted being dragged into being Secretary-General of the UN. It's not my scene. I am not a political dealer.'

Whatever the reason, Mary knows that the South American

trip marked a nadir in her relationship with the press and with the Department of Foreign Affairs. She had not been forgiven by Dick Spring, she feels, for her comments on the Framework Document.

Dick Spring denies that he or his department took any pleasure in Mary's South American troubles. 'Mary Robinson was representing Ireland and in fairness to her 95 per cent of that was excellent, and you are bound to run into a few stray problems and South America was one.'

As for his department's doing more to represent her: 'The President always handled her own PR. She didn't need any great direction or advice or assistance, and of her own preference that's the way she operated.'

The truth is that, for whatever reason, in South America Mary and Bride allowed the media coverage of the visit to get out of their control. They were far away and press queries were being handled by an overrun Foreign Affairs press office in Iveagh House which often couldn't even contact the President.

Her toughest critics, Independent Newspapers, were making hay at home. In South America she was exposed to the cold gaze of *Irish Times* veteran foreign correspondent Conor O'Clery. O'Clery set a cracking pace followed smartly by RTE's Eileen Whelan and her crew. The press had got used to Mary's determined adherence to her chosen agenda. When the requirements of a state visit pushed that agenda out of focus, the press pursued Mary herself. 'Her usual subtle ways of dissent were not articulated as well as they might have been been,' says Ed Mulhall. 'The people who criticised her were the very people she should have been going to see.'

Mary's own assessment, and indeed that of Foreign Minister, Dick Spring and his department, was that the visits were generally a success, that they developed excellent trade links, particularly in Argentina and Chile from which Irish companies are still benefiting, and established even deeper cultural and political friendships with Chile and Brazil. But the media perception was different. For them, Mary needed to keep on taking risks, the sort she didn't feel able to take in South America. For once, she hadn't kept journalists in hot pursuit. For once, she had stopped to draw breath and they had caught her.

21

'I FELT SHAMED'

RTE's Charlie Bird and his camera crew were leaving the Áras when Bride Rosney stopped him. 'Stick around,' said Bride. So Charlie and his crew waited at this special briefing by the aid agencies on the famine in Somalia to hear the President ask innocently: 'What can I do to help?' To which Father Aengus Finucane, head of the agency Concern, responded: 'Why don't you go there yourself, President?'

It was a matter for government, said the President, but personally she wished to go. Charlie had his story.

Father Finucane's question was inspired. It was inspired in advance by Mary and Bride Rosney. The Finucane brothers, Fathers Aengus and Jack, were related to Bride through marriage and were happy to play their part in Mary's careful set-up. 'Nothing she ever said,' says Jack Finucane admiringly, 'was innocent.'

'I took the initiative,' says Mary, 'because the situation in Somalia was so desperate.' It was 1992 and Mary had been discussing with Nick and Bride her need to fulfil her inauguration promise 'to contribute to the international protection and promotion of human rights'. She said to them: 'If it's not possible in a context like this (Somalia) then it's not ever going to be possible. This is exactly what I was talking about.'

For seventeen years, Somalia in the horn of Africa had been

torn apart by war, first with Ethiopia, then by the civil war which began in 1989, prompted by President Mohamed Siad Barre's increasingly repressive regime. Barre was overthrown but the clan-based rebel movements could not agree among themselves. Bitter fighting broke out after an internal split in the United Somali Congress between USC chairman, General Farah Aideed and interim President of Somalia, Ali Mahdi.

Over a million refugees left Somalia during the civil war, tens of thousands had died of starvation. By autumn 1992 out of a total population of 7.8 million, 1.5 million were in immediate danger of death from starvation and a further 2.5 million were seriously at risk.[1] This was the situation Irish Foreign Minister, David Andrews, found when he visited there in the early autumn. This was the situation Mary felt the world still hadn't listened to.

So she asked the agencies involved – Concern, GOAL, the Red Cross – up to the Park and had herself invited to Somalia.

Somalia was a dangerous place to visit in 1992. Despite a UN-brokered ceasefire, sporadic fighting continued. John O'Shea of GOAL, who was delighted at Mary's readiness to go there, began to worry. 'I had qualms of conscience that we were walking her into certain death and I contacted the government and got agitated and did whatever I could to stop her from going,' he says. 'At that time in Somalia, gun rule was the only rule. People were shot for a sixpence. Aideed was on one side, Mahdi on the other. Kids were running around with Kalashnikovs. She was the first foreign leader to come in, so what better way to make your mark than to shoot her? She ignored all that. She showed bravery over and above the call of duty.'[2]

Mary says she will always be grateful to Albert Reynolds for allowing her to go. 'I spoke very openly to Albert. I said, "I believe if I go as Irish head of state it can make some difference." And he said, "Well, my security people are not happy about it."' But she persuaded him that this was something that Ireland, as a neutral country with a good track record in the third world, could usefully do. 'He could have played it safe,' she says. 'Albert had a formula to refuse me permission on security grounds if he had wanted to, so I give him full credit.'

She urged that not only should she go to Somalia, but then that the government should let her go to tell the story of the displaced and the starving at the UN – that way she could be effective.

'I wanted to support those who were supporting the people patiently waiting with dying children at the feeding stations. I was also very conscious of the limited and artificial nature of a short visit, the voyeur element. I was praying that I would achieve a practical measure of real support by being able to highlight the situation.'

From the moment the public knew she was going to Somalia, money rolled into the Áras. 'It frightened the life out of us,' she says. She channelled it through the Irish agencies and, conscious always of Northern Ireland, through Christian Aid in Belfast. When she arrived with Nick in Baidoa in Somalia on 3 October 1992, the Irish agency heads were waiting for her including John O'Shea of GOAL. 'For years I'd been trying to get our government to be the real leader of poor nations – Lynch, FitzGerald, Reynolds. And suddenly here was our President coming off the plane. I was in tears when I walked out to meet her.'

O'Shea's description of Baidoa as the 'cockpit of death' is apt. Father Aengus Finucane says in September alone Concern had provided shrouds for 3,500 people who had starved to death – and these were just the bodies which had not been claimed by relatives.[3] Before communal burial, the bodies would be washed and placed in shrouds according to the Islamic tradition. The day Mary arrived 140 bodies had been picked up. That morning the editor of the Sunday Tribune, Vincent Browne, had been out when the bodies were collected and noticed that a little girl left lying beside adults was still alive. She was brought back to the feeding centre, but it wasn't clear how long she would survive. At one stage, says Aengus Finucane, he saw Browne turn into a corner to cry.

For all the Irish travelling with Mary, it was a shocking experience and a moving one. She describes one small incident in her own account of the visit. She had started to shake hands with the children in the feeding line at the GOAL centre and then they all wanted to shake her hand.

'One young boy winced when I took his hand, and I looked and saw the open sores and began to draw my hand back lest I hurt him further, but he put out his hand again and smiled at me. It was much more important to be touched.'[4]

At an Irish Red Cross and Somali Red Crescent centre she talked to emaciated women who had waited for hours and would wait as long again to get food for themselves and their babies. She has written about breaking out of her shock to talk to them. 'I moved to the next woman. Her baby looked very sick. I asked could I hold the child. The baby was very light and frail and began to cry as I lifted it, and then stopped. I became aware that none of the babies was crying. They simply didn't have the energy. As I held the tiny baby, I heard the Irish photographers saying. 'Look this way, President,' and just that time I did. Just for that moment I held the baby for the cameras and then I realised that while they must take their photographs, I was here to talk to and listen to the Somali people. This was not going to be easy, it was going to need my intense concentration, a concentration which was the least I could give to the people sitting on the ground here before me, in the flies and the dirt and the pungent smells.'[5]

That moment was a turning point in Mary's relationship with the cameras. How could she use the power of the press without demeaning the very people she was trying to help? 'I turned for the photograph and then I remember feeling absolutely horrified at how inappropriate it was to have any regard for the photographers. I felt that awful voyeur, PR difficulty and realised that I had to do a different job.'

From then on, in Somalia and elsewhere, says Bride, she went deaf to photographers. 'After that, it didn't matter what they said, she didn't hear them.'

Bride herself took a more active role with the cameras, as one photographer in Somalia has reason to remember. 'He had one camera up to his face, the other on his back and he was so busy getting his picture that he swung back and the camera hit a skeletal woman and she crumpled in on herself, holding her child. She collapsed. I just lit on him. I nearly killed him.'[6]

Everywhere people asked Mary to tell the world that they needed food, clean water, medicine, shelter. At the Trócaire agency's camp Mandera (Trócaire means Mercy), over the border in northern Kenya, in a letter of welcome, M.J. Jakub of the Somali Refugee Society told her: 'We have no President. We have no government. We benevolently need you to be our voice at the international community and convey the suffering of our people to those who can improve our situations. We need you to tell the UN to immediately send troops to protect us and all in Somalia.'[7]

It was through the efforts of Algerian-born UN representative, Ambassador Mohammed Sahnoun, whom Mary came to admire greatly, that she met the leaders of the USC warring factions. After a tense journey over the crossfire line in Mogadishu she met Ali Mahdi, the Provisional President of Somalia, and later she met General Aideed. They both assured her that they wanted an end to violence. All through these difficult meetings, Mary says, she was supported quietly and skilfully by Foreign Minister David Andrews who had made a similar trip on his own in September.

Despite the horror of what she saw, she was, she says, 'completely on top of my emotions'. She walked straight into the stink of gangrene in an operating theatre in Mogadishu where limbs were being amputated – Bride, she remembers, had to leave. 'In Northern Kenya I experienced the terrible living conditions of people, families of nine or ten in a small space, the stench of illness – none of that threw me. It was telling the story afterwards at the press conference – then it came over me like a wave.'

There are politicians who will cry at will. Mary isn't one of them. As a barrister, as an advocate now on behalf of the Somali people, she felt it was 'not appropriate' to let emotions show. When she broke down during her press conference in Nairobi, she hated herself. 'I felt I had blown it and I felt utterly disgusted with myself that I hadn't been able to keep my composure.'

Even as she began the press conference, her anger showed. She said to the assembled press: 'I cannot be entirely calm speaking to you because I have such a sense of what the world must take responsibility for.' She spoke as a mother seeing other mothers starving beside their dying children. 'I have an inner sense of justice. It has been offended by what I've seen in the last three days – deeply offended.' Her voice breaking, she said: 'I felt shamed by what I saw, shamed, shamed. On behalf of the European world and the American world and the developed world generally. What are we doing that we have not got greater conscience for it?'

She hoped to be more composed, she said, when she spoke to the UN Secretary-General. As she left the room, journalist Vincent Browne, one of her sharpest critics, passed her up a note that said: 'You were brilliant.'

'That confirmed for me,' says Bride Rosney, 'that she was as good as I thought she was. And I remember going up to her bedroom and she was so angry with herself that we had words. I remember the words that went over and back that night.'

Mary was angry that she had lost control of her emotions, and Nick was upset that he had not been sitting closer so as to support her. 'She was angry she'd broken,' says Bride. 'I was angry that she'd been angry with herself, because she had been brilliant. I feel there's a time when you are a human, not a President.'

The raw emotion of that press conference made an enormous impact. It was carried again and again on television news bulletins. But Mary was happier with the more considered interviews she did in the United States, and with her visit to the UN Secretary-General. She also wrote a personal diary of her trip with unforgettable photographs contributed by the accompanying cameramen: *A Voice for Somalia* published by O'Brien Press. The proceeds went to Somalia. 'She sent the book and a letter asking for action on Somalia to every head of state of the UN Security Council, the European Union, the Council of Europe, and indeed every head of state she met.

Personal letters of support came back from most of them including a particularly warm response from the Dalai Lama, from President Mitterand of France and from 'Your good friend, Elizabeth R'.

Mary says: 'There was a dramatic shift in the degree of attention and follow-up.' The agencies credit Mary with helping to influence directly the UN-authorised intervention by US marines and French Foreign Legion troops in December 1992 in Somalia which at least ensured that food supplies got to the hungry and starving. 'Whatever you think about the US intervention,' says John O'Shea, 'without it hundreds of thousands more people would have died.'

Mary still has nightmares about what she saw in Somalia. Flying to the UN to tell the story, she describes how she closed her eyes and wept quietly for a long, long time. It hurt her deeply and, for her personally, it had two outcomes. It persuaded those who thought her cold of the true depth of her compassion. And it was a pointer for the future.

'It was a turning point,' says Bride. Somalia was not something Mary was going to be able to walk away from. 'She now knew that she wanted to help with development work in some way.'

The third-world agencies knew they had found a real champion and she became a hot property to be fought over. Justin Kilcullen of the agency Trócaire admits cheerfully that he created a bit of a scene in the Foreign Affairs Department in 1994 when he heard Mary was going to visit the camps run by other agencies at the borders of war-torn Rwanda. The Hutu-dominated government had been overthrown after the genocide of a million Tutsis and moderate Hutus earlier that year. The minority Tutsis now led the government and about 1.5 million mainly Hutu refugees had fled to camps over the border. Mary had decided to visit the camps after state visits in October 1994 to Tanzania and Zimbabwe.

'I went in banging the table in the Department of Foreign Affairs,' says Kilcullen. 'I said, "She's going to Goma in Zaire where GOAL is. She's going to Ngara in Tanzania where Concern is. She has to go to Rwanda itself where Trócaire is."'[8]

There had been some unseemly jostling for publicity between the agencies during Mary's Somalia visit and the department was conscious of that. Rival agencies had turned up at one another's camps, wearing their publicity tee-shirts and vying for the attention of the cameras. The government wanted to avoid a repetition of this.

But Kilcullen was making a deeper point. He was arguing that it was only within Rwanda itself that a long-term solution would be found, that real progress could come only by engaging with the regime in power. Trócaire had come to believe that attempts by agencies to remain politically neutral were pointless. Even in refugee camps, there were dominant political affiliations, and to concentrate aid efforts on refugee camps alone was too short-term.

It was a controversial view, one with which the Department of Foreign Affairs was nervous. The Rwanda government had been in power only since July, had come to power through force of arms, and did not represent the majority of the people. But both Mary and the government accepted what Trócaire was saying from its investigations in Rwanda, and key people in the Development Aid section of Foreign Affairs, such as Ronan Murphy and Barbara Jones, supported the reasons for Mary's stance. 'That Rwandan government was the only show in town,' says Justin Kilcullen. 'The alternative was worse – the return of the previous government. This one had to be engaged with.'

When Mary arrived in Rwanda, she visited a site chosen by Trócaire where thousands of people had been murdered under the previous government. She insisted on meeting local workers, not just the Irish agencies. In the Milles Collines hotel in Kigali she gathered members of five local human rights organisations and discussed the situation with them in French. 'They'd never had access to anyone like her to talk to about their work, about the trauma of genocide. She motivated them,' says Justin Kilcullen.

No one of her stature had visited Rwanda since the genocide and there was some criticism internationally that she had taken sides. But she didn't back off. She went on to see the mainly Hutu camps in Goma and in Ngara over the border, but in a speech praising the work of the Irish agencies, she said she had heard that while considerable aid was going to help the refugees, very little help was being given to the penniless new government.[9] The world could materially assist the new government to run its public services and investigate the killings, she said.

After her visit, Mary was critical of the UN, critical of its failure to commit the same level of resources to Rwanda as had been committed to the Gulf War, critical of their failure to support and co-ordinate the work of their own agencies or to set properly about the job of gathering evidence of genocide and sending in enough monitors to stop genocide happening again.[10]

On her second visit to Rwanda in October 1995 she was even more critical, warning that the world needed to act soon to defuse 'the time bomb situation',[11] resulting from the 1994 genocide. Once again she visited a site at Nyarabuye where unknown thousands had been murdered and asked the deputy prosecutor of the international genocide tribunal why it was taking so long for the tribunal to proceed with its work. 120,000 people were being kept indefinitely in prison – she visited a horrendously crowded prison in Butare – but no trials were forthcoming.

Because the international community hadn't dealt with the question of genocide, she warned in Goma, the situation was frozen into a 'cycle of impunity'.[12]

Mary was preaching a new gospel on development aid, one that governments and even the UN were resisting. She was arguing that every situation had a political context. One had to engage with that to do any long-term good. It was unfair to expect aid agencies to perform miracles with short-term humanitarian aid if they weren't getting the necessary back-up from the international authorities to address the causes of the disasters.

Rwanda had taught her hard lessons and she listed some of them in a keynote speech on humanitarian crises in December 1996.[13] 'These lessons include how aid agencies might have worked more closely with the government of Rwanda. How more lives might have been saved through better contingency planning and co-ordination. Why compassion demanded that aid agencies engaged with camp leaders, whose refugee status was doubtful because many were intimidators, in order to ensure that aid reached what have come to be known as "ordinary refugees". Why for so long the needs of refugees dominated the agenda to the exclusion of the psychological and material needs of the forgotten survivors of the genocide within Rwanda itself. As a result of these reflections, aid agencies are asking why ethical responsibility for confronting the intimidators of ordinary Rwanda refugees was left with the aid agencies and not taken up by the international legal and political community.' Complex political crises, she said, could not be resolved by short-term humanitarian responses alone.

She was right, says Justin Kilcullen of Trócaire. The days of 'humanitarianism unbounded' where one did not address the political context, were over. 'She was pinpointing the dilemma for agencies. Who were you feeding?' In the context of the camps outside Rwanda, he said, it was known that the former army was regrouping and arms were being brought in. 'Agencies who came in, innocently wanting to feed people, were wide open to manipulation. It's not that you shouldn't do it but you should know what you are doing.'

Mary tried not to let the international community off the hook on Rwanda and she had planned her second visit there to get maximum effect. First, despite some resistance, she got the Irish government to agree that she would make Ireland's formal speech at the UN 50th anniversary session in October 1995. Only then did she tell them she wanted to go to Rwanda first and then to the UN, 'so as to bring the issues to that table in a very public way'. She couldn't be too specific in her formal speech but she used the publicity surrounding her visit to the US, as well as formal speeches in Stanford and Yale Universities, to focus sharply on Rwanda.

She spoke of her anger at the world's failure to respond, and said what she saw there defied her powers of articulation. So, as she often did, she made the connection with the Irish memory of famine, and quoted Seamus Heaney's poem, *For the Commander of the Eliza*:[14]

> . . . O my sweet Christ
> We saw piled in the bottom of
> their craft
> Six grown men with gaping
> mouths and eyes
> Bursting the sockets like spring
> onions in drills
> Six wrecks of bone and pallid,
> tautened skin.

The publicity that Mary gave to development projects in Africa and India was invaluable to the aid agencies. She had become their advocate. She invited them up the Áras, not only on Development Day in December, but regularly for briefings from them and from their visitors from the third world. Father Jack Finucane says: 'She was driving the Department of Foreign Affairs, who had to put more money into projects in places where she was going. They wanted to be seen to be involved. We got much more money from DFA because of her visits.'

John O'Shea of GOAL said she made it a plus to be Irish when operating abroad. He remembers meeting an Arab doctor one day on a plane leaving Baidoa. 'Ah, Ireland,' said the doctor, 'the caring nation.'

Trócaire say her impact was profound. She changed a whole political climate. 'Since 1973 when Trócaire was founded we had been arguing that the Irish aid budget was inadequate.' At that time Irish aid accounted for 0.07 per cent of GNP whereas the UN target is 0.7 per cent of GNP, ten times higher.

In 1982 Charles Haughey actually did away with the post of Minister for Development, dismissing it as superfluous. The official climate in the eighties was not generous. Dick Spring and Labour helped to change that. It was only in 1993, when the Labour–Fianna Fáil coalition came into office, that Foreign Affairs Minister Dick Spring demanded, as a condition of government, a commitment to increase aid by an annual 0.05 per cent to reach a target figure of 0.4 per cent. All governments have continued that commitment and it is now, in 1998, at 0.33 per cent. 'The fact that it happened within her presidency, after the visit to Somalia and the profile she gave it, is more than a coincidence,' says Justin Kilcullen. 'TDs saw there was a public interest and that rather than being criticised for raising the aid budget, they would get credit.'

She also created a more sophisticated understanding of aid and of human rights. She tied the issue of development aid and human rights together, says Justin Kilcullen, defining human rights as including economic and social as well as political rights. 'We now have a Minister for Development Aid and Human Rights whereas the title used to be just Minister for Development Aid.' The push to put human rights on the agenda came from the Labour–Fianna Fáil and Labour–Fine Gael governments, and was highlighted in Dick Spring's White Paper on Foreign Policy which foreshadowed the setting up of the Oireachtas Standing Committee on Human Rights which includes the third-world agencies.

'But that was also done in the context of Mary Robinson's widening the public mind to a fuller understanding of human rights. She helped to create the right political climate,' says Justin Kilcullen.

Mary's commitment to human rights in Africa went back to long before the presidency. Since the 1970s she had been a leading member of the Irish Anti-Apartheid Movement, active in marches and protests, and one of her sweeter moments in office was when she attended the inauguration of Nelson Mandela as President of the new democratic South Africa in 1994. She returned for a state visit in March 1996 and was welcomed by her old colleague in the Trinity Law Department, Kadar Asmal, head of the Irish Anti-Apartheid Movement and the Irish Council of Civil Liberties for years, now Minister in the new government. Mary had always admired him for his enthusiastic commitment and his radicalism. 'He has the right values which is why I'm delighted he's done so well politically. But when it came to lecturing, he never used one word where four hundred would do,' she says.

Kadar made an enormous fuss of her, introduced her to Mandela in the parliament, 'so by the time Mandela got up to speak at the state dinner we were among friends'. Nelson Mandela began to speak in his slow, deliberate way. 'We know that President Mary Robinson had the privilege of being lectured by Professor Kadar Asmal. And we know, too, that her husband, Nicholas Robinson, had the privilege of being lectured by Professor Kadar Asmal . . . As we now in cabinet have the privilege also of being lectured by Professor Kadar Asmal.' The whole place exploded with laughter. Afterwards Kadar exclaimed. 'President! I don't lecture at cabinet.' And Mandela said, 'Kadar, you heard the reaction!'

For Mary, it was a night to celebrate. She told the President she would love to meet the musicians playing in a gallery above them and Mandela brought her up. 'It was quite a climb and he leaned on my arm – the old pins are very unstable. I remember the sheer emotion of the moment. First of all, we greeted the white musicians. I remember their shining faces for their President – and then even more so with the black choir on the other side, the incredible pride and worship in their eyes for Mandela.'

The President asked them to sing a song and they did. 'And Mandela started to move and I started to move and we danced. And the people at the dinner started to clap. And Charlie Bird from RTE had already gone off to send his tape and later said incredulously to Bride, "Is it true she danced with Nelson Mandela?"

'I can get quite emotional. I could feel the tears flowing down my cheeks from the emotion of those young people and their feeling for Mandela, and his ability to respond – because I had felt the weight of him going up the stairs . . . He's a lovely man.'

The ease with which Mary now moved in international circles, and her deep commitment to the human rights agenda, had fuelled further widespread speculation that she would take up a UN post. The third-world agencies hoped she would – they believed she would get things done. The media were convinced she would and discussed it endlessly – her admirers because they thought she would do it well, her critics because they wanted to accuse her of using the presidency as a springboard to an international career.

There was plenty of circumstantial evidence to link her with the UN. She was a regular visitor to UN headquarters – almost every time she went to New York she visited there. The UN – its potential, its failures, its future – was a frequent theme of her speeches and interviews.

Speaking at Harvard she said the United Nations needed to see the world as a single whole, where people listened, shared their prosperity and empowered one another.[15] In her speech on the fiftieth anniversary, she said the UN was in crisis – that 'its authority was uncertain, its financial situation dire'. It needed 'a new strength of purpose, a new sense of direction'.[16] In a speech to the US Foreign Policy Association in New York[17] she warned of the need to strengthen the UN financially as well as every other way and to create what she called a 'global ethic' to guide UN affairs. Speaking to the UN Association of New York in October 1996, she said the United Nations system was 'under threat' and called for its revitalisation.[18] This woman was interested in the UN.

Irish Times editor Conor Brady says he was delighted when she agreed to address the Irish Times–Harvard Colloquium. 'But I don't think any of us could have misinterpreted the alacrity with which she took up the invitation to make a very important address at Harvard and the tenor and tone of the address. It was a visionary statement on the future of the UN and on its potential. And she obviously elected to take this very high profile platform with guaranteed and extensive media coverage – the speech was carried live by RTE – with a view to making a statement of intent with regard to the United Nations, and the future role she could play there.' Brady feels the South American visit had a similar aim. 'Looking back on the South American visit now, it was a very conscious geographic spread of her presence, and looking at her subsequent ambitions, she needed to garner as much support as she could from that quarter. I don't know if we rationalised the thing like that at the time. We put it down to bad judgement, bad staffwork, stretching herself too far. I don't think any of us were too surprised or under any illusion as to what her long-term agenda was.'

Mary's response is that hindsight is perfect.

The rumour that she might succeed UN Secretary-General

Boutros Boutros-Ghali was constantly in the Irish and US papers from 1994. The British *Observer* and *Independent* pushed the idea heavily in 1996 despite the issuing of a public denial by the President. After a phenomenally successful US state visit in June 1996, it was clear that she would be Bill and Hillary Clinton's favourite candidate for almost any post she wanted.

But Foreign Minister Dick Spring backs up her own claim that she did not seek the Secretary-General's job. 'If she had told me she was interested, it would have warranted a secure, confidential discussion between us,' he says. 'But it was difficult to find out if she wanted to do it because even if she said she was available, it would have had implications for the presidency.'

His understanding from the Foreign Ministers' grapevine was that the job wasn't going to go to someone from Europe, anyway. 'It wasn't available because it wasn't Europe's turn. She would have known that.'

Mary repeats, with an air of weariness, that she would always have resisted being put forward for the Secretary-General's job. 'I never wanted, looked for, or thought about the very political, manoeuvring job of being Secretary-General of the UN.'

Once she had left the Labour party she had abandoned the thought of any political job, she says. She knew that if she didn't run for another term as President, she would have to look for something equally fulfilling and outside Ireland. 'The options were limited, but I knew there must be the possibility of a job with a purpose, the purpose being to work with others, to change the inequalities and to work in the area of human rights. The UN wasn't in that conscious form centrally involved. There were various potential options.' One of those, she says, was the International Labour Organisation which had made approaches to her. 'The ILO had put out feelers through the unions – the position was that of Director-General.' She decided against it.

People associated her with the UN because of her constant visits there and her constant references to it. But you can't avoid the UN, argues Mary, if you are trying to achieve anything in the area of human rights.

'I did visit the UN a lot by presidential standards. I had a great interest.' If she wanted to use the presidency to talk about humanitarian issues, then the UN was important in institutional terms, she said. 'The importance of going to Somalia was not just going to Somalia but then going on to the UN. It was important to talk at Harvard about reforming the UN. It was important to go to Rwanda and then to the UN. If you were really going to have a voice at the international level, then that was where to have it.'

SURVIVING THE ÁRAS

'I tolerated the Park,' says Nick Robinson, 'meaning the whole apparatus, the task. We all have our way of protecting ourselves. Mine was to be as private as I could.' In fact Nick became as important a public symbol as the light in the window. He never said anything, but he radiated gentlemanly goodwill. He bulked behind Mary in West Belfast, in Rwanda, an immensely reassuring figure. Nothing very dangerous could happen, people felt, with Nick around.

He was Albert to her Victoria. He protected her from the public. He protected her from herself. 'I used to call him Old Fud because many's the time he would say, "No, think about that, now." He was always more conservative on issues than I was, instinctively, and having to justify to him what I was doing meant having to clarify issues for myself. And sometimes I went ahead, but sometimes I didn't on the basis of Old Fud's view. He always told me the things I didn't want to hear.'

He has the old Protestant ethic, Mary says. He always insisted that she be true to herself. He was more conservative than she was, particularly on economic issues, but he shared her natural sympathy with the underdog. There was perhaps something of the eighteenth-century Whig about them both, a sense that privilege brought its own responsibilities, that they must champion the rights, as Mary's grandfather Bourke put it, of the 'small man'.

Nick had always taken on the big guns on behalf of the citizen – Dublin Corporation over Wood Quay, King's Inns over the sale in England of rare Irish books, the developers over Georgian Dublin. Mary and he might differ in style, but their hearts were in the same place.

The family called him the German Ambassador, partly because of his distinguished-looking beard, partly because he was punctual and punctilious, the sort of man, says his friend Dr Edward McParland, who liked to see postage stamps fixed on straight. His eye for detail extended to Mary's clothes, to the presents she would bring with her on foreign trips – Nick recommended gifts from a range of Irish crafts on which he is expert – to the last-minute additions she needed to make to major speeches. He and/or Bride would always accompany Mary on trips abroad. He was automatically included on state visits. On working visits, where Mary was running from business breakfasts, to tourism promotions, to social events, it was often Nick who would pick up the local references she needed for her speeches. He was a stickler, too, for grammar and syntax, and monitored her constantly. He curbed her tendency to speak too long – he would cough pointedly and Mary would wind up. 'Nick's cough,' she says, 'became an important part of the presidency.' And he was precious company. 'Official trips are quite lonely things because you work flat out until eleven at night and then you're in a hotel room,' Mary says.

Much of the time, on state visits, Nick got sent off with the spouses to be amused or educated at galleries or gardens or the theatre. He was a great addition to these female-dominated groups, and conversed easily in English and French. Without either language, conversations could get a bit sticky, he says, particularly on long shared car journeys. He enjoyed meeting world figures and building a balanced view from people with different perspectives.

'To meet Mario Soares in Portugal, and then to talk to Jim Callaghan about the assistance Britain gave Soares when Portugal moved to democracy in the seventies – it was all so interesting. To enjoy a sparky chat with Castro, or Arafat, at a UN gathering of world leaders where eighty egos criss-crossed New York – it was wonderful for a cartoonist. The cartoonist in me rescued me from many a terrible state dinner. The cartoonist was hovering above the table when I was caught with people who had no word of English.'

Nick looked imposing enough to be the President and people often assumed that the President had to be a man. In Perth, Australia, Mary and Nick were visiting a public park and a jogger passing by asked Mary's secretary, Ann Lane, what was going on. Ann told him the President of Ireland was visiting. 'Which one is he?' asked the jogger, looking over at Nick and the entourage surrounding the President. 'He's the one,' said Ann Lane with some asperity, 'in the black dress with the red spots.' On one visit to the Kilosa region of Tanzania, Mary and Nick were watching a performance by Masai dancers – the women danced with elaborate necklaces and the men made great leaps in the air. At the end of the dance, Mary was presented with a necklace by one of the women dancers. 'And then I could see a Masai warrior with the chieftain's stick. I could see he had been told to give it to me. I could see him standing and looking at me and looking at my husband, and then he came and gave it to me with enormous difficulty. He gave it with goodwill but it was an extraordinary moment for him psychologically.'

Nick made room for Mary's career, but he did more. He always made a wholehearted personal investment in it. He accepts the central part work plays in her life. He says simply: 'She's very good at it.' He was the one who really encouraged her to run for President.

They are both, he says, generous people. 'Generosity is one of the elements of a successful woman's career where the man is still around after twenty-seven years,' he says. Nick gave up his job as director of the Irish Centre for European Law when Mary became President.

'I felt I was earning enough,' says Mary, 'and there was a supportive role to be played. It is the extraordinary strength of a trusted pair of additional eyes and ears and a brain that you can benefit greatly from when you're doing a bit more than you have stamina for.'

Nick, in any case, was busy. He wrote a very well-received book on the life of Edmund Burke as told through eighteenth-century cartoons.[1] He devoted more and more time to his real enthusiasms, the preservation of historic buildings, big and small and, just as important, the preservation of their records. All his life, Nick had fought a particular enemy, the official amnesia about whole chapters of Ireland's past. Sometimes it was more than amnesia, it was hatred. The mindset that burned the great Anglo-Irish houses in the 1920s was still allowing the destruction of Georgian Dublin, the stripping of Countess Markievicz's home at Lissadell, the selling abroad of Irish books, works of art and antiques in the sixties and seventies. The colonial past was indeed another country and nationalist Ireland cherished no reminders of it.

Nick had for years been prominent in An Taisce, the Irish equivalent of the British National Trust.[2] A crucial report 'Heritage at Risk' that he helped produce in 1977 led to a new governmental appreciation of the state's need to give tax breaks and grants to the owners of historic houses.[3]

He chaired the working party that established the Heritage Trust, a charity that raised funds for conservation projects, and subsequently became its executive chairman. But perhaps his lasting contribution will be the Irish Architectural Archive. Nick's friend, Dr Eddie McParland of the History of Art department in Trinity College Dublin, had helped mount a photographic exhibition of the magnificent Georgian houses in Parnell Square. Nick was helping him to dismantle the exhibition and suggested that there should be an archive to preserve this wonderful photographic record.

Eddie says his own ambitions at that time extended to a few filing cabinets full of photographs but Nick, he says, thought big and in May 1976, the Archive came into being.[4] Nick and the Archive's first director, Nicholas Sheaff, and secretary Rose Dunne, gathered their material by raiding skips outside architects' offices, and making emergency sorties down the country to rescue what they could. Once the owner of a country house rang to say she was selling up and needed to clear out a roomful of documents, some of which seemed to be architectural. Could the Archive take what they wanted and she would burn the rest? Nick and Eddie did a mercy dash in a van and found a fine collection of architectural drawings dating back to the eighteenth century. Indeed, there was such a treasure trove that the lady of the house said at one point: 'Oh, Dr McParland, you must leave me something to burn!'[5]

The Archive, which is now based at 73 Merrion Square, has a fine collection of drawings, models and manuscripts as well as photographs. Nick helped to write some of the books it has published: *The Vanishing Country Houses of Ireland* by the Knight of Glin, David J. Griffin and Nick Robinson[6] and a monograph with Sean O'Reilly, *New Lease of Life – The Law Society's Building at Blackhall Place*.[7]

You can immediately spot any book Nick has had a hand in, says Eddie McParland, right down to his original pamphlet on the Architectural Archive. 'The way in which that booklet is produced, the sheer rightness of it, the elegance of it, the polish of it,' says Eddie McParland, 'he always outpaced me in the business of seeing that things were absolutely right.'

Nick was chairman of the Archive for years, and a board member until 1995. In 1992, still in the Áras, he helped set up the Irish Landmark Trust, a charity that rescues small architectural gems – lighthouses, gate-lodges, follies – and hires them out as holiday homes. He is still its chairman. In all his enterprises, he had fun. He involved his friends, or sometimes his new colleagues became his friends, and convivial lunches were not unknown. Just as he collected caricatures and seashells, says Eddie, he collected friends.

Nick was precisely the man to appreciate the architectural pleasures of living in an interesting and historic house like Áras an Uachtaráin. He is proud of what he calls 'the invisible mending' done by the Board of Works during Mary's presidency. Major rewiring was done, and the public rooms were upgraded, incorporating some of Nick's ideas. He agreed with the Board of Works' view that the refurbishing should be as authentic as possible – for example, removing the carpet in the elegant front hall and relaying flagstones. He suggested that the Velasquez copy hanging in the state reception room wasn't suitable and should be replaced by an original painting. He and Eddie McParland noticed that two of the low pedestals in the corridor should be holding not busts, but urns, and found the original urns and put them in place. Nick is also proud of the attention paid to the grounds, the lake, and particularly the trees by the Chief Superintendent of the Park, John McCullen, 'one of the unsung heroes of modern Irish conservation'.[8]

It was Nick who decided the Robinsons would live in the older eighteenth-century part of the house, not in the west wing added in the nineteenth century and reconstructed in the twentieth century, where President Hillery had lived and where the present President now lives. He always makes those sorts of decisions, says Mary. 'I'm to a fault a very abstract person. I relate to people not places.' It was natural that he would choose. 'But his main concern was not the architectural aspect but the fact that we would live over the shop and take control and enjoy. He kept saying to me at the beginning – he needed to say it – "We're going to enjoy this. We have to get our minds right." So we wanted to achieve two things. To live there as a family over the shop and to be private. Having an upstairs that was separate from the staff in the house was so important. I can't tell you how important that was. Aubrey, for instance, could come up, take off the shoes. That was utterly vital as far as I was concerned. I am somebody who needs that private space.'

The staff did not live in at the Áras. Apart from family, there was only the security staff at night. The rooms, which ran in one long suite, were medium-sized, low-ceilinged. and very simply furnished. They looked out on to the gardens and the Phoenix Park where every tourist bus slowed down at a gap in the hedge to see the emigrants' light burning in Mary's kitchen window. The kitchen, where the light burned day and night, was under the main portico, as was the family sitting-room, the children's bedrooms and Nick's study. Nick chose the strong colours for the walls – rust, aquamarine, yellow. The kitchen was converted from what used to be the flag room – soldiers climbed up through a hole in the ceiling to lower and raise the flag.

Mary and Nick organised breakfast for the family. Often if she came in late at night, she had soup and sandwiches there, or she had friends in for meals in the evening. William and Tessa had the odd party in the private dining-room or upstairs. 'Sometimes,' says Mary, 'I'd come up from work and there would be a whole gang of young people there.' Aubrey was banished from the state rooms downstairs early on, says Mary. He and his friends had had a paper chase and visitors the next day were startled to find mysterious messages down the sides of their chairs saying: 'Do not sit here.' It wasn't easy to explain.

Aubrey had friends to stay overnight and if his mother and father were away, Tessa often came out from her flat in town – she was at Trinity studying history of art. William went to study architecture in Glasgow.

The children kept out of Mary's public life, and Nick insisted on living life as much as possible as he always had. 'I kept on walking around town and meeting friends for lunch. I didn't let the presidency derail me, but it did stop Mary doing that sort of thing. She went into bookshops, but people would rush up to look at the last book she had put down – it could have been anything at random.'

Mary became isolated. She knows she became cut off from old comrades-in-arms such as Senator Mary Henry, formerly her Senate election agent, and Nell McCafferty with whom she had fought many a women's rights campaign. 'Nothing was more important than having close friends and family in order to be completely relaxed and unpompous – "unprotocolled" – but I had a sense of being less relaxed with people such as Nell, because you're not just responsible for yourself, you are in a position of high office and it does impose that kind of constriction.' Both Nell and Mary Henry were public people, she says, a journalist and a politician respectively. 'And Dublin is a very small place.' Nell had been invited to lunch but declined, saying she would have preferred if Mary had rung herself. They might not have been able to relax together in the way they used to, says Mary. 'We have been informal with each other but not completely relaxed on either side.'

Mary was careful to keep her distance from the press. 'It was my style that I didn't mix with journalists and others. That was a deliberate decision, a personal matter of style.' Unlike President Hillery, when away on a state visit she didn't come down at night to join the accompanying reporters at the bar for a drink. Often, she would have enjoyed the company rather than go to her hotel room at the end of a long working day, but she felt that in making the presidency active and adventurous, she had to be especially careful to maintain its dignity. Anything that undermined the authority of the presidency made it less effective for the people she was trying to help. 'I was very conscious therefore of the need for a certain distance as well as a pro-active approach. It is open to my successor to take a very different approach!' she says. 'So I was precluded from sitting around at the bar at night which could have been a very relaxing way of ending the day. The danger was that you would have done it with some and not with others.' Bride's job was to be with press and politicians, says Mary. Her job was to be with the people.

The small group she now relaxed with included the Bourkes and Robinsons – they are close families on both sides. Mary enjoys her food and wine and liked to share them with a trusted few. As well as enjoying their friendship, she knew she could trust totally their discretion.

'I got closer to certain friends and relied on them greatly and had a real sense of confidentiality,' she says. 'When you're written about a lot in the newspapers regarding everything you do or say or think or wear, you begin to value the very small space of privacy that's left.' Her very jokes, she said, would come back to her in four or five different versions.

When she found she had to appoint an official, state-paid chaplain to the Áras, she quickly chose Enda McDonagh, Professor Emeritus of Moral Theology at Maynooth. 'I quickly said I'll have Enda in case I got inflicted with anyone else. I wanted the fun of his being chaplain to reinforce our friendship.' In fact, Mary's appointment of Enda was as deliberate as almost everything else she did. It had a private and a public significance. Enda was an ideal chaplain for Mary, who was comfortable with his radicalism, his persistent questioning of Church tradition and precedent. She was comfortable with his view that true spirituality was inspired by a sense of justice, of idealism and of beauty, that without that ethical and aesthetic sense, traditional religion was barren. When Enda looked for spiritual inspiration, he looked to the women's movement, to those who worked for social justice, to the environmental movement, to poets and musicians, as his words demonstrate:

> Today, in Ireland at least, Catholic Christianity may have to adopt a much humbler stance as it seeks dialogue with artists and women, as it seeks in the name of religion to join the traditional triad of aesthetics, ethics and religion. The fundamentalist temptation to flee those worlds of artists and woman (justitia as well as femina) must be vigorously resisted. Only in dialogue and interaction with the moral and artistic, as they flourish today, can the religious hope to renew religion.
>
> As Eavan Boland notes in her analysis of women and women poets, the margin may be the very best place from which to understand a society. For followers of Jesus Christ, this ought to have great resonance.[9]

This was a definition of creative spirituality that Mary could recognise. It respected the ethical basis of her own morality, her need to question, something that traditional Catholicism with its emphasis on blind obedience could not encompass. McDonagh had won the respect of many frustrated Irish Catholics who asked why such an inspirational thinker had not been recognised by his own Church. For them, at least, his appointment as chaplain to the President was an important gesture of recognition. It wasn't a bishopric, but then Enda was probably more comfortable with his thoughts and his holy cardigan than with a mitre and crozier.

He became as close a friend to Mary's youngest, Aubrey, as to Mary and Nick, and when the Robinsons bought their house in Massbrook, Co. Mayo, Mary asked Enda to take the gate-lodge at the bottom of the avenue. There, as in the Áras chapel, Enda would say mass for the family.

Massbrook was bought in 1994 for £350,000. It is a nineteenth-century fishing lodge, bright and comfortable, with views out over Lough Conn. Its 120 acres are overrun by rhododendrons and that's the way Mary likes it. 'It's a sanctuary for me,' she says. She hopes it will become a sanctuary for the local wildlife as well, because even though it has some of the best fishing and shooting in the area, she doesn't allow any guns on the estate.

Massbrook is now the Robinsons' home in Ireland. 'The bank still owns most of it,' she says a little defensively, 'but we're hanging on for the moment.' Down there, she lives in her jeans. She walks the dog, a golden Labrador called Jammet (after Howard Robinson's favourite Dublin restaurant), and goes proudly down to the well beside the boat jetty every morning to get fresh spring water. An old tennis court set in the middle of tall woods was recently cleared of undergrowth but she's not going to revive it. 'I think I'd rather just stand here looking up at all the trees,' she says.

Massbrook with its seclusion allowed Mary to come home to Mayo on her own terms. 'I was always escaping Mayo until we bought Massbrook.' She sees her family down there constantly and knows that they paid a price, too, for her time as President. 'It restricted our lives,' says her brother Henry, a barrister based in Galway. 'You had to be what you possibly were not. You had the feeling people were watching you. It was inhibiting. Things get into the press domain so quickly.' Mary was always acutely aware of the office of the presidency and of ensuring that no one could accuse her, or her family, of abusing it. 'If I asked her to come and address some organisation it would be scrutinised very carefully and Bride would be very aware of it,' says Henry.[10]

Mary knew she had complicated life for her family. Her brother Adrian had considered contesting a Trinity seat in the Senate at one stage but was prevailed upon not to run. 'He was President of the Law Society and that double thing of being Law Society President and brother of the President was enough public strain. But the one I was most worried about was my father, until I realised that he was committing the sin of pride every single day! He weathered it well because for him it was a more positive experience than otherwise. But all of my family were not keen that I do a second term. Their attitude was. "You've done that now!"'

For Mary's children, there was a sense of relief when she chose not to stand again. William, in Glasgow, no longer had to field questions as to what his parents did. He was now able to say to friends, some of whose parents were unemployed: 'They're both between jobs.' The friends would nod sympathetically.

Aubrey, the boy who went to school from Áras an Uachtaráin, put it best. 'At last,' he said, 'I can have an address.'

23

TIME TO GO

Mary Robinson's greatest achievement was to be popular – in the real sense of that word. She was the President of the people and they confirmed that in every opinion poll. Her 82 per cent rating in June 1991 had risen to 92 per cent in April 1995 and rose even higher.[1] She earned that support week after week in every corner of the country. People trusted her, so they came to trust what she stood for.

After all, it was a time of great uncertainty. The power of the Church suddenly crumbled. Attitudes to sex and marriage had relaxed. But there was still a large number of conservative Irish people offended by the rate of change. Polls showed the country was still deeply split on issues like abortion and divorce. There was a large conservative constituency out there and yet a liberal President got overwhelming national endorsement.

Mary had perfected the political lesson that you can successfully send out contradictory messages at the same time, you can simultaneously win two different constituencies. She did it constantly. For instance, she never backed off her liberal views on divorce, but her solid family life reassured traditionalists. She was the Unionists' friend, but she shook hands with Gerry Adams. Her presidential style was conservative, but her agenda was radical. She shared Labour's political agenda but made a public issue of her distance from them. She moved easily on the world stage, but was a familiar figure in the smallest village hall in Ireland.

Mary deliberately set up these contradictions and they worked, but they worked only because people saw for themselves the effort she put in on the ground. It was at the local community level that she won respect. Then she used it to change things.

She had broadened her base in the election campaign and tried to broaden it even further as President, so that even conservative Irish people would be comfortable with the things she stood for. There is no doubt that this had an impact on the divorce referendum: 'I would try also to be the President of very conservative elements in the country who might then be more inclined to open to the issues that I clearly stood for.' Her visits to the Rape Crisis Centre, to women's rights groups, to travellers' groups, she said, made it clear what she supported. There could be no mistaking that. 'But my way of being President was to try deliberately to be acceptable to, and to coax in, all groups.'

It wasn't just the more traditional women's organisations like the Irish Countrywomen's Association that she forged links with, she says. In the years before the divorce referendum, she made a big effort to be in touch with those most likely to be hostile to divorce. 'I invited Nora Bennis (the leader of the conservative National Party) from Limerick up to the Park.'

She attended anniversary celebrations at All Hallows' seminary in Dublin and St Patrick's Maynooth, made visits to St Patrick's College Carlow, and invited the major superiors of the Congregation of Christian Brothers and of the Columban Missionary Society up to the Park. She met hundreds of priests 'and then I kept meeting them all over the world! Quite consciously and not hypocritically, I had a desire to persuade them through being somebody they could identify with, and then to have them think, maybe it's not so impossible to envisage a society where people have different attitudes and approaches.' People who didn't agree with her views had voted for her as President, and that alone was a sign of a more pluralist society. 'Very often you are talking about people who have one view – the church-determined view – on issues, and I wanted to have them comfortable with me as someone who really represented them as President, but also clearly someone who on significant issues differed from them. And that shouldn't be a real problem. We should be able to differ and maybe even think about it and not differ quite so much.'

So did she think her presence as President influenced the outcome of the divorce referendum? 'Yes, I think it probably did.'

A major factor in the acceptance of divorce was that Fianna Fáil, the biggest party, had this time supported the referendum, urged on by their liberal deputy leader, Mary O'Rourke. O'Rourke knew her party had to move with the times, and accepts that perhaps Mary Robinson made it politically safer to be liberal. 'Maybe unconsciously she made it easier, less dangerous to address the liberal agenda. By being a good President, a solid person, she lent texture to the debate and maybe gave a respectability to the liberal agenda.'[2]

In the days when she clashed with cardinals, it is unlikely that Mary Robinson ever saw herself stepping into the vacuum left by the decline of the Catholic Church and other institutions, but that to a certain extent is what her presidency did. The erosion of the Church's moral authority had been accelerated by a series of sexual abuse scandals, just as accusations of corruption had undermined the authority of politicians. The presidency became a focus for unity, powerful only because of its moral authority. And Mary was scrupulously careful that no whisper of scandal or abuse of privilege would reduce that authority – that was why she finally sued Independent Newspapers.[3] Added to that was the fact that the presidency worked. It was one of the few democratic institutions which had become *more* responsive to the people, not less.

Local government representatives in Ireland are powerless, national governments are increasingly accountable to Brussels which would not necessarily be a problem if the European Union's own institutions were properly democratic, but, as the EU itself recognises, they are not. Ordinary people found that at least when you wrote to the President, you got an answer and often she came herself and she listened, even if she couldn't do very much.

Mary's popularity and the new vigour of the presidency met with frank hostility from Charles Haughey, but there was some small degree of institutional jealousy present with all other Taoisigh, as there was bound to be. Presidents and governments, after all, are political competitors. They compete for popular acclaim and international recognition, if not for actual political power. By expanding the presidency to its full potential, Mary was reclaiming territory ceded to other public figures in the field. The tensions that arose from time to time with governments and with the civil service were evidence that both the presidency and the executive were now alive and kicking.

It was with Haughey, however, that Mary fought and won her major territorial wars. She speaks of him as one warrior speaks of another. 'In a peculiar way, I always found Haughey a most interesting Taoiseach. Without being unfair to Albert, there was no comparison in the discussions we had.' She says it was 'highly interesting fencing with Haughey and not without humour, and he was a good acceptor of the situation and changer of the subject. We always left each other courteously. When he came up to the Áras the last time to resign, we had quite a long, and, I would say, a warm discussion,' she says. 'We said goodbye as two people who had a mutual respect for one another. He was complex and resourceful, always interesting though ruthless.' Charles Haughey's private view of Mary is known to be far less generous, but he has never cared to put it on the record.

Taoiseach Albert Reynolds, the man who ousted Haughey, was one of the Dáil's few businessmen. In his shrewd way, he judged that Mary was no great threat to him because she was dominating a different segment of the political market – one that Haughey coveted, but not Albert. Albert wanted to be in the backroom, striking political deals. He was perfectly happy for someone else to strut the world stage. Mary wasn't a competitor, she was a corporate ally, someone with whom he could strike up a strategic alliance. In business terms, he saw her as a resource to be used for the best interests of Ireland Inc. 'The increased presidential allowance was a small price to pay for the return we got on her,' he says. 'When I visited the US looking for trade and investment, I used to hear at first hand the impression she was creating. My view was that every time the President was on the international media, it had to be a plus. I had no ego problems.'

Mary appreciated the trust Albert put in her and found aspects of him fascinating. 'That gambler instinct, that going for broke. It was wonderfully successful in the bringing about of the ceasefire and devastatingly dangerous in the bringing down of the government.'

The events that led to the fall of that government marked the low point in Albert's and Mary's relationship. Albert appointed Attorney-General Harry Whelehan as president of the High Court and in protest the Labour party walked out of cabinet on 11 November 1994. When a controversy arose, a few days later, as to what Albert told the Dáil about the handling by Harry Whelehan's office of allegations of sexual abuse against a priest, Labour leader Dick Spring withdrew his support and Reynolds resigned on 17 November. On 16 December 1994, a new coalition came into office led by opposition leader John Bruton of Fine Gael and including Dick Spring's Labour party and Proinsias de Rossa's Democratic Left. By this time Harry Whelehan had resigned from his new post.

Mary Robinson felt strongly that judicial appointments should not be made in this way and had made clear her distaste for the whole charade when Albert had rushed Whelehan up to the Park on 11 November so she could sign his warrant of appointment.

Harry Whelehan and Mary are friends. 'We dine privately from time to time. But I was horrified at this manner of appointment to a senior judicial office. I was aware of the walk-out by Labour from the cabinet at the time and I thought: this is terrible! You did not appoint a president of the High Court in those kinds of circumstances. I had a sense that this was a very inappropriate attitude towards a serious and important institution of state. The president of the High Court is the second most senior judicial office. I was absolutely horrified.'

She is still indignant. 'There was a quick phonecall. Would I be available to appoint the president of the High Court? The protocol of a judicial appointment is that the judge and everybody else wears formal dress. Nothing like that happened. That's an irrelevant detail, but it shows how sudden and inappropriate the whole thing was.'

Mary was in casual clothes when the call came through and changed in such a hurry that it was only later she noticed she was wearing one black and one brown shoe. Government press secretary, the inimitable Sean Duignan, describes how the Taoiseach's party was received at the Áras that dark November evening. 'Áras only needs tapers and guttering torches to resemble some Hollywood horror set. Midnight in the crematorium, matched by her (President Robinson's) smile "like moonlight on a tombstone",' writes Duignan in his diary account of his two years as Albert's spokesman. '"Extraordinary haste," says Bride Rosney. The nightmare coming true. He's president of the High Court and we're all off to the boneyard.'[4]

Mary's thoughts were as grim as her smile that evening. She believed fiercely in the independence of the judiciary. 'If you have a kind of political ready-up as this was, it's playing with very serious issues. I was also conscious that Albert had that gambler's look on his face. You know . . . "There! I said I'd make you president of the High Court and I have." I possibly felt Harry had been unwise to let the matter go on for so long and that maybe a good month earlier, he should have taken himself out of the running.'

But Albert, she said, was a generous Taoiseach to deal with. He never thought she was stealing his thunder. 'He was a very pragmatic man, not someone you would have a deep philosophical discussion with on any issue I can think of. But he did talk a lot about the Northern Ireland situation once it had developed.' She saw the bringing about of the IRA ceasefire as one of Albert's great achievements. 'As a businessman, he had been prepared to broaden his contacts in a quite remarkable way. He was definitely prepared to see from a businessman's perspective the Unionist viewpoint. It was a peculiarly pragmatic and insightful way of looking at it.'

She was a nice woman, says Albert, and she was kind to him the day he went up to resign. 'She said she was sad at the way things had turned out, that we had worked well together. And we had.'

'I was conscious,' says Mary, 'that I had been very unreceptive when he had come up at the time of Harry Whelehan's appointment. I wanted him to realise that not only did I have sympathy for the mill he'd had to go through, but also a warmth for the personal relationship we'd had.'

John Bruton, she says, was 'the most frank of all the Taoisigh'. He had, after all, been to school at Clongowes with her brothers, and she had an open and easy relationship with him. 'He had the enthusiasm and commitment of someone who had unexpectedly become Taoiseach and was therefore more open about some of the difficulties he faced.' Bruton was her third Taoiseach, and Mary was conscious of being more secure and at home in her position at first than he was. Bruton in turn admired her, for her efforts to include those on the margins of society and for her understanding of Northern Unionists, though he never changed his view that she was wrong to shake Gerry Adams's hand before an IRA ceasefire.

'At an earlier stage, he had been very hurt not to be appointed to the Council of State,' she says. Opposition leaders were usually appointed to the Council, but Mary had chosen instead to appoint Fine Gael's liberal former TD, Monica Barnes. Then when Bruton became Taoiseach and automatically joined the Council, Mary asked Monica Barnes to make way for Fianna Fáil's deputy leader, Mary O'Rourke. Again John Bruton was 'less than happy', but Mary was consciously including someone who was not only the leading liberal on the Fianna Fáil benches and a woman, but also the sister of Brian Lenihan. Despite opposing Mary as presidential candidate, Lenihan had been gracious and totally supportive of her as President.

Nothing was ever said of her reasons for making the appointment, but Mary O'Rourke knew what was meant. 'I felt, and I wonder if she felt, since there were others she could have chosen, that she was making a gesture – not making amends, but equalling the situation.' It was an honour, said Mrs O'Rourke. 'And it was very welcome because, even in opposition, I now felt part of the state's business.'

Bertie Ahern knew Mary for only a few months as Taoiseach, but he'd had a good relationship with her since the Gerry Adams handshake and he always admired her for one particular gesture at the All-Ireland Hurling Final between Clare and Offaly in 1995. It had been a magnificent match, with the outcome unclear up to the last dramatic minute. Clare won for the first time since 1914 and the sheer emotion of that victory was there to be seen on every Co. Clare face. The face Bertie remembers is that of former President and Clareman, Paddy Hillery, sitting in the stands up behind Mary Robinson. 'Paddy Hillery was weeping. And she waved to him and brought him down to the front and he was crying.' Dr Hillery stood beside Mary as she presented the Cup to the winning team and he then shook hands with all the players. Clare had never won while he was President. 'He couldn't have come forward unless she brought him down. It was a really nice thing for her to do.'[5]

Reynolds, Bruton and Ahern had few personal tensions with Mary. Haughey and Tánaiste Dick Spring had many, because for both of them she was a direct competitor. With Haughey, it was mostly vanity – she dashed his dreams of being a presidential Taoiseach. With Dick, the Minister for Foreign Affairs, it was more substantial. A President developing a role on international issues and on Northern Ireland was always in danger of straying on to his patch. Their major stand-offs were all about Northern Ireland or the UN. She stole some of his thunder as the liberal, socially caring face in Irish public life, but he never complained about that. It was when she seemed to touch on his departmental territory that he objected.

The problem for politicians was that Mary was almost untouchable. She did her job superbly and was careful to defer to the government on political issues. But she also had the luxury of being aspirational, pointing up the need for change without ever having to deliver the political goods. Sometimes she did stray over the edge, but what were they to do? Her popularity was her strength. In most of her confrontations with government, the people sided with Mary. 'You don't argue,' says Albert Reynolds, 'with 92 per cent.'

Some tensions between the presidency and the politicians arose over the strict sense of protocol during Mary's presidency. The country's first liberal woman President was determined to maintain her authority by running a tight ship. Aides attest to this, including secretary Ann Lane. 'When Mary was under pressure, everyone was under pressure. She wasn't expecting it to be three-quarters right, but totally right.' In 1995, official guidelines by the Department of Foreign Affairs, to which Bride Rosney contributed, were sent to Ministers about their duties to the President when on visits abroad. They stressed the supportive nature of the accompanying Minister's role. They stated that Ministers should be ready to leave five minutes before the President came down from her room, and that they should not issue statements that might contradict hers. Some Ministers took offence.

The guidelines were simple common sense, according to Bride Rosney. 'She was very punctual. There were a couple of occasions when she was already in the lobby and the Ministers hadn't arrived down. It was embarrassing all round. If you are the President and you are abroad and the Foreign Minister and other dignitaries of the host country are present and your own Minister isn't there, it's very embarrassing,' says Bride.[6] Michael D. Higgins, whose long involvement with Central and South America made him an obvious Minister to accompany Mary on her trip to Argentina, says he didn't mind the new guidelines.

'Some people found them helpful. What I found crazy was the nonsense of the entourages,' he says. The President, he maintains, was overprotected by security provided by the host country, with as many as nine cars in a cavalcade and the accompanying Minister in car six. When she arrived somewhere, she was immediately surrounded, and Ministers had to battle their way through a crowd to get into the building. It was undignified for Ministers, he said. 'In Paris, people were hanging out of the windows of cars, screaming. I had made up my mind that I was never again going to find myself in the position where someone said: "We have to run, now," and I think to have an ambassador and a Minister trotting along the pavement trying to get into a building is an insult to the country – but that's not Mary's fault.'[7]

Higgins praised Mary's handling of meetings and press conferences abroad and said she was skilful and generous in deferring to accompanying Ministers. 'She made it easy for me and invited me into the discourse.'

Mary tried hard and usually succeeded in having a fruitful relationship with politicians and with the civil service. The Department of Foreign Affairs in particular worked very closely with her on her human rights missions, and on state visits.

Mary remembers with particular affection the Head of Protocol during much of her period as President: the imperturbable John Burke, later to be Irish Ambassador to Portugal. Mary's very active presidency involved an unprecedented number of visits abroad and of return visits to Ireland by foreign heads of state. Burke was the man who prepared the ground meticulously for all these events at home and abroad. When he died suddenly in November 1997, Mary, in an appreciation in the *Irish Times*, paid full tribute to the role he played in helping her do her job as President.

Civil servants like John Burke gave her the support she needed in making the presidency more active. Sometimes, however, it was the civil service who opposed any new departure. She remembers particularly the official nervousness with which she was given permission to be rapporteur-general at the Council of Europe's interregional preparatory conference for the Vienna Conference on Human Rights. They were worried that she might be seen to be getting involved in policy issues. 'I think there was more civil service and Foreign Affairs resistance than any political resistence. The politicians couldn't care less.'

In drawing up the report of the conference, she says, she was helped by Michael O'Boyle of the Council of Europe and held a number of bilateral meetings with key human rights experts from different regions including the Australian, Philip Alston, chairman of the UN Committee on Economic, Social and Cultural Rights. In the corridor outside, there were Irish civil servants from the Department of the Taoiseach, the Department of Foreign Affairs, the Permanent Mission to the UN, and the Irish embassy in Luxembourg. When Alston came out of the room, he was met by a bevy of anxious officials. 'What did she say? What happened?' They seemed to be terrified at how the report would go down in Strasbourg and when there was widespread applause they almost fainted with relief and began to clap, too.

Mary knew the limits on her powers as President, but she also knew the value of the expressed wishes of heads of state – particularly, as she saw on a state visit to France, when one of those heads of state was President François Mitterrand.

Mary is unashamedly romantic about France. It was where she first felt truly at home as a teenager, the country and the culture that opened her mind to the world of ideas and shaped her intellectually. It was where she had spent the beginning of her honeymoon.

French media interest in Mary was enormous. She was intellectual, a woman, a Francophile. Her obvious enthusiasm for everything French was disarming, and François Mitterrand laid on a magnificent welcome for her on her state visit in May 1992.

The student who had careered around Paris on the back of a motor-cycle, now made a triumphant entrance to the city, with a mounted guard of one hundred French soldiers before and behind her. She had to pinch herself to make sure it was really happening. 'Today,' she said incredulously to Bride, 'we stopped the traffic on the Champs-Elysées.'

At a meeting with President Mitterand at the Elysée, he spoke glowingly of Irish culture and the Celtic tradition, but Mary pointed out to him in French that he didn't know modern Irish culture, that Ireland was a young country and that the French view was very nostalgic. 'Mitterand turned and said to his Foreign Minister, "Il faut faire quelque chose," and we began to talk about the possibility of an exhibition. David Andrews was equally enthusiastic.' When Mitterand proposed the organising of an extended season of contemporary Irish arts and culture in France, she immediately confirmed it in writing, as did he, and she reopened the matter in discussions with his successor, Jacques Chirac.

It now gained momentum. Both governments made significant contributions to it, the Irish government for their part dedicating one and a half million pounds to it. The result was a celebration of the arts which ran from April to July 1996, called *L'Imaginaire Irlandais*. It comprised concerts, recitals, readings, exhibitions. In May Mary and President Chirac performed the official launch of the major contemporary art exhibition at the École Des Beaux Arts in Paris, and of the Abbey Theatre's production in the Théatre de L'Odéon of Frank McGuinness's play *Observe the Sons of Ulster Marching towards the Somme*.

It was in France, above all, that Mary wanted recognition of the new renaissance in the arts in Ireland. Doireann Ní Bhriain, the Irish Commissioner and organiser of *L'Imaginaire*, says it is a measure of her confidence in the quality of Irish writers, artists and musicians that she wanted to expose them to the most critical public in the world. It worked, says Ní Bhriain, and the long-term effect was as important as the short-term. 'It was of huge benefit to Irish artists who went over, a lot of them taking up residencies in cultural establishments in France. Networks were established which still exist.'[8]

Mary's strategic sense never deserted her during the presidency. All round her she could see how fast Ireland was changing. With Church influence fading, Ireland was no longer Catholic in the way it had been. With the development of the peace process in Northern Ireland, Ireland was no longer aggressively nationalist in the way it had been. The two traditions which had defined Ireland for so long were fading and here was a chance for generous new thinking.

The decline of the Catholic Church in Ireland did not have to mean that there was now no ethical code, no spirituality. Those who criticised Mary as 'immoral' during her confrontations with the Catholic Church on social issues would have been surprised to find her leading the search for an international moral and ethical code. When Mary went to visit the Pope in 1997, she saw him as a crucially important religious and spiritual leader but not the only one who mattered. 'The importance to me is a spirituality which deepens and enhances and changes our relationships as human beings. I expressed that through being a Catholic, but I have very little sense, which I know the Pope has, that Catholicism is the true belief and that others aren't. So when I meet the Dalai Lama I have genuinely as much respect for his spirituality and the fact that he has reached an extraordinary stage of being up in the highest levels of mind and morality. And that has made me both value the role of religions, and be relaxed about a sense that there are many routes to a higher spirituality. But it is that spiritual, ethical connection that makes all the sense out of humanitarian and human rights concerns.'

She spoke to the Pope about the priests and nuns in Ireland who had become a radical force for the poor and for a fairer society. That commitment to justice, for her, is the basis for her own spirituality. Mary has been in touch with religious leaders all over the world about the development of a universally acceptable ethical code, and has been aware of the work on this subject by the Swiss theologian and rebel Catholic, Hans Kung, who visited her at the Áras.

'One of the areas I am very interested in, and have written on and talked to Hans Kung about, is trying to develop the concept of a global ethic, drawing on the religions of the world and on humanism – the ethical strands and connections through history – in order to relate them to the consumer-driven, short-term, selfish global world. Without that ethical dimension we are greatly impoverished,' she says.

She has contributed to a series of essays Kung produced on the global ethic. It was a theme she returned to again and again as President and the London *Independent* in June 1996 led its front page with her plea: 'We need a global ethic.' She told the *Independent*: 'In a world that seems to have lost all spiritual cohesiveness, many people feel we need an ethical basis that values religions, that values a secular tradition and is thoughtful about others.'[9]

Mary's thinking on Northern Ireland has been prescient. In resigning over the Anglo-Irish Agreement, she rightly saw that Unionists had to be included as they now have been in the Good Friday Agreement. In her controversial visit to West Belfast, she foresaw that in order to bring peace one had to reach out to all groups in the North. But now she wanted nationalists to start thinking the unthinkable, to ask how they would feel if the essence of their nationalism – the total break with Britain – was diluted, just as they expected Unionists to dilute their position – the total break with the Republic. It was her last major comment on Northern Ireland, delivered to the Merriman Summer School on 22 August 1997, weeks before she resigned as President.

Once before, when speaking of Unionist insecurity about proposed all-Ireland institutions, she had asked Southerners how they would feel if they were faced with rejoining the Commonwealth.[10] She put that challenge again. 'If somebody posed the question: "Should Ireland rejoin the Commonwealth?", just think of your reaction. It is a good way of assessing the insecurities we still have after seventy-five years,' she said. 'I pose it so that each of you can think of your reaction and understand the insecurity and the emotion that there is underneath the surface.'[11]

The indignant reaction from some of her audience indicated that there was indeed insecurity and emotion beneath the surface. The idea was considered early on and briefly at the recent Northern Ireland negotiations, according to Irish government sources, but was regarded as a proposal for the longer-term.

As President, Mary made Irishwomen visible. Everywhere she went she would ask why there were not more women on the platform, on the committee, in the executive group. It was a question women began to ask and to answer. A small indication of how she changed public attitudes was that four of the five candidates in the election to choose her successor were women. Before Mary Robinson there had never been a woman presidential candidate.

Mary decided to leave because she knew she couldn't remain a fresh voice for another seven years. 'If it had been for another three years, I would have gone forward again', she says.

'I'm not sure whether or not I was influential in her decision not to run again,' says Nick. 'The cautious thing again! My view was, get out while you're ahead. I was aware of other political leaders seeming to pass their sell-by date.' Mary decided to resign and then announced it. Subsequently she told Taoiseach John Bruton she was interested in the Commissioner for Human Rights job which had been made vacant by the sudden return to Ecuadorean politics of her predecessor, José Ayala-Lasso. Tánaiste Dick Spring personally lobbied the US President as did Taoiseach John Bruton. 'We put a whole campaign in place and put top diplomats on to it to lobby in every capital where we could usefully do so on her behalf,' says Bruton.[12] She appreciated it very much. 'I had a lot of discussion with her on it and briefed her on what was being done,' says Bruton.

Mary completed her final official engagement as President of Ireland on 12 September 1997. Like her first, it was to do with the homeless – she opened a housing project for Focus Ireland and her friend, Sister Stanislaus Kennedy. She finished simply with the Irish words: 'Sin é.' ('That's it.')

That was it for Peter Ryan, to whom Mary had become particularly close, who had worked loyally for her through a turbulent presidency he could never have expected, and who had gone faithfully with her on foreign trips despite his fear of flying. Peter returned to the Taoiseach's office.

That was it for Ann Lane, Mary's secretary for twenty-eight years. Mary could not bring her to Geneva and Ann had in any case decided she would not have stayed on at the Áras. 'I found it isolating,' she said. Ann now works as personal assistant to Attorney-General, David Byrne.

That was it for Laura Donegan, Mary's housekeeper whom Mary and Nick encouraged to set up in a florists' business – Laura used flowers from the Áras's own gardens to do most of the flower arrangements during the presidency.

The only staff concession the UN had made was for Bride, who would go to Geneva on a year's contract. Having helped Mary into and through the presidency, Bride now had to help her out of it.

It wasn't easy. Early on at the UN, Bride remembers, they went to New York. 'For the previous seven years, every time we went to New York there were people everywhere to support the President.' This time, they had to fend for themselves. They came out of their hotel and hailed a cab. 'She didn't even know where she was going,' says Bride. 'We got into a lift and she just stood there. God forbid that she'd press a button! So I just stood there and we just stood there and nothing happened and I said. "Press the button!" Then we got out of the lift and she follows the person in front of her because that's what she's done for the last seven years!' Bride shakes her head. 'She's been institutionalised. Like a prisoner. You know, the guest of the nation.'

Bride detached herself little by little as Mary found her feet in Geneva. Mary had a hard beginning, catapulted straight from work and emotional goodbyes in Dublin. 'After the last emotional event with Sister Stan at the housing project, the signing of my resignation, the short speech, the getting into the plane, I was absolutely exhausted,' she says. She hadn't yet seen her new house. Her son Aubrey had started at school in Geneva a week earlier.

'And then I had to start on a Monday morning in an absolutely utterly demanding, intensely difficult job in an intensely difficult context with a staff whose morale was at rock bottom, some of whom felt they had been abandoned by Ayala-Lasso who had left the previous March, who were part of a structure that had been an office of the High Commissioner for Human Rights, and a Centre for Human Rights, with a High Commissioner who didn't speak to the Director of the Centre and with the staff divided between them!' Mary had a job on her hands. The position of High Commissioner for Human Rights had been created only in 1993. Relations between Mary's predecessor and his second-in-command, the Director of the Centre for Human Rights were, it was said, strained to the point of silence.

Mary would have to give new leadership to the staff of about 400, and turn the tide with a job budget of $22.5 million from the UN, and up to $50 million which comes from voluntary sources and could therefore be strategically withheld by donors who might not want too vigorous a human rights policy. The High Commissioner's office had a poor reputation. Mary's predecessor had been criticised severely by Amnesty International for failing to deliver.

'On top of all that,' says Mary, 'I had to learn to work within the UN system which is terribly bureaucratic. For the first couple of months I wasn't helped by the fact that there were barriers to doing everything and nobody seemed to be talking values. Here was this UN. What was it about? That's why I said in a speech at Oxford in November that the UN seemed to have lost the plot,' she says.

'There were huge expectations when I arrived and a sense of disappointment when I didn't wave a magic wand. I suffered an enormous sense of culture shock for a couple of months because every time I said I have a problem, this is what we'll do, they'd say, "No, you can't do that. You can't bring new people in. You can't have this. You can't change that. You can't. You can't. You can't."'

New Secretary-General Kofi Annan, she says, made all the difference. 'It was Kofi Annan in his reform package who said human rights must be mainstreamed. He gave the leadership. He didn't just back me. He promoted actively what I was doing and it worked dramatically.'

By March, Mary had established a sense of teamwork and her whole outlook had changed. She no longer looked gaunt, preoccupied, as she had in the first three months. 'I feel now that along with my colleagues I can make a difference. That's why the adrenalin is flowing and I'm not wasting my time.' That same month, she held a special forum in Geneva where all the UN agencies discussed the mainstreaming of human rights in the UN. It was addressed by Kofi Annan himself and by Czech President Vaclac Hável. It was getting to the heart of the problem, making sure that human rights was now accepted as a major focus and an integral part of the UN's work.

Mary knows that a lot of her energies in this new job will go into persuading people and that the new warm person who blossomed during the presidency will be able to do that. 'I got more than I gave by coming out of my shell. I won't go back,' she says. But she understands, too, that the ready welcome she got as President of Ireland won't always be extended to a Human Rights Commissioner who has to speak out against injustice. She's already braved the wrath of Algeria and Rwanda. But she's long known the price of speaking out. As long as you show you care, she says, you can afford to be awkward.

'I was an awkward voice before becoming President of Ireland. Maybe I'm going back to being an awkward voice.'

NOTES

CHAPTER 1

1 On 27 May 1993.
2 Interview with Mary Robinson. This book is based primarily on a long series of exclusive interviews by the authors with Mary Robinson. Her voice is clearly identified in the text, thus it has not been necessary to cite each of the hundreds of direct quotations from the subject in the end notes.
3 Tony Donohoe, 'The Crossmolina Conspiracy 1880 to 1884', *Blian Iris, The North Mayo Historical Journal*, Vol. 1., No 3, (1985), pp. 18–21.
4 Interview with Dr Aubrey Bourke.
5 The Literary and Historical Society, the premier debating society in UCD.
6 Interview with the late Mr Bertie O'Donnell.
7 Interview with Henry Bourke.
8 Interview with Adrian Bourke.
9 Interview with Mother Stephenson, one of Mary's key teachers at Mount Anville.

CHAPTER 2

1 An Irish Catholic temperance organisation.
2 An introductory French textbook used in Irish schools of the 1950s and 1960s.

CHAPTER 3

1 Interview with Ciaran McGonigal.
2 J.H. Whyte (quoting Bishop Browne of Galway), *Church and State in Modern Ireland*, 2nd edition, (Gill & Macmillan, Dublin, 1980), p. 258.
3 Ibid. p. 312.
4 Ibid. p. 307.
5 Interview with Dr Bourke.
6 Interview with Senator Shane Ross.
7 Interview with Malcolm Argyle, Veterinary Surgeon.
8 Interview with Eavan Boland.
9 Interview with Senator David Norris.
10 Interview with Ruth Buchanan.
11 Interview with Dr Bourke.
12 Interview with Mother Stephenson.
13 Mary Bourke, 'Law and Morality,' unpublished paper, read at the Inaugural Meeting of the Dublin University Law Society, February 1967.
14 Ibid.

CHAPTER 4

1 *Keesing's Contemporary Archives*, Vol. xvii, (London, 1969–70), p. 2373
2 Senate Election 1969, *Election Address of Mary T.W. Bourke to the Electors of Dublin University*, p. 2.
3 Ibid. pp. 2, 4–5.
4 Jonathan Bardon, *A History of Ulster*, (The Blackstaff Press, Belfast, 1992), p. 669.

CHAPTER 5

1 Interview with Howard Robinson.
2 Interview with Adrian Bourke.
3 Interview with Henry Bourke.
4 Interview with Nick Robinson.
5 Jonathan Bardon and Stephen Conlin, *One Thousand Years of Wood Quay*, (Blackstaff Press, Belfast, 1984), p. 30.
6 Olivia O'Leary, *Irish Times*, 25 September 1978.
7 Attorney-General (Martin) v Dublin Corporation, High Court Unreported, 12 February 1979; Supreme Court Unreported, 7 March

1979; [1983] IRLM 254; Application No.8569/79 European Commission of Human Rights.

8 Olivia O'Leary, *Irish Times*, 25 September 1978

9 Ibid.

10 Interview with Dr Pat Wallace, Director of the National Museum.

11 Webb v Ireland [1988] IR 353; [1988] IRLM 565.

12 Interview with Bride Rosney, Special Adviser to the President.

CHAPTER 6

1 J.H. Whyte, op.cit. p. 257.

2 Personal communication to one of the authors.

3 Michael Solomons, *Pro Life? The Irish Question*, (Lilliput Press, Dublin, 1992), p. 12.

4 Ibid. p. 10.

5 Ibid. p. 12.

6 Interview with Mary Maher, *Irish Times* journalist and a founder member of the Irish Women's Liberation Movement (IWLM).

7 John Horgan, *Mary Robinson – An Independent Voice*, (The O'Brien Press, Dublin, 1997), p. 35.

8 Interview with Dr Garret FitzGerald, former Taoiseach and Leader of Fine Gael.

9 *The Furrow*, March, 1971, pp. 244–5.

10 *Irish Times*, 29 March 1971

11 Ibid.

12 John Cooney, *Magill*, November 1997, p. 48.

13 As reported to the authors.

14 June Levine, *Sisters*, (Ward River Press, Dublin, 1982), pp. 174–182.

15 Senate Debates, 14 November 1973, cols. 3–12.

16 Senate Debates, 20–21 February 1974, cols. 205–406.

17 J.J. Lee, *Ireland 1912–1985*, (Cambridge University Press, 1989), p. 479.

18 Ibid. p. 498.

19 Irish Family Planning Association v Ryan (1979) IR 295.

20 Interview with Maura O'Dea, founder of Cherish.

21 Michael Viney, 'No Birthright', *Irish Times*, Dublin, 1964 (series).

22 Ibid.

23 Interview with Anna Lee, social worker.

24 ECHR, Case of Johnston & Others v Ireland, decision 1986, Series A No. 112.

25 Keegan v Ireland, ECHR Reports (18) 1994. Mary Robinson being President at this time could not herself take this case in Strasbourg. It was completed by Dervla Browne, Junior Counsel.

26 Eileen Conway, unpublished PhD thesis UCD, in preparation.

27 Fr Colm Kilcoyne, RTE, Lenten Series, *What Really Matters*, 20 February 1997.

CHAPTER 7

1 Interview with Nell McCafferty.

2 Irish Women's Liberation Movement, 'Chains or Change', pamphlet, 1971, 32 pages.

3 Pat Brennan, *Magill*, April, 1979.

4 Interview with Máirín de Burca.

5 de Burca v Attorney General [1976] IR 38.

6 *Irish Times*, 10 May 1970.

7 Murphy v Attorney General [1982] IR 241.

8 Hyland v Minister for Social Welfare [1989] IR 624; [1989] IRLM 196; [1990] IRLM 213.

9 Murphy v an Bord Telecom Éireann [1986] IRLM 483; [1989] IRLM 53; [1988] CMLR 879; [1988] ECR 673.

10 Interview with Minister Mary O'Rourke, TD.

11 Mary T.W. Bourke, *Election Address*, 1969, op.cit. p. 5.

12 Lorna Siggins, *Mary Robinson, The Woman Who Took Power in the Park*, (Mainstream Publishing, Edinburgh, 1997), p. 95.

CHAPTER 8

1 Interview with Dick Spring, TD, former leader of the Labour party.

2 Ibid.

3 Interview with Ruairi Quinn, TD, current leader of the Labour party.

4 Interview with Brendan Halligan, former general secretary of the Labour party.

5 Interview with Dr Garret FitzGerald.

6 Interview with Ruairi Quinn.

7 *Irish Times*, 26 March 1982.

8 Interview with Michael D. Higgins, TD.

9 Interview with Brendan Halligan.

10 Twelve candidates stood for the three Trinity seats in the Senate in 1981. Conor Cruise O'Brien topped the poll with 1,245 votes; Trevor West was 2nd with 1,057 votes; Mary Robinson 3rd with 900 votes. In 1973, she had topped the Trinity poll with 1,472 votes.

11 Interview with Mervyn Ennis, social worker.

12 Mc Donald v Feely, City and County Manager, unreported judgement, Supreme Court, 23 July 1980, (196–1980).

13 Housing Act, 1988, s13.

CHAPTER 9

1 Billy Hutchinson of the Progressive Unionist party (PUP), on the *Rodney Rice Saturday View*, RTE, 12 April 1998.

2 Purcell & Others v Ireland, Application No. 15404/89, *Year Book of the European Convention on Human Rights*, (Kluwer Academic Publishers, The Netherlands), pp. 90–102.

3 Senate Debates, 10 August 1971, col.72.

4 Senate Election 1973, *Election Address of Mary T.W. Robinson*, pp. 4–5.

5 Senate Election 1977, *Election Address of Mary T.W. Robinson*, p. 4.

6 *New Ireland Forum Proceedings*, 12, (Stationery Office, Dublin, 1984). Opening Statement from Dr Cathal Daly, 9 February 1984, p. 2.

7 Ibid. p. 21.

8 Ibid. p. 19.

9 Ibid. p. 32.

10 Interview with Dick Spring.

11 *New Ireland Forum Report*, (Stationery Office, Dublin, 1984), p. 29.

CHAPTER 10

1 Attorney General v X & Others, IR [1992] 1. Section 58 of the Offences against the Person Act, 1861, was the original legislation outlawing abortion in Ireland.

2 Interview with Ed Mulhall, *Irish Times*, 24 November 1977.

3 *Irish Independent*, 15 August 1983.

4 *Irish Times*, 29 March 1971.

5 The Pro-Life Amendment Campaign was launched on 27 April 1981.

6 The 8th Amendment to the Constitution (art. 40.3.3)

7 Senate Debates 4 May 1983, cols. 509–67. Her contribution to this

debate continued on 27 May 1983, cols. 1095–1185 and on 26 May 1983, cols. 1231–1331.

8 Senate Debates 4 May 1983, cols. 543–5.

9 Ibid. col. 559.

10 Senate Debates, 25 May 1983, col. 1176–7.

11 Ibid. col. 1182

12 Ibid. col. 1120.

13 John Horgan, op.cit. p. 104.

14 SPUC v Grogan [1989] IR 753; [1990] ILRM 350; [1992] IRLM 461.

15 Judgement of Mr Justice Hamilton, President of the High Court, 19 December 1986, cited in ECHR, Open Door Counselling and Dublin Well Woman Centre v Ireland, judgement of 29 October 1992, Series A, no 246–A.

16 Ibid. As Mary Robinson had become President, this case was completed by Adrian Hardiman SC and Brian Murray JC, instructed by Barbara Hussey, solicitor.

17 *Irish Times*, 20 February 1992.

18 X case, op.cit.

19 12th Amendment to the Constitution reads: 'It shall be unlawful to terminate the life of an unborn unless such termination is necessary to save the life, as distinct from the health, of the mother where there is an illness or disorder of the mother giving rise to a real and substantial risk to her life, not being a risk of self destruction.' 13th Amendment to the Constitution reads: 'This section shall not limit freedom to travel between the State and another state.' 14th Amendment to the Constitution reads: 'This subsection shall not limit freedom to obtain or make available in the State, subject to such conditions as may be laid down by law, information relating to services lawfully available in another state.'

20 Interview with Clara Clark.

21 ECHR, Johnston & Others v Ireland, decision of 23 January 1986, Series A no. 112.

22 Personal communication from the Central Statistics Office.

CHAPTER 11

1 Criminal Law (Sexual Offences) Act, 1993.

2 Norris v Attorney-General & Ireland [1984] IR 36; judgement of 26 October 1988, Series A no.142.

3 Offences against the Person Act, 1861, ss 61 & 62.

4 Interview with Ger Philpott.

5 As summarised in Norris v Attorney-General, op.cit.

6 Luke J. Clements, *European Human Rights*, (Sweet and Maxwell, London, 1994), 1–11; 104–6.

7 Interview with Lord Lester of Herne Hill, QC.

8 ECHR, Airey v Ireland, judgement 9 October 1979, Series A, no 32.

9 Norris v Attorney-General, op.cit.

10 Mr Justice Rory O'Hanlon, *Irish Times*, 20 May 1998.

11 Interview with Paddy MacEntee, SC.

CHAPTER 12

1 The first President of Ireland, the scholar, Dr Douglas Hyde, was a non-party agreed nominee. The five presidents between him and Mary Robinson: Sean T. O'Kelly, Eamonn de Valera, Erskine Childers, Cearbhall O'Dalaigh and Patrick Hillery, were all Fianna Fáil nominees.

2 Mary Robinson was nominated by twenty members of the Labour party, seven members of the Workers' party and two Independent members of the Oireachtas, Senators David Norris and Brendan Ryan.

3 Since Patrick McCartan in 1945 no one had ever successfully gone the route that Dana, Rosemary Scallon and Derek Nally went in 1997, i.e. getting four county councils to nominate them.

4 Interview with Dick Spring.

5 Interview with Eoghan Harris.

6 Harris document as quoted in Emily O'Reilly, *Candidate; The Truth behind the Presidential Campaign*, (Attic press, Dublin, 1991), pp. 19–56.

7 Interview with Anne O'Donnell.

8 Interview with Mairin de Burca.

9 Interview with Brenda O'Hanlon.

10 Interview with Cecily McMenamin.

11 Gay Byrne Show, RTE, 28 September 1990.

12 *Sunday Tribune*, 4 November 1990.

13 *The Star*, 2 October 1990.

14 *Today Tonight* RTE 1, 1 November 1990.

15 Seamus Brennan, Fianna Fáil Minister for Tourism and Transport, 5 November 1990.
16 *Hot Press*, 4 October 1990.
17 As quoted from Wexford People, November 1990, in *Mary Robinson – a president with a purpose* by Fergus Finlay (O'Brien Press, 1990), p. 129.
18 Interview with Bertie Ahern TD, now An Taoiseach.
19 *Rodney Rice Saturday View*, RTE, 3 November 1990.
20 Interview with Alan Dukes, TD, former leader of Fine Gael.
21 Interview with Albert Reynolds, TD, former Taoiseach.

CHAPTER 13

1 Mary Robinson, Inauguration speech.
2 Early in Mary 1970, when the troubles in Northern Ireland were intense, the Taoiseach, Jack Lynch, sacked two of his Ministers, Charles Haughey and Neil Blaney. On 28 May they were arrested and charged with conspiracy to import arms and ammunition. Both men were subsequently acquitted by the courts, but the crisis split the Fianna Fáil party.
3 *Scrap Saturday*, RTE Radio 1, 26 January 1991.
4 Interview with Kevin O'Driscoll, trade union official and former programme manager in the Department of Arts, Culture and the Gaeltacht.
5 The McCracken Tribunal was set up in 1997 to enquire into payments made to politicians or to political parties by Mr Ben Dunne or Dunnes Holding Company between 1986 and 1996.
6 Interview with Ruairi Quinn.

CHAPTER 14

1 Letter to President Robinson from Michael Hare Duke, Bishop of St Andrews, 11 January 1991 and from Archbishop Donald Caird of Dublin, 9 January 1991.
2 Letter in May 1991 from Joe McNulty, secretary of Bundoran Waterworld Ltd.
3 Letter from President's office confirming that the invitation had been withdrawn for the reasons stated.

4 Letter from President's office confirming her withdrawal for reasons stated.

5 *Sunday Tribune*, 4 November 1990.

6 'You'll be speaking Irish?'

7 Interview with Martin Dully, former head of Bord Fáilte, the Irish Tourist Board.

8 Memo from cabinet office to President's office.

9 Senate Debates, 18 January 1989, cols. 1698–1704.

CHAPTER 15

1 Figures in this paragraph supplied by Department of Finance, July 1998.

2 The President's salary is linked to that of the Chief Justice, plus 10 per cent. It was £79,592 per annum at the start of Mary Robinson's presidency and £115,276 per annum when she left office. Her pension is £56,000 (half her salary), payable immediately. Her UN salary and living allowance is 235,000 Swiss francs or about £110,000 Irish.

3 Interview with Chris McCarthy.

4 Interview with Jim Rodgers.

5 Interview with Margaret McLaughlin.

6 Interview with Rose Fellowes.

7 She had proposed to deal with the same subject in the Dimbleby lecture that Charles Haughey refused to let her make in the UK. To avoid similar difficulties, the UK-based Allen Lane Foundation moved the venue to Ireland.

8 Interview with Father Sean Healy.

9 Interview with John Lonergan, Governor of Mountjoy Prison.

10 Poem quoted by kind permission of Chris McCarthy.

CHAPTER 16

1 Article 2 of the Constitution then claimed that Northern Ireland was part of the national territory of Ireland. That has since been amended by referendum on 22 May, 1998, to become an aspiration to unity rather than a territorial claim and will come into effect at the same time as the full Good Friday Agreement (1998).

2 Living standards in Britain were almost twice those in Ireland in the

1960s, but by 1991 the gap was closing rapidly and in 1996, Irish living standards outstripped Britain's for the first time, Paul Tansey, *Ireland at Work*, (Oak Tree Press, Dublin, 1998), Table 1.8, p. 31.

3 The Irish Constitution, Article 4, provides that the name of the state is 'Ireland' in English and 'Eire' in Irish. The Republic of Ireland Act, 1948, describes the state as 'The Republic of Ireland' but common official usage is 'Ireland'.

4 Interview with Colin Parry.

5 Memo from cabinet office to President's office, 15 February 1993.

6 Interview with Albert Reynolds.

7 *Irish Independent*, 3 June 1995.

8 Interview with Major Grogan, British Legion, Republic of Ireland Head Office.

9 *Irish Times*, 11 November 1980.

10 Interview with Kevin Myers.

11 Excerpt from *The Redress of Poetry*, by Seamus Heaney (Faber and Faber, 1995), p. 202, quoted by kind permission of Faber and Faber.

12 Interview with An Taoiseach, Bertie Ahern TD.

CHAPTER 17

1 As reported to the authors.

2 Five were killed in Guilford, 5 October 1974; two in Woolwich, 7 November 1974; twenty-one in Birmingham, 21 November 1974, McKee and Franey, *Time Bomb*, (Bloomsbury, London, 1988), pp. xiii–xiv.

3 Interview with Pat O'Neill of the Irish Community Forum, Birmingham.

4 Paul Tansey, *Making the Irish Labour Market Work*, (Gill and Macmillan, Dublin, 1991), p. 7.

5 Interview with Michael Forde, Irish World Heritage Centre, Manchester.

6 Patrick J. Bracken, Liam Greenslade, Barney Griffin, Marcelino Smyth, 'Mental Health and Ethnicity: an Irish Dimension', *British Journal of Psychiatry*, 172, 1998, pp. 103–5.

7 Donall McAmhlaigh, author of *Dialann Deoraí* (*An Irish Navvy*), (An Clochomhar, Dublin, 1960), was a regular columnist in the *Irish Times* during the 1970s. Patrick MacGill, author of *Moleskin Joe*, (Caliban Books, London, 1983).

8 Frank Millar, *Irish Times*, 8 July 1996.

9 Interview with Sister Elizabeth Cahill, Irish Community Care, Manchester.

10 London *Independent*, 4 June 1996.

11 Quoted in John Horgan, op.cit. pp. 176–7.

12 Interview with Bertie Ahern.

13 Interview with Alan Dukes.

14 Paul Byrne, 'Emigration: The Great Non-Issue', *The Furrow*, April, 1995, p. 227.

15 *Irish Times*, 13 June 1998.

16 Interview with Dr Mary Hickman, Director of the Irish Studies Programme, University of North London.

17 Kevin Cullen, *Boston Globe*, 21 October 1991.

18 Interview with Lena Deevy, Director of the Irish Immigration Centre, Boston.

19 Kevin Cullen, *Boston Globe*, 4 October 1996.

20 Boyle and O'Grada, as quoted in Cormac O'Grada, *Ireland a New Economic History, 1780–1939*, (Clarendon Press, Oxford, 1994), p. 179, confirm this view.

21 Cecil Woodham Smith, *The Great Hunger*, (Four Square Books), pp. 321–2.

22 Speech at Grosse Ile, Quebec, Canada, 20 August 1994.

CHAPTER 18

1 Interview with Inez McCormack, regional Secretary of UNISON, a public sector union.

2 Interview with Eileen Howell, Director of the Falls Community Centre.

3 Interview with Gerry Adams, President of Sinn Féin.

4 Interview with Albert Reynolds.

5 Interview with Dick Spring.

6 Sean Duignan, *One Spin of the Merry Go Round*, (Blackwater Press, 1997), p. 107.

7 Interview with Bertie Ahern.

8 *Irish Independent*, 26 June 1993.

9 Memo from cabinet office to President's office re British Ambassador's visit, 11 June 1993.

10 Memo from cabinet office to President's office re 25 June visit,

initiated by British Ambassador to present his government's concerns and proposals.

11 Charlie Bird interview with Dick Spring in his documentary *President – Mary Robinson 1990–1997*, RTE, 8 October 1997.

12 *The Newsletter*, 21 September 1993.

CHAPTER 19

1 Interview with Dick Spring, op.cit.

2 Sean Duignan, op.cit. p. 107.

3 Joe Carroll, *Irish Times*, 28 February 1995.

4 Chris Glennon, *Irish Independent*, April 1995.

CHAPTER 20

1 Interview with Bride Rosney.

2 Interview with Eric Luke, *Irish Times* photographer.

3 Interview with Cecily McMenamin.

4 Martha Duffy, *Time Magazine*, 29 June 1992.

5 Anthony Lewis, *New York Times*, reprinted in *Irish Times*, 1993.

6 *Vanity Fair*, July 1992,

7 Quoted in Martha Duffy, op.cit.

8 Jack O'Sullivan, London *Independent*, 4 June 1996.

9 Interview with Conor Brady, Editor, *Irish Times*.

10 Interview with Ed Mulhall, Director of News, RTE.

11 Eamon Dunphy, *Sunday Independent*, 20 June 1993.

12 Interview with Aengus Fanning, Editor, *Sunday Independent*.

13 Tom Brady, *Irish Independent*, 15 June 1994.

14 Liam Deegan letter, *Irish Independent*, 23 June 1994.

15 Conor O'Clery, *Irish Times*, 23 March 1995.

16 Interview with Conor O'Clery, *Irish Times*, Foreign Correspondent.

17 *Irish Times*, 29 March 1995.

18 *Irish Times*, 27 March 1995.

19 *Irish Times*, editorial, 1 April 1995.

CHAPTER 21

1 Mary Robinson, *A Voice for Somalia*, (The O'Brien Press, Dublin, 1992), pp. 94–5.

2 Interview with John O'Shea, Director of GOAL.

3 Interview with Father Aengus Finucane.

4 Mary Robinson, op.cit. p. 20.

5 Ibid. p. 17.

6 Interview with Bride Rosney.

7 Mary Robinson, op.cit. p. 82.

8 Interview with Justin Kilcullen, Director of Trócaire.

9 Ed O'Loughlin, *Irish Times*, 15 October 1994.

10 Olivia O'Leary, *Sunday Tribune*, 13 November 1994.

11 *Irish Times*, 14 October 1995.

12 Ibid.

13 Churchill Lecture to the English Speaking Union, 'Humanitarian Crises: Prevention, Response and Rehabilitation, The Guildhall, London, 3 December 1996.

14 *For the Commander of the Eliza* by Seamus Heaney (from *Death of a Naturalist*, Faber and Faber, 1966 page 21), quoted by kind permission of Faber and Faber.

15 Mary Robinson's Address to the Irish Times/Harvard Colloquium: 'We the Peoples of the United Nations . . . renewing that determination', *Irish Times*, 14 March 1994.

16 Mary Robinson's Address to the Special Commemorative Meeting of the General Assembly at the 50th Anniversary of the United Nations, 22 October 1995.

17 Address to the US Foreign Policy Association in New York, 11 June 1996.

18 Acceptance speech on receiving the Global Leadership Award of the UN Association of New York, *Irish Times*, 9 October 1996.

CHAPTER 22

1 Nicholas K. Robinson, *Edmund Burke, A Life in Caricature*, (Yale University Press, New Haven & London, 1996).

2 An Taisce is the Irish word for treasure chest.

3 An Taisce Report, *Heritage At Risk*, Dublin, 1977.

4 Interview with Dr Edward McParland, Trinity College, Dublin.

5 *Drawings from the Irish Architectural Archive*, Introduction by Nicholas Robinson, (Irish Architectural Archive, Dublin, 1993).

6 The Knight of Glin, David J. Griffin, Nicholas K. Robinson, *Vanishing Country Houses of Ireland*, (Irish Architectural Archive & The Georgian Society, Dublin, 1988).

7 Sean O'Reilly and Nicholas K. Robinson, *New Lease of Life – The Law Society's Building at Blackhall Place,* (Irish Architectural Archive and The Incorporated Law Society of Ireland, Dublin, 1990).

8 Interview with Nick Robinson.

9 Enda McDonagh, *Faith in Fragments*, (Columba Press, Dublin, 1996), p. 46.

10 Interview with Henry Bourke.

CHAPTER 23

1 IMS/Independent Newspapers Polls, 19 June 1991 and 12 April 1995.

2 Interview with Mary O'Rourke, TD, Minister for Public Enterprise.

3 See Chapter 20.

4 Sean Duignan, op.cit., p. 155.

5 Interview with Bertie Ahern.

6 Interview with Bride Rosney.

7 Interview with Michael D. Higgins.

8 Interview with Doireann Ni Bhrian, organiser of *L'Imaginaire Irlandais.*

9 London *Independent*, 4 June 1996.

10 Joe Carroll, *Irish Times*, 28 February 1995.

11 Frank Connolly, *Sunday Business Post*, 31 August 1997.

12 Interview with John Bruton, leader of Fine Gael and former Taoiseach.

CHRONOLOGY

21 May 1944	Mary Bourke born in Ballina, County Mayo.
1949–54	Attends a private junior school, Miss Ruddy's, in Ballina, with her brothers.
1954–61	Convent of the Sacred Heart, Mount Anville, Dundrum, Co. Dublin.
September 1961–June 1962	Attends finishing school in Paris.
October 1963–September 1967	Trinity College Dublin and the King's Inns: BA Moderatorship in Legal Science, first class honours, LLB, first class honours, Honourable Society of King's Inns, Dublin, Degree, Barrister at Law, first class honours.

Harvard University

1967	Fellowship to the Law School
1967–8	LLM first class honours.
Autumn 1968	Joins the Law Library in the Four Courts, Dublin, and becomes a junior barrister on the western circuit.
October 1968–June 1969	Tutors in the Law Faculty at UCD.
1969	Joins the Irish Council of the European Movement in Dublin and shortly afterwards is appointed to its executive committee.
1969–75	Reid Professor of Penal Legislation, Constitutional and Criminal Law, and the law of Evidence (1888). The title was changed in 1975.

June 1969	General election. Decides to run for one of th Dublin University seats in Seanad Éireann, th Irish Senate.
	Seanad Éireann – The Irish Senate
2 August 1969	Elected to Seanad Éireann on the second count
2 December 1969	Maiden speech in Senate on lack of direction i government policy and gross under-use of Senat by government.
November 1970	At a meeting of the newly established Irish Famil Planning Rights Association in Dublin, announce her intention of introducing a private member Bill in the Senate to repeal laws banning sale an importation of contraceptives in Ireland.
12 December 1970	Marries Nicholas Robinson.
1971–2	Appointed by the European Commission as Iris representative on Vedel Committee to advise o enlargement of the European Parliament.
3 March 1971	M.R.'s private members' bill to change the law o contraception placed on order book of the Senate
7 July 1971	Bill given a first reading without any prior notice Defeated by 25 votes to 14.
July 1971	Given leave to introduce another private mem bers' Bill, amending the 1952 and 1964 Adoptio Acts to make couples in mixed marriages eligibl to apply to adopt a child.
10 August 1971	Speaks in Senate against introduction of intern ment in Northern Ireland
August 1971	Fights in Senate against the Forcible Entry Bill. Invited to become first president of the Women' Progressive Association, (later The Women's Poli tical Association).
May 1972	Member of inter-denominational working party o the Irish Theological Association which identifie discrimination in the Constitution and legislatio and makes many radical recommendations on th preamble to the Constitution, its religious clauses the ban on divorce, marriages laws and laws bannin contraceptives.
June 1972	M.R.'s private members' Bill, Adoption Amen

ment Bill 1971, given its second reading. When the Minister for Justice promises the government will bring its own Bill to deal with discrimination against mixed marriages in adoption matters, M.R. withdraws her private members' Bill. Subsequently takes the M v An Bord Úchtala case, which challenged the constitutionality of the religious clauses in the Adoption Acts and wins the case, leading to the passage of the Adoption (Amendment Act) Act 1974, which removes the offending clauses.

1972–79	Vice Chairman, Irish Council of the European Movement, and in October 1972 is appointed to the policy committee of ICEM.
October 1972	Starts teaching European law in TCD, in addition to her Reid Professorship lectures.
2 October 1972	Tessa Robinson born.
1 December 1972	Two bombs go off in Dublin killing two people and injuring 127. Offences against the State (Amendment) Act 1972 goes through the Dail late at night.
2 December 1972	During its passage through the Senate, M.R. tries to have amendments made to Offences against the State Bill that would have put a time limit on the powers given by the act and more protection to the rights of people arrested under it.
7 December 1972	Referendum to amend the Constitution: a) to reduce the minimum age for voting from 21 to 18; b) to remove from the Constitution article 44 which recognises the special position of the Roman Catholic Church and also refers to some other religions, both passed by a large majority.
31 December 1972	At midnight Ireland, Britain and Denmark become members of EEC.
1973–1990	President of Cherish, a new self-help organisation of single mothers.
8 February 1973	General election; FF defeated after sixteen years in power. Fine Gael and Labour form a coalition government, with Liam Cosgrave as Taoiseach, Brendan Corish as Tánaiste.

3 March 1973	Dr Tessa Bourke dies suddenly at their house in Westland Row, while helping with M.R.'s election campaign for the Senate.
1 May 1973	Senate election. Ten candidates for three Trinity seats. M.R. heads poll and is elected on first count.
July 1973	Called to the Bar of the Middle Temple, London.
1973–1989	Member of the Oireachtas Joint Committee on EC Secondary Legislation.
14 November 1973	Introduces her second private members' Bill to reform the laws banning contraception. Senate agrees by 27 votes to 12 that her Bill should proceed to the second stage.
19 December 1973	Supreme Court ruling on McGee case upholds Mrs McGee's right to import contraceptives by finding, by four to one majority, s17(3) of the Criminal Law Amendment Act 1935 unconstitutional.
1973–1979	Executive Member of the Tri-Lateral Commission.
11 January 1974	William Robinson born.
27 March 1974	Debate on M.R.'s 1973 Family Planning Bill defeated by 32 votes to 10.
May 1974	Introduces The Illegitimate Children (Maintenance and Succession) Bill in the Senate. Bill withdrawn when government promises to introduce its own Bill – The Family Law (Maintenance of Spouses & Children) Act 1976, which tackles some of these issues.
16 July 1974	Government's attempt to reform laws on contraception fail when Taoiseach Liam Cosgrave and his Minister for Education vote against their own bill.
17 December 1974	M.R.'s third Family Planning Bill (1974) granted first reading and published. Finally defeated by 23 votes to 20.
December 1975	Supreme Court finds law regarding women on juries unconstitutional. M.R. acts for plaintiffs, Máirín de Burca and Mary Anderson.

1975–1990	Part-time lecturer in European Law at Trinity.
April 1976	M.R. and Nick join Friends of Mediaeval Dublin to try to preserve Viking site at Wood Quay.
July 1976	Joins Labour party.
1976–79	Member of Executive Committee of newly formed Irish Council for Civil Liberties.
1976–90	Member of the advisory board of *The Common Market Law Review*.
September 1976	Opposes government's Emergency Powers Bill and Criminal Law Bill.
October 1976	Joins Irish Transport and General Workers Union.
June 1977	General election. M.R. stands for Labour party in Rathmines West. Eliminated on eighth count.
18 August 1977	Senate Election. Mary elected third.
November 1977	David Norris, represented by M.R., issues summons in High Court, claiming ss61 and 62 of the Offences against the Person Act, 1861 inconsistent with the Constitution. Eventual repeal of 1861 Act follows.
2 October 1979	Josie Airey, with M.R. as her counsel, wins case against Ireland in the European Court of Human Rights, Strasbourg, when the state is found to be in breach of the European Convention for the Protection of Human Rights due to its failure to provide free legal aid in a family law matter. After this judgement the Irish government moves to put in place a limited scheme for civil legal aid.
1979–83	Member of Dublin City Council; the City of Dublin Vocational Education Committee and Comhairle le Leas Oige.
1980	Called to the Inner Bar
April 1980	Divorce Action Group formed in Dublin. Mary participates in their campaign and drafts Bill to remove constitutional ban on divorce.
3 May 1981	Aubrey Robinson born.
11 June 1981	General election. M.R. fails to win seat in Dail.
September 1981	Senate election: comes second in election for three Trinity seats.
April 1982	Anti-Amendment Campaign on abortion estab-

	lished; Mary takes a public stand against proposed amendment to the Constitution.
1982	Visiting Professor, University of San Francisco Summer Programme.
1982	Two general elections (February and November), Mary holds Trinity seat in the Senate in both.
1983–84	Labour party representative on New Ireland Forum.
January 1983	Resigns from Dublin City Council.
February 1983	Re-elected to the Senate on the Trinity panel.
1984–90	Member of advisory committee of INTERIGHTS, the International Centre for the Legal Protection of Human Rights, London.
1984	Patron of the Liam Maguire Trust for disabled people.
1985	Resigns from Labour party over Anglo-Irish Agreement.
28 February 1985	Welcomes The Health (Family Planning Amendment) Bill.
1985–1990	Patron of the Marriage and Family Institute.
18 December 1986	European Court of Human Rights in its judgement on the Johnston and Others v Ireland (with M.R. acting for the plaintiffs) does not find that the European Convention guarantees the plaintiffs a right to re-marry, but does find that Irish law does not afford sufficient respect to the rights of their illegitimate daughter. Subsequent to this judgement, the Irish government passes the Status of Children Act in 1987, which abolishes the legal status of illegitimacy.
19 December 1986	SPUC (Society for Protection of the Unborn Child) wins High Court case against the Dublin Well Woman Centre and Open Door Counselling to prevent them from offering help and advice to Irish women seeking an abortion, with M.R. acting for defendants. Supreme Court upholds this verdict but the European Court of Human Rights in 1992 finds Ireland in breach of the Convention on Human Rights by depriving people of access to information.

February 1987	General election. M.R. retains her seat in subsequent Senate election.
1987–90	Member of the International Committee of Jurists, Geneva.
1987–89	Chairs the Legal Affairs Sub-committee of the Oireachtas Committee on EC Secondary Legislation.
1988–90	Founds, with Nick, Irish Centre for European Law in Trinity.
1989–90	Member of Chambers, 2 Hare Court, London.
1989–90	Member of Euro-Avocats, Brussels.
May 1989	Announces that this is her last term in the Senate.
26 April 1990	Administrative Council of Labour party votes 4 to 1 for M.R. as their nominee for the presidency, running as an independent candidate.
May 1990	M.R., accompanied by Nick and Bride Rosney, commences her election campaign in Limerick.
9 November 1990	Wins presidential election.
3 December 1990	Inaugurated as President of Ireland in Dublin Castle.
22 March 1991	Defies Taoiseach to meet Dalai Lama.
5 April 1991	Allowed her first visit to England for opening of the European Bank for Reconstruction and Development.
4 February 1992	First working visit by an Irish President to Belfast
10 February 1992	President accepts resignation of An Taoiseach Charles J. Haughey, and later in the day gives seals of office to An Taoiseach, Albert Reynolds, and his Ministers.
May 1992	State visit to France.
8 July 1992	First Address to the Houses of the Oireachtas on Irish Identity in Europe.
6 October 1992	Visits Somalia and then UN headquarters in New York to brief them on horrors of Somali famine and plight of refugees in the horn of Africa.
7 April 1993	Attends memorial service in Warrington, England, for two boys, Jonathan Ball and Tim Parry, killed by IRA bombs in Warrington.

27 May 1993	Has afternoon tea with Queen Elizabeth II in Buckingham Palace.
18 June 1993	Visits the West Belfast Community Festival and local community groups, where she meets and shakes hands with Joe Hendron of the SDLP, Gerry Adams of Sinn Féin and other local leaders.
November 1993	First President to attend Memorial Day Service for World War Dead in St Patrick's Cathedral.
March 1994	Official visits to the UN Headquarters, to New York, Philadelphia and Boston,
May 1994	Attends inauguration of Nelson Mandela as President of the new South Africa.
August 1994	Working visit to Canada.
September–October 1994	State visits to Republic of Zambia, Republic of Zimbabwe and Tanzania, during which M.R. includes a visit to Rwandese refugee camps at Ngara, Benaco and Lumasi.
October 1994	Working visit to Rwanda.
2 February 1995	Second Address to the Houses of the Oireachtas: Cherishing the Diaspora.
February–March 1995	State visits to Japan, Brazil, Argentina and Chile.
1–4 June 1995	Prince Charles visits Republic of Ireland for the first time and has lunch at Áras an Uachtaráin.
October 1995	Second visit to Rwanda.
24 November 1995	15th Amendment to the Constitution, which abolishes the constitutional ban on divorce.
25–29 March 1996	State visit to the Republic of South Africa.
4–7 June 1996	Official visit to Britain.
1 June 1996	State visit to the United States, one of many U.S. visits M.R. made during her presidency.
6 July 1996	Visits Manchester in a gesture of 'friendship and solidarity' with the people of a city devastated by an IRA bomb three weeks earlier.
1–3 March 1997	Returns to Rwanda for her third visit there.
6–9 March 1997	Visit to Italy and to the Vatican to meet the Pope.
12 March 1997	Announces that she will not stand for second term in presidency.

8 September 1997	Last visit to Northern Ireland as President of Ireland.
12 September 1997	Opens new housing project for Focus Ireland, her last public engagement as President of Ireland; returns to Áras an Uachtaráin to bid farewell to her staff, then catches flight to Geneva to take up new post as High Commissioner for Human Rights at the UN.

INDEX

Note: in the index MR stands for Mary Robinson.

318